Good
Book

Good Book

THE BIZARRE, HILARIOUS, DISTURBING, MARVELOUS, AND INSPIRING THINGS I LEARNED WHEN I READ EVERY SINGLE WORD OF THE BIBLE

David Plotz

HARPER

An Imprint of HarperCollins*Publishers*
www.harpercollins.com

HarperCollins books may be purchased for educational, business, or sales promotional use. For information, please write: Special Markets Department, HarperCollins Publishers, 10 East 53rd Street, New York, NY 10022.

FIRST EDITION

Printed on acid-free paper

Library of Congress Cataloging-in-Publication Data is available upon request.

ISBN: 978-0-06-137424-1

09   10   11   12   13   WBC/RRD   10   9   8   7   6   5   4   3   2   1

For my parents, the best argument
in the world for the Fifth Commandment

Contents

Good
Book

Introduction

In the Beginning

I've always been a proud Jew, but never a very observant one. I believe in God, but only in a please-*please*-desperation-prayer kind of way. I say the Lord's name only to take it in vain. I don't have any other gods before Him, but mostly because I haven't looked for any. I rarely remember the Sabbath day, and never keep it holy. I go to the synagogue about as often—and with about as much pleasure—as I go to the DMV.

But not long ago, I made one of those rare visits to the synagogue for my cousin Alina's bat mitzvah. As usual, I found myself confused (and bored) by a Hebrew service I couldn't understand. During the second hour of a ceremony that would last as long as an NFL game plus overtime, I picked up a Torah from a rack on the pew, flipped it open at random, and started reading the English translation.

I had landed at Genesis, Chapter 34. I was immediately engrossed—and horrified—by a story I didn't know. It begins with a young man named Shechem raping Dinah, who's the daughter of the patriarch Jacob. (Someone *is* in the kitchen with Dinah.) After the rape, Shechem realizes he actually loves Dinah, speaks to her "tenderly," and decides he must marry her. He and his father, an idol-worshipping chieftain named Hamor, pay a conciliatory visit to Jacob and his sons, Dinah's brothers. Hamor pleads: *My son loves Dinah and yearns to marry her.* Hamor and Shechem offer to share their land with Jacob's family, marry off the women of their clan to Jacob's sons, and pay any bride price if only Dinah will be Shechem's wife. (I should note that Shechem and Hamor aren't suckers: they're also eager for the marriage so that they can get their hands on Jacob's land.)

Jacob's sons pretend to agree to their proposal, but insist on one condition: Shechem, Hamor, and all the men of their town must be circumcised before the marriage. Shechem and Hamor accept this. They and their fellow townsmen get circumcised. And here the story turns macabre. Three days after the townsmen's circumcision, "when they [are] in pain," Jacob's sons Simeon and Levi descend on the settlement, spears drawn, and murder all the incapacitated men. Then Jacob's other sons plunder the town, seize the livestock and property, and take the women and children as slaves. Jacob, who hasn't said a word up to this point in the chapter, complains to Simeon and Levi that, because of the massacre, neighboring tribes won't trust him anymore. "But they answered, 'Should our sister be treated like a whore?'"

Needless to say, this isn't a story they taught me at Temple Sinai's Hebrew school in 1980. The Garden of Eden, David and Goliath, Noah's ark, sure. But the founding fathers of Israel lying, breaching a contract, encouraging pagans to convert to Judaism only in order to cripple them for slaughter, massacring defenseless innocents, enslaving women and children, pillaging and profiteering, and then justifying it all with an appeal to their sister's defiled honor? Not on the syllabus. And the tale of Dinah isn't hiding way in the back of the Bible, deep in Obadiah or Nehemiah or one of the other minor-league books no one ever reads. It is smack in the middle of Genesis, the one book of the Bible even ignoramuses think they know.

Like many lax but well-educated Jews (and Christians), I had long assumed I knew what was in the Bible—more or less. I read parts of the Torah as a child in Hebrew school, then attended a rigorous Episcopalian high school in Washington, D.C., where I had to study the Old and New Testaments. Many of the highlights stuck in my mind—Adam and Eve, Cain versus Abel, Jacob versus Esau, Jonah versus whale, forty days and nights, ten plagues and commandments, twelve tribes and apostles, Red Sea walked under, Galilee Sea walked on, bush into fire, rock into water, water into wine. And, of course, I absorbed other bits of the Bible elsewhere—from stories I heard in churches and synagogues, from movies and television shows, from tidbits my parents and teachers told me. All this left me with a general sense that I knew the Good Book well enough, and that it was a font of crackling stories, Jewish heroes, and moral lessons.

But the tale of Dinah unsettled me, to say the least. If this story was strutting cheerfully through the heart of Genesis, what else had I forgotten or never learned? What else had Rabbi Lippmann neglected to teach us on Saturday morning? What other juicy bits did the Reverend Mr. Bowen leave out of Bible class? When I got home from Alina's bat mitzvah, I complained to my wife, Hanna, "How can I be thirty-five years old and still so uneducated?" I found myself obsessed with the story of Dinah. At a party, I was introduced to a woman named Dinah and spent an awkward half hour enlightening her about the source of her name. I met an Orthodox Jew named Dinah who told me about her lifelong quest to make sense of her namesake's story. I mentioned Dinah to a friend who was born Muslim. He then described to me how he was circumcised as a teenager—a squirm-inducing story that brought home the agony suffered by Shechem and his townsmen. I learned about various interpretations of the story, how some commentators—whose views have been dramatized in Anita Diamant's *The Red Tent*—think Dinah went with Shechem willingly. By contrast, an evangelical Christian friend told me that when she was a girl, her parents and pastor taught her Genesis 34 as a cautionary tale about female modesty: Dinah never should have gone out where Shechem could accost her. This version appeared to make a horrendous story even worse: now Dinah was *asking* for it!

I soon realized that I needed to read the Bible—*really* read the

Bible—for the first time in my life. I would begin with "In the beginning," and see how far I got. I decided I would write about it as I went along—not learned exegesis or spiritual essays, just my immediate responses. That is the origin of *Good Book*.

For the millions of Jews and Christians who know the Bible intimately, this project may sound presumptuous or even absurd: why should a numbskull beginner interpret the Bible stories that you know by heart? I didn't intend any kind of insult. My goal was not to find contradictions, or to mock impossible events, or to scoff at hypocrisy. I was reading out of genuine curiosity and fascination. I needed to understand the book that has shaped my religion and my world.

I also knew enough to know that Judaism and Christianity aren't just the Bible. Judaism is built on thousands of years of commentary, interpretation, and law. This library of wisdom was totally unfamiliar to me, and I couldn't hope to compete with it. I also knew I was coming very late to the game. There are books to tell you why the Bible is literally true, others to advise you how to analyze it as history, and still others to help you read it as literature. There are experts standing by to teach you how to approach the book as a Jew, a Catholic, an evangelical Protestant, an archaeologist, a historian, a feminist, a lawyer, an athlete, or a teenager.

So what could I possibly do? I had one—and only one—advantage over the experts: the book was fresh to me. I didn't know what I was supposed to know. My goal was simple. I wanted to find out what happens when an ignorant person actually reads the book on which his religion is based. I was in the same position as many other lazy but faithful people (Christians, Jews, Muslims, Hindus). I loved Judaism; I loved (most of) the lessons it had taught me about how to live in the world; and yet I realized I was ignorant about its foundation, its essential document. So what would happen if I approached my Bible empty, unmediated by teachers or rabbis or parents; if I ignored commentary and learned experts; if it was just me and the word(s)? What would delight me? What would horrify me? How would the Bible relate to the religion I practice, and to the lessons I thought I had learned in synagogue and Hebrew school? How would it change me? Would it make me more faithful, or less? I have small children: would it teach me how to teach them about God?

HOW TO READ THIS BOOK

Good Book is a chapter-by-chapter tour through the Hebrew Bible. You can read it in various ways. You can start with the chapter on Genesis and go straight through to the end of 2 Chronicles. Or you can dip into it, a little Genesis here, some Job there, and Esther for dessert. You can read *Good Book* as a Bible study companion, following the text along with me, comparing my take on the book of Judges with your own. Or, if you don't have the time or inclination to read the Bible, you can just read *Good Book* instead. It will give you a rapid (and entertaining, if not necessarily theologically sound) biblical education, without your having to suffer through a single "begat." *Good Book* is unlike the Bible in one very significant way: you can, without feeling guilty, keep it in the bathroom.

> *Note on translation:* I can't read the original Hebrew of the Bible, obviously, so I'm stuck with translations. My wife, charmed by my new biblical obsession, gave me a wonderful Jewish Publication Society translation of the Hebrew Bible for Hanukkah. That's my number one source. I dishonored my father and mother (and broke another commandment, too) by stealing a copy of the King James Bible from their house. So I will also dip into the King James Version, because it's a wellspring of our language and literature, and the foundation of all subsequent English translations. And I will occasionally consult and quote from other modern translations, particularly the New International Version and the New Revised Standard Version.

ONE

The Book of Genesis

God's First Try

In which God creates Earth and pretty much everything else, including Adam and Eve; Adam and Eve are expelled from the Garden of Eden; Cain kills Abel; God floods the sinful Earth; Noah survives; God chooses Abram, renames him Abraham, and promises him the Holy Land; God incinerates the sin cities of Sodom and Gomorrah; Abraham almost sacrifices his son Isaac; Isaac's son Jacob tricks his older twin brother, Esau, out of their father's blessing; Jacob wrestles an angel, is renamed Israel, and has twelve sons; the older sons sell Joseph into slavery; Joseph becomes prime minister of Egypt, saves his brothers during a famine, and reconciles with them; all the Israelites settle in Egypt and fail to live happily ever after.

CHAPTER I

You'd think God would know exactly what He's doing at the Creation. But He doesn't. He's a tinkerer. He tries something out: *What happens if I move all the water around so there's room for dry land?* He checks it out. Yes, "this was good." Then He moves on to His next experiment: *How about plants? I'll try plants.*

Creation is haphazard, like any do-it-yourself building project. For example, God tackles the major geological and astronomical features during the first two days—light, sky, water, earth. But day three is a curious interruption—the creation of plants—that is followed by a return to massive universe-shaping efforts on day four with the formation of the sun, moon, and stars. The plant venture is a tangent, like installing the refrigerator before you've put a roof on the house.

Does the Lord love insects best? They're so nice He makes them twice. On day five, He makes "the living creatures of every kind that creep." A day later, He makes "all kinds of creeping things of the earth." "Creeping" is all over Creation, in fact. When God tells His newly made man and woman that they rule over the Earth's creatures, He specifies that their subjects include "every creeping thing that creepeth upon the earth." What a phrase, perfect for bugs and babies.

CHAPTER 2

Two chapters in, and I'm already confused. Chapter 2 gives us an entirely different account of Creation, with different methods and in a different order. In Chapter 1 (first Creation), God makes man and woman at the same time on day six, after he has made everything else. But here in Chapter 2 (second Creation), He forms man, but not woman, *before* he makes plants and animals. Only later, *after* the plants and animals arrive, does God create woman, from Adam's rib. And while man and woman are created equal in the first Creation, here in the second Creation the woman is made explicitly to be man's "helper." Which is the real story? I'll take the first Creation, any day.

As it happens, just as I'm reading about Creation, my five-year-old daughter has arrived at the age when it becomes necessary for her to ask impossible questions, such as "Where do people come from?" She drops that on me one night at bedtime, and I find myself flummoxed. I briefly consider trying to explain the evolution of *Homo sapiens* and chimpanzees from a common ape ancestor over millions of years but then decide that's way too complicated to throw at her. So for lack of any better idea, I flop back to the Genesis story. After all, I figure, it's had a 3,000-year run. I tell her that long ago, even before Granny was born, God created the world and made people. I feel ashamed of myself as I gaze into her blue eyes and say this, but I find a way to rationalize it: the Genesis story is simpler and easier for a five-year-old to understand, and I can always tell her the scientific version later.

But I get what I deserve: my skeptical wife, Hanna, overhears us and rebukes me for telling a story I don't believe. And my daughter, who's a little rationalist, right down to her pinky toes, doesn't buy it, either. As kids always do, she intuits that I'm lying. She asks the same question a couple of nights later, a sure sign that she was dissatisfied with my creationist story. This time I give an evolutionary explanation, and she's very enthusiastic. She asks me a few follow-up questions about apes, then goes happily to sleep. She never again asks me about where people come from.

Before God creates Eve in Genesis 2, He parades the animals past Adam—cattle, wild beasts, and "all the birds of the sky"—so that Adam can name them all. This episode captures something fundamental about the male brain: our obsessive need to categorize. The bird-watcher, the stamp collector, the guy trying to visit every Starbucks in America— we are all reenacting in a small way Adam's introduction to the animals.

CHAPTER 3

The Lord—not so good at follow-through. In Genesis 2, He is clear as can be: He commands man *not* to eat from the tree of knowledge of good and evil, "for as soon as you eat of it, you shall die." No wiggle room there. *As soon as you eat of it, you shall die.* But when Eve and Adam eat the fruit at the beginning of Genesis 3, do they die? Nope. God merely punishes Eve with "most severe . . . pangs in childbearing" and curses Adam by making the soil barren. Any parent knows you have to follow through on your threats, or your children will take advantage of you. God made a vow He didn't keep. Instead He delivers a halfhearted punishment that will actually encourage His children to misbehave. Is it any surprise that we sin again? And again? And again, all the way down to the present day? You can call this "original sin," but maybe it's just lax parenting.

In Genesis 1, God was the mighty and remote king of the universe, shaping the galaxies and pouring the ocean. But now He is increasingly like a father—or should I say like a dad? He's an exasperated, down-to-earth deity. He peevishly hunts all over the Garden of Eden to find Adam and Eve, more like a frustrated parent who has lost his kids at the mall than all-knowing, all-powerful Yahweh.

When God finally locates the first couple and quizzes Adam about eating from the tree, Adam immediately sells out Eve. Adam says, "The woman You put at my side—she gave me of the tree, and I ate." What kind of husband is this? Adam's supposed to be her master, but he won't even take responsibility for his own sin and just blames her instead.

Oh, and that fruit from the tree? We've been duped. It's *not* an apple. The Bible just calls it a "fruit." According to a history of the apple I happen to be reading, it actually couldn't have been an apple, because there weren't any apples in that part of the world in those days. So what was it? A fig? A pomegranate? Me, I'd risk divine punishment for a really great mango.

CHAPTER 4

The first murder—that didn't take long. Cain offs Abel. I never realized there was a vegetarian angle to the killing. Cain presents God with an offering of fruits and veggies, while Abel brings the choicest meat. God scorns Cain's vegan platter, so Cain jealously slays his carnivorous brother.

The story of Cain and Abel suggests a more charitable interpretation of God's parenting style. Maybe He's not lax. Maybe He's laissez-faire. His job is to prod His kids in the right direction, but ultimately, He understands that they must be free to make mistakes. When God rejects Cain's green offering, He doesn't threaten Cain, but instead advises him about self-improvement. "Sin couches at the door; its urge is toward you, yet you can be its master." Not that Cain pays attention: he kills his brother in the very next verse.

God's advice would be more persuasive if He actually gave Cain any incentive to master sin. On the contrary, Cain gets off scot-free after his fratricide, and goes on to a happy life as the father of all mankind. In fact, rather than punish Cain, God gives him special protection, the "mark of Cain" on his skin. I always thought the mark of Cain signified disgrace. But it's the opposite: the mark indicates that God is looking out for Cain and will take "sevenfold vengeance" on anyone who harms him.

CHAPTERS 6–10

The story of Noah that I remember from school and from kids' television is pretty jolly: Dr. Doolittle grows a beard and takes a cruise, and then it rains. But it turns out that the actual Bible tale is so much grimmer than the Sunday school version that I'm astonished anyone manages to teach it at all.

As it begins, God is deciding man's wickedness is so great that He's got to kill us all and start over. (The animals will be collateral damage.) This immediately presents us with a mystery (an urgent mystery if you're a person who wonders if God might do this again). The mystery is: what did humans do that was so terrible? It has been a very short time since the Creation—how much evil could man have learned? Why would God give up on man so easily? The Bible is frustratingly vague about the nature of our sin, but let's try to figure it out. Earlier chapters suggest that men had learned agriculture and metalwork and built cities. Perhaps, as they mastered the world, they felt they didn't need God. They came to see their laws, achievements, and prosperity as their own, accomplished independently of God. Perhaps the point of the Flood is not to restore ordinary moral behavior—day-to-day decency, law, etc.—since Genesis offers no evidence that such everyday social morality has failed. The Flood must instead be intended to restore faith, or at least fear. We thought we didn't need God, and that was what made Him angry. Noah is a good man—the *only* good man—yet even he finds himself subjugated to God's awesome power. The Flood is supposed to remind us (or at least to remind the one righteous man permitted to live) that we are *never* independent of God, but always floating alone, vulnerable, at His mercy.

Somehow I do not find this reassuring. When I have quizzed Christian friends about Noah and the planetwide devastation, they have given me some version of this answer: The Flood is just God teaching a lesson; He's giving us a powerful reminder to obey Him; etc. But aren't there more efficient ways to "send a message" than global genocide? Until now, God has been a little scatterbrained and inconsistent. But now I'm wondering if He's just cruel.

My favorite detail: All Earth's creatures except those on the ark have died. But what is the very first thing Noah does after landfall? He makes an animal sacrifice.

Then Noah plants the first vineyard and naturally soon becomes the first person to get falling-down drunk. He passes out naked on the floor of his tent. His youngest son, Ham, sees this sorry spectacle but doesn't do anything to help Dad. The two elder sons, Shem and Japheth, cover Noah up. Noah curses Ham, proclaiming that Ham's descendants (the Canaanites) will be slaves to his brothers' descendants. This is just the first of many Bible stories about children disappointing their parents and parents embarrassing their children.

CHAPTERS 12–17

Here come the patriarchs. God calls Abram—soon to be Abraham—and announces: "I will make of you a great nation, and I will bless you."

Why Abram? There is no obvious reason. Unlike Noah, he's not a "righteous man." He's seventy-five years old and hasn't done anything with his life. He isn't pious, rich, or accomplished. He's not a king, a chief, a prophet, a genius, or a warrior. He's completely ordinary, and I suppose that's the point. Abram isn't special: it is God's choosing him that makes him special. He is a regular man touched by God—just as any of us could be.

Abram and his wife, Sarai, travel to Egypt to avoid a famine. To trick Pharaoh, Sarai pretends to be Abram's sister. The Egyptian ruler, clearly hoping to score, admires Sarai's beauty and presents her and Abram with livestock. At this point God, perhaps warming up for the ten Egyptian plagues to come, "afflict[s] Pharaoh and his household with mighty plagues on account of Sarai." This seems unfair of the Almighty. It's Abram and Sarai who tricked Pharaoh—why should the Egyptian get punished for ogling Sarai? A few chapters later, the couple (now Abraham and Sarah) pull exactly the same "she's my sister" con: This time the mark is King Abimelech. He's about to seduce Sarah when God appears to him in a dream and tells him that Sarah and Abraham are actually married and Abraham is a prophet. Abimelech begs forgiveness and buys off Abraham and Sarah with land, livestock, and silver. (Not explained—why would Abimelech want to seduce Sarah, who is at that point nearly ninety years old?)

God makes a covenant with Abraham, promising him "all the land of Canaan, as an everlasting holding." God is a kind of celestial Donald Trump: He can't go a chapter without a new real-estate deal. By my count, He promises land to Abraham at least four times, and each time the boundaries are different. (Promised land, indeed.)

The covenant imposes only one obligation on Abraham and his heirs: circumcision. That's it. That is God's single requirement. It's an inspired choice. Circumcision is painful enough that no one will undertake it lightly. It's visible, and so it obviously demarcates you from others. And it's irreversible.

CHAPTER 18

Wait a minute: Jews had the three wise men before Jesus! Three strangers visit Abraham, and he welcomes them hospitably. One of the strangers—who are God's messengers—announces, "I will return to you next year, and your wife Sarah shall have a son." So the story of the Nativity is a rip-off. In the popular Christmas tale, it's impossible for Mary to have a child because she's a virgin, but she does, and the messengers herald the miracle birth. Here it's impossible for Sarah to have a child because she's postmenopausal (as we are told very directly: "Sarah had stopped having the periods of women")—but she will, and three supernatural visitors herald the event. The big difference: We Jews do not have any good songs about this incident.

Later the Lord stops by Abraham's tent to let the patriarch know that He's considering the destruction of Sodom and Gomorrah, because "their sin [is] so grave!" (I love the way God just drops in, like a nosy neighbor in a sitcom.) The king of kings is very enthusiastic about His plan, but then Abraham starts rebuking Him: "Far be it from You to do such a thing, to bring death upon the innocent as well as the guilty, so that innocent and guilty fare alike. Far be it from You! Shall not the Judge of all the earth deal justly?" Abraham asks if the Lord should destroy Sodom and Gomorrah if even fifty innocent people are living there. The Lord grudgingly agrees that He must spare these twin cities if there are even fifty innocents. What if there are forty-five, Abraham demands? OK, not if there are forty-five, either, God says. Forty? asks Abraham. No, God concedes. Thirty? Twenty? Ten? God agrees that if there are even ten innocents, he will spare Sodom and Gomorrah.

I can't tell you how happy this story makes me. I came to the Bible with the notion that it was overflowing with righteous heroes, but so far Genesis has been one evil act after another, from the murder of Abel to the Flood to Abraham and Sarah's grifting. But in this tale Abraham emerges as a moral hero, unafraid to challenge even Almighty God to do right. Isn't something upside down when God is the villain of holy scripture and man is the hero? To my modern eyes, though perhaps not to the Bible's authors, collective punishment is the great moral conundrum of the Torah (the Flood, the Tower of Babel, Sodom and Gomorrah, the Egyptian plagues, etc.). And God is always on the wrong side of the question.

CHAPTER 19

This chapter makes *The Jerry Springer Show* look like a Cabbage Patch picnic. God does destroy Sodom and Gomorrah, despite his conversation with Abraham, and Genesis 19 tells how it happens. Two male angels visit Lot's house in Sodom. A crowd of men ("Sodomites," natch) gather outside the house and demand that the two angels be sent out, so the mob can rape them. Lot, whose hospitality is greater than his common sense, offers up his virgin daughters instead. Before any virgin-raping can be done, the men in the mob are blinded by a mysterious flash of light. In the confusion, the angels escort Lot, his wife, and their daughters out of the city, and God destroys Sodom and Gomorrah with brimstone. Lot's wife looks back and is turned into a pillar of salt. (God may have listened to Abraham's criticism in the preceding chapter, but He surely didn't heed it. What of all the innocent children murdered in Sodom and Gomorrah? What of Lot's innocent wife?)

And the horror show isn't over. After the attempted gay gang rape, the father's pimping, the urban annihilation, and the uxorious saline murder, it looks as if Lot and his daughters are finally safe, holed up in a cave in the mountains. But then the two daughters—think of them as Judea's Hilton sisters—complain that cave life is no fun because there aren't enough men around. So, one night they get Lot falling-down drunk, have sex with him, get pregnant, and bear sons: Moab, who becomes the patriarch of the Moabites; and Ben-Ammi, the patriarch of the Ammonites. This is a fantastic in-joke: the Bible's Israelite authors are tracing the ancestry of enemy tribes to father-daughter incest. Even so, Genesis 19 poses what I would call the "Sunday-school problem"—how do you teach this in Sunday school? What exactly is the moral lesson here?

CHAPTER 22

Over and over Genesis reminds us that the only thing Abraham wants is to have a son with Sarah. Isaac's birth is a miracle, foretold by angels. Isaac is always described as Abraham's "favored" one. So when

God tells Abraham to take Isaac to Mount Moriah and sacrifice him, the command seems impossibly cruel. The precise, cinematic detail of the story compounds its horror. This bit of dialogue between father and doomed son as they walk up the mountain is particularly stunning:

> *Then Isaac said to his father Abraham, "Father!" And he answered, "Yes, my son." And he said, "Here are the firestone and the wood; but where is the sheep for the burnt offering?" And Abraham said, "God will see to the sheep for His burnt offering, my son."*

As a father, I find this nearly impossible to read. The repetition of "my son" is devastating. Abraham does not try to distance himself from Isaac, to separate himself from the child he must kill. Isaac remains "my son," "my son."

My initial reaction to the near-sacrifice was: How cruel and manipulative of God! How jealous He is of human love! But that indignation has mellowed into something slightly more resigned. After all, testing fealty by demanding the most painful sacrifice is an ur-idea, running through myths, religions, and fairy tales from the beginning of civilization till today. Since God is offering the greatest of rewards to Abraham (His love), why shouldn't He demand that Abraham prove his complete faith? And the Lord does let Isaac live, providing a ram at the last minute to replace the boy.

This is, of course, another story adopted and repurposed in the New Testament; but in the Christian version, God *does* sacrifice the son. I'm a sucker for a happy ending, so I'll take the Genesis tale, complete with the deus ex machina and the spared child.

CHAPTER 23

Sarah dies, a passing that's taken care of in two quick verses. These are followed by eighteen verses explaining Abraham's protracted, confusing negotiations to buy a burial site for her in Hebron. Real estate, again! It is the strangely dominant theme of Abraham's life. Nearly every chapter about him is crammed with details about land—who owns it, who can buy it, whether God is giving it, whether it's a temporary deal or a permanent one. There's more about real estate than there is about the Lord.

And how little has changed in 3,500 years. The burial site Abraham purchased—called the Cave of the Patriarchs—remains the most contentious spot on the West Bank. Jews consider it the second-holiest place on Earth, but Hebron is an Arab town. Hebron's few ultra-religious Jewish settlers and thousands of neighboring Palestinians live cheek by jowl, always unpleasantly, often violently. In 1929, Arabs massacred sixty-seven Jews in Hebron. In 1994, a Jewish settler slaughtered twenty-nine Palestinians at the Cave of the Patriarchs.

CHAPTER 25

Abraham dies at age 175, "a good ripe age, old and contented." Why do people live so long in Genesis? Before the Flood, they routinely live more than 600 years. After the Flood, they still live at least 100 years. Ishmael, for example, dies later in this same chapter at age 137, which is just about the youngest age at which anyone dies. The obvious answer, and the one I believe, is "It's not true, that's why." But I wonder why the authors of the Bible *believed* it to be true. At the time Genesis was written down, 1,000 years after Abraham was supposed to have lived, the Israelites who drafted it had normal life spans. Why did they credit their ancestors with such superhuman health? Was their theory that man got weaker the farther he got from the Creation? Modern scholars of folklore would probably attribute the exaggerated life spans to the normal process of mythmaking. As stories tumble down through the centuries, the heroes grow grander and grander and their achievements more and more extraordinary. Their towers reached the sky; they fought giants and met angels; and they lived almost forever.

Of course such a theory of exaggeration doesn't satisfy biblical literalists. Modern-day Bible fundamentalists, who are among the most imaginative people I've ever met, have concocted some extremely ingenious explanations for the long lives in Genesis. My favorite of these is the "vapor canopy." Before the Flood, according to this theory, enormous amounts of water in the atmosphere protected Methuselah et al. from disease and life-sapping solar radiation. The Flood washed out the canopy, shortening our lives to three score and ten. I don't know about you, but I'd happily take a few very cloudy days if it added eight centuries to my life.

CHAPTERS 25–26

In the middle of Genesis 25, a verse announces: "This is the story of Isaac." But it's not. The "story of Isaac" is actually the stories of his wife, Rebekah, and his twin sons, Esau and Jacob—of everyone except him. Isaac is a cipher, the Harpo Marx of Genesis. During a long and dramatic chapter about Abraham's effort to find a wife for Isaac, for example, the groom himself doesn't say a word. He has a bit part in his own marriage. He shows up only at the end, to silently escort his bride, Rebekah, home. After Esau and Jacob are born, Isaac again disappears as the boys take the limelight. Almost all we hear about Isaac is that he preferred Esau to Jacob, because Esau was a hunter and Isaac "had a taste for game."

The Lord appears to Isaac only once—while Abraham was chatting with God daily. And when He does appear to this minor-league patriarch, it's clear that Isaac doesn't really matter to Him. God promises Isaac prosperity, but not because of anything Isaac has done—it's only because his father, Abraham, had obeyed the Lord. Isaac doesn't even get to think up his own tricks. He and Rebekah pull exactly the same ruse on King Abimelech—"She's my sister"—that Abraham and Sarah pulled on both Abimelech and Pharaoh.

CHAPTER 27

My son Jacob is still too young to understand Bible stories, but I've been looking forward to the day when I can talk to him about his namesake. There's something solid and decent about the name Jacob.

My wife's family name is Jacob. My boss is a Jacob. You can trust a Jacob. The biblical Jacob I remember from childhood wrestled an angel, fathered the twelve tribes of Israel, adored his children, honored his mother, and made peace with his wicked brother. This is why I'm finding the real story of Jacob so incredibly disturbing. It turns out I have saddled my son with a blight of a name, because the original Jacob actually had no moral compass, no filial feeling, and the heart of a con artist.

Jacob's very first act, in Genesis 27, is to rip off his older twin, Esau. He gives his hungry brother a bowl of lentil stew, and demands Esau's birthright in exchange. Then Jacob and his mother, Rebekah, devise an elaborate scheme to bamboozle Isaac and further dispossess Esau. Isaac, blind and dying, is preparing to issue his paternal blessings. Rebekah proposes to trick Isaac into mistaking Jacob for Esau and blessing him instead. At first, Jacob is reluctant to help with his mother's scam, though not for ethical reasons—he just fears he will get caught and "bring a curse" upon himself. But Rebekah, the original Lady Macbeth, shushes him, and says, "Just do as I say." While Esau goes hunting, she cooks goat stew for Jacob to give Isaac, since Esau was instructed to bring meat to his father. She concocts the idea of covering Jacob's hands and neck with goat skins, so he will feel as hairy as Esau. Jacob warms to the fraud as it continues, eagerly playing the role of Esau. When Isaac asks him how he hunted down the animals for the stew so quickly, Jacob cavalierly invokes God with his lie: "Because the Lord your God granted me good fortune." Isaac, believing Jacob is Esau, grants him his grand blessing—making him master over his brothers and promising him wealth and power. When Esau returns, there are no backsies. In a heartbreaking moment, poor, innocent, stupid Esau weeps and begs, "Bless me, too, Father!" But Isaac can't undo his prime blessing and offers Esau only a lame substitute benediction instead.

I've never read anything on the relationship of brothers that's as grim as Genesis. Cain and Abel; Ham, Shem, and Japheth; Isaac and Ishmael; Esau and Jacob; and soon Joseph and his brothers. Brothers are purely antagonistic: they battle for inheritance, God's love, their father's respect. They conspire against each other, rat on each other, murder each other. There's not a single act of love or kindness between brothers so far. Brothers are only enemies. Was nomadic life so difficult that only one son in any family could hope to prosper?

And if brothers are bad, women are worse. The story of Isaac's blessing is a reminder of just how uncharitable the Bible is toward the fair sex. God is like Norman Mailer on a bad day. The women of the Bible have so far been either invisible, foolish, or vindictive. Eve is suckered by the serpent. Noah's wife doesn't even get a name. Sarah is tricky (pretends to be Abraham's sister) and cruel (exiles the concubine Hagar and Hagar's son, Ishmael, to the desert). Lot's wife dies because she lacks self-control. Lot's daughters rape him. Rebekah hoodwinks her husband, Isaac, and punishes her older son. Why are the women so unappealing? Partly, I suspect, this portrayal reflects the patriarchal, tribal culture from which the Bible sprang, a culture where control of female sexuality was of paramount importance. In such a society, women who wished to exercise power would have to do it slyly and in the private sphere. This situation produces either invisible women, or semi-heroines like Rebekah and Sarah, who are domestically wily because that is their only way of exercising power.

But Rebekah, with her icy cunning, does embody a more important lesson of Genesis: God doesn't suffer fools. It's clear that Esau's chief failing is that he's dumb. He loses his birthright because he's impatient for lunch, and loses his father's blessing because he's not smart enough to recognize that Jacob might steal it. Jacob and Rebekah, for all their faults, are smart. Abraham, Rebekah, and Jacob, the three great brains of Genesis so far, get what they want and earn the Almighty's blessing because they finagle, cajole, argue, deceive, play mind games, and even misuse God to advance their lies. And the Lord seems to love it.

This may explain the ambivalent attitude toward Isaac in Genesis. Isaac is at the heart of two of the Bible's most vivid stories. As a child he is almost sacrificed, and as a dying man he is tricked by Jacob and Rebekah. In each story he is the passive victim. He never speaks up for himself: He doesn't chastise his father or punish his son. He's easily manipulated by his wife and gulled by Jacob. All the while, he appears just to want a simple life, kicking back in the tent, having a barbecue. He's the accidental patriarch. Is it any surprise that God and the author of Genesis are so much more interested in Abraham and Jacob?

CHAPTER 28

God appears to Jacob in a dream. God says that Jacob's descendants will prosper and multiply—the promise He made to Abraham and Isaac. The Lord also makes a new *personal* commitment to Jacob: "Remember, I am with you: I will protect you wherever you go and will bring you back to this land. I will not leave you until I have done what I have promised you."

My wife and I have many evangelical Christian friends, and one thing that strikes me about them is that they share Jacob's sense that God is interested in their lives. Like Jacob, they feel that God, or Christ, is with them and that He will not leave until He has done what He promised them. But I don't know any Jews who feel this way. It could be that I am friends with the wrong Jews, but the Jews I know don't act or talk as if they have a personal relationship with God. They pray to God and may even feel that God works in the world, but they don't believe that God takes a personal interest. I sure don't think He's watching me. Why would He bother? I'm not even interested in myself most of the time, so why should He be interested in me?

I wonder if there's a scriptural explanation for this difference between Christians and Jews. A Christian armed with the rather gentle New Testament has a very agreeable God and Savior to spend time with. You wouldn't mind having Jesus micromanage your life. Jews face a more difficult proposition. Can you imagine the Old Testament God, with all His caprice, vindictiveness, and violence, acting directly in your life? I can't. It would be like wearing a "Smite Me" sign taped to my back. Better to imagine an abstract, detached creator than worry that the God of Genesis is watching my every move.

CHAPTERS 29–31

Let the Bible soap opera begin! Jacob falls in love with his cousin
Rachel and works seven years for his uncle Laban to win her, but on their
wedding day, Laban sends Rachel's elder sister Leah down the aisle.
When Jacob finally lifts the veil, it's too late: the vows have already
been spoken. Turnabout is fair play: Laban has tricked Jacob into marrying the wrong sibling, just as Jacob duped his father into blessing the
wrong sibling. Jacob works seven extra years and marries Rachel, too.
Jacob starts fathering sons left and right with Leah. This makes the
barren Rachel despondent, so she dispatches her maid Bilhah to Jacob.
After Bilhah pops out a couple of boys, Leah sends *her* maid Zilpah to
Jacob's bed. (The poor guy must be exhausted!) Two more sons result.
Then Leah has another son, and finally Rachel gets into the act and
gives birth to Joseph. During this whole time, Leah and Rachel feud
like contestants on a reality show.

What with having a dozen sons, Jacob needs cash. He decides to go
into business for himself. As compensation for his fourteen years of
service, Jacob asks for all of Laban's streaked and spotted goats and
sheep. Laban agrees, but then secretly culls the streaked and spotted
animals from his flocks. Jacob, realizing he has been fooled, tricks
Laban back. He separates out the healthiest animals from the herd and
breeds them to be streaked and spotted, leaving the feebler animals
for Laban. It's like a David Mamet movie, with two all-time great
tricksters crossing and double-crossing each other.

I guess that "one God" concept hasn't really caught on yet. When
Jacob and his family leave Laban's house, Rachel steals her father's
"household idols." How does the Lord feel about these teensy domestic rivals?

CHAPTERS 32–33

Jacob wrestles with and defeats an angel, then forces the angel to bless
him. The wrestling match wins Jacob a new name (Israel), and it also
gives him a new identity. Until now, Jacob has been the mama's boy, a

metrosexual (without any metro). Esau went out hunting; Jacob stayed
home cooking. Esau was hairy and manly, an animal. Jacob's hairless-
ness suggested weakness. Esau was strong; Jacob was cunning. Yet
when the angel wrenches Jacob's hip, the patriarch fights through the
pain and crushes the angel. He's the original tough Jew.

Immediately after the wrestling match, Jacob reconciles with
Esau. When last seen, Esau was vowing to murder his birthright-
cadging, blessing-stealing younger twin. So Jacob is understandably
cautious in approaching his estranged, wronged brother. Jacob mus-
ters every defense he has, both human and divine. He prays to God to
protect him. He divides his livestock and followers into two camps,
so that if Esau attacks one group, the other can escape. He sends hundreds of animals to Esau as a present, explicitly hoping to bribe him
off. But none of this is necessary. Esau, proving again that he is the
mensch of the family if not the brains, sees Jacob and immediately
runs to him, embraces him, and kisses him. Jacob insists on giving
Esau the animals, and it's clear that Jacob views this as buying back
his brother's goodwill. But the present doesn't seem to matter to
Esau, who grants forgiveness for nothing. Yet between Esau's morality and unconditional love and Jacob's strategy, it's obvious which
God prefers.

That's why this is a story I'm not sure I want to teach my own Jacob. Beneath its surface of filial forgiveness is a deplorable moral: don't
bother treating loved ones right, since the suckers will always forgive
you. The good guy is played for a fool.

CHAPTER 34

Dinah. Enough said.

CHAPTER 35

Jacob's getting old. His firstborn son, Reuben, sleeps with Jacob's
concubine Bilhah. This is an obvious "screw you" to Dad, but Jacob
doesn't protest or chastise. His powers are fading.

Riddle me this: Isaac was blind and near death when Jacob stole the blessing, eight chapters and more than twenty years ago. Yet he does not die until this chapter.

CHAPTER 37

The biggest, nastiest fraternal rivalry of them all: Joseph versus his ten elder brothers in a no-holds-barred battle to the death (or slavery). I forgot or never knew that Joseph is actually a nasty little tattletale. He sends "bad reports" of his brothers to Jacob. Then he lords it over them by telling them his dreams, recounting one in which he and his brothers are sheaves of wheat, and they bow down to him, and another in which they are stars and bow down to him.

Of all people, Jacob should know that favoring one son rips a family apart, but he can't help it. Because Joseph is the first son of his beloved wife Rachel, Jacob singles Joseph out as his darling. He gives Joseph the special present of a "Technicolor dreamcoat" (oh, wait, I mean "ornamented tunic"). Given Joseph's twerpiness and Jacob's favoritism, is it any surprise that the older brothers "could not speak a friendly word" to Joseph? Can you blame them?

So they make a plan. The brothers say to each other, "Here comes that dreamer! Come now, let us kill him and throw him into one of the pits; and we can say, 'A savage beast devoured him.'" Whose idea is the murder? We know the firstborn, Reuben, isn't to blame, because he immediately tries to stop it. The next two brothers in age are Simeon and Levi. Aha! There is an ugliness to those two: they are the villains of Dinah's story, scheming to slaughter Shechem and Hamor. Presumably it's they who seek to murder Joseph, too.

Judah, the fourth-born son, saves Joseph's bacon by suggesting they sell him into slavery instead. "After all," Judah says, "He is our brother, our own flesh." What a line! This is the Genesis philosophy of brotherhood: he's our brother, so let's not kill him—let's just sell him into slavery. (They get twenty pieces of silver for Joseph. Even I know that Judas sells out Jesus for thirty pieces of silver. Another New Testament swipe?)

The brothers smear the tunic in goat's blood and show it to Jacob. This is Jacob's second comeuppance for the trick he played on his own father, Isaac. It's brilliantly parallel—each father is fooled by his own senses. Blind Isaac tasted his son's stew and felt his hairy hands and thus believed he was blessing his beloved Esau. Jacob examines the tunic and sees the blood, and thus believes his beloved Joseph has been killed by wild animals.

CHAPTER 38

Genesis mysteriously interrupts itself, leaving Joseph in a slave caravan, to tell a fascinating story of sexual malfeasance. Judah marries a Canaanite girl, who bears sons named Er and Onan. Er marries Tamar, but Er is "displeasing to the Lord" and dies. Judah orders Onan to do his duty to his dead brother by marrying Tamar and getting her pregnant. Onan, knowing the child would be treated as Er's and not as his own, "let the seed go to waste whenever he joined with his brother's wife." This annoys the Lord, who smites Onan.

Stop right there! Why on earth has Onan's story been read as a condemnation of masturbation? It has nothing to do with masturbation. God smites Onan to punish his crime against a dead brother. Onan has sex with Tamar, but spills his seed. This is coitus interruptus. So Onan's sin, "onanism," is not masturbation, it's birth control.

The story takes an even pervier turn. Now that her husbands, Onan and Er, are dead, Tamar moves back into her father's house. One day, her father-in-law, Judah, walks by. Tamar, who's sitting at the roadside, covers her face with her veil to conceal her identity. Judah assumes she's a whore and asks to sleep with her. She insists that he leave his seal and staff with her, then obliges him (and thus has now slept with every man in the family). Three months later, Judah hears that Tamar had "played the harlot" and is pregnant because of it. With the Near East's usual tolerance for female sexual misbehavior, he orders her burned. Before this can happen, she reveals Judah's staff and seal. He revokes the execution order, but doesn't seem the least bit embarrassed by or ashamed at what he did.

I love the Onan-Tamar-Judah-Er rectangle. It's exciting and smutty. It has given us a wonderful word, "onanism," and a misinterpreted sexual prohibition. Even so, I have no idea what the story is doing in this part of Genesis. Why interrupt the tale of Joseph for this digression?

Biblical literalists will argue from Sunday to Sunday that the Bible is perfectly organized and internally coherent. But reading Genesis 34–38 in one sitting, I get a sneaking suspicion that the book has no plan at all, that it's just a mess. Here's what I mean. From Genesis 34 to 38, we read about, in this order: the rape of Dinah, Simeon and Levi's slaughter of their newly circumcised enemies; Jacob building an altar; Jacob's son Reuben sleeping with his father's concubine; the birth of Benjamin; the death of Isaac; the genealogy of Esau; Joseph feuding with his brothers and being sold into slavery; and the sexual misbehavior of Judah, Tamar, Onan, and Er. How on Earth do these bits connect to each other? How does one lead to the next?

After I finished the whole Bible, I went back and read some biblical theory, because I was so confused by the apparent incoherence. The chaos of these five chapters goes right to the core of the debate about the authorship of the Bible. Most scholars—at least those who aren't literalists—doubt that a book like Genesis was composed by a single writer. Rather, it was written, edited, and redacted by various scribes over hundreds of years. James Kugel, author of *How to Read the Bible*, famously calls the Bible a work of "junk sculpture," meaning that various random bits have been soldered together and thus turned into a new piece of art. The separate stories that make up the Bible had their own individual meanings. But welded together in a "book of Genesis," the stories take on entirely new meanings, because the juxtapositions create significance never intended by the authors.

Professor Jacques Berlinerblau of Georgetown extends Kugel's argument. In a fascinating book, *The Secular Bible*, Berlinerblau contends that all biblical interpretation rests on a false premise of the Bible as a coherent whole. Rather, he says, we must recognize that the book is a pastiche of accidental juxtapositions. Any meaning we ascribe to those juxtapositions is artificial, and was never intended by the author—because, in fact, there was no author, merely a series of editors separated by centuries and often working at cross-purposes. We impose meaning on these disjointed stories to serve our own religious, spiritual, political, or literary purposes, says Berlinerblau, but we're deluding ourselves if we think that our meanings are intended by the book.

Let's apply Kugel and Berlinerblau's reading to these chapters. Scholars sympathetic to the Bible would say that Genesis 34–38 is thematically linked, that it intentionally explores the consequences of sexual misbehavior and highlights the dangers of family conflict. But in fact, this is not even remotely clear on the page, at least as I read it. After all, there are forty-three verses of genealogy chunked into the middle, a birth, a death, the building of an altar, etc. Berlinerblau's view is that these passages were thrown together by the Bible's compilers for reasons we can't possibly know now. We find meaning in them only because humans have an extraordinary capacity for pattern recognition. We are very good at finding artificial order in chaos—*Ah, these chapters are about sexual misbehavior and its consequences*—but it's like seeing pictures in the clouds.

CHAPTER 39

Back to Joseph, who is now enslaved to Potiphar in Egypt, and yet another story about sex. Joseph's encounter with his Egyptian slave-mistress is pure *Desperate Housewives*. Joseph is "well built and handsome"—the Middle Kingdom's version of the cabana boy. Over and over, Potiphar's predatory wife demands, "Lie with me." Over and over, Joseph rebuffs her. He doesn't succumb even when she threatens to frame him for rape. And it's not as if Joseph is being faithful to a nice little wife back home. The kid has no wife—he just has character. The chapter reminds us four times that "the Lord was with Joseph" while he was enslaved. Joseph's willpower, in other words, is rooted in his faith and God's love. So far Genesis has described straight rape, attempted gay rape, father-daughter incest, coitus interruptus with a dead brother's wife, sex with one's own wife, sex with the wrong wife, sex with a concubine, sex with dad's concubine, and sex with a prostitute who is also a daughter-in-law. In any situation in which sex is available, men seize it. What's remarkable about Joseph is that he is the first person to resist sexual temptation. He's the best—or perhaps the only—biblical argument for abstinence-based sex education.

CHAPTERS 40–41

Joseph is a Sammy Glick—always ingratiating himself with powerful men and angling for the next job. He quickly makes himself indispensable to Potiphar and takes charge of Potiphar's house. Then, when the Desperate Pyramid-wife sends him to prison on a trumped-up charge of rape, he immediately becomes the warden's right-hand man. In jail, he's asked to interpret the dreams of two fellow prisoners: Pharaoh's cupbearer and baker. He tells the cupbearer that his dream means he'll be free in three days and back in Pharaoh's favor. And he tells the baker that his dream means he'll be executed in three days.

Both dreams, of course, come true. Two years later, when Pharaoh has dreams his sorcerers can't interpret, the cupbearer remembers Joseph's talent and urges Pharaoh to have him interpret the dreams. Here's what follows:

> *Thereupon Pharaoh sent for Joseph, and he was rushed from the dungeon. He had his hair cut and changed his clothes, and he appeared before Pharaoh.*

He stops for a haircut! What a detail—the touch of a genius, an astounding storyteller. It suspends the story for just a moment. It holds the tension, delays the encounter with the king just long enough to make a reader nervous. And it tells us everything we need to know about Joseph: his attention to his public appearance, his awareness of status, his ambition, his gift for seizing the main chance, and his engagement with the political world as much as the spiritual.

Joseph explains that Pharaoh's dreams of seven fat cows and seven gaunt cows, and seven plump ears of grain and seven shriveled ones, mean Egypt will enjoy seven rich years followed by seven years of famine. With his eye on the brass ring, Joseph says that Pharaoh needs to hire "a man of discernment and wisdom" to coordinate Egypt's homeland security, to store the bounteous crops during the fat years, and to ration the surplus during the lean years. And who, pray tell, is such a man? How about, um, Joseph?

Pharaoh picks Joseph not for his obvious intelligence or moxie, but because he recognizes that Joseph has "the spirit of God" in him. Pharaoh is a polytheist and animal worshipper, but he's a canny enough monarch to appreciate God's power. (This perceptive pharaoh is obviously supposed to be contrasted with the detestable pharaoh to come in Exodus, who is so thick-skulled that it takes ten plagues before he acknowledges the Lord.)

Another incident also suggests Joseph's strength of character: Pharaoh gives Joseph an Egyptian name, "Zaphenath-paneah," and orders him to marry a high-ranking Egyptian girl. But when his two sons are born, Joseph gives them Hebrew names: Ephraim and Manasseh. Joseph hasn't forgotten where he came from, or what God he worships.

CHAPTER 42

Let me digress for a moment about a peculiar subject: Egyptian public policy during Joseph's administration. Joseph is Pharaoh's viceroy during the fat years and the famine. To hear Genesis tell it, he's the best viceroy Egypt has ever seen. But to a modern reader, Joseph is appalling. During the seven fat years, he gathers the entire national grain supply in warehouses. When the famine comes, he sells grain to the hungry Egyptians and to foreign buyers. No problem, so far. But as the famine worsens, Egypt's peasants return to Joseph to beg for help. So Joseph sells them more grain, collecting "all the money that was to be found in the land of Egypt . . . as payment for the rations." The people are still hungry. Joseph again feeds them, but now seizes their horses, sheep, cattle, and donkeys as payment. The famine continues. The Egyptian people, having given their money and livestock to Pharaoh, come back to Joseph once more. This time, Joseph demands all their land in exchange for grain: "Thus the land passed over to Pharaoh." Joseph explains the new deal to them: they will be sharecroppers, and will hand over one-fifth of their harvest every year to Pharaoh, keeping the balance for themselves. They reply, "We are grateful to my lord, and we shall be serfs to Pharaoh."

So our hero Joseph abolishes private property, turns freeholders into serfs, and transforms a decentralized farm economy into a command-economy dictatorship. This is bad economics and worse public policy. This is China in 1949. Joseph is Chairman Mao. If you want to speculate, you could even argue that the centralized dictatorship established by Joseph is what made possible the Israelites' enslavement in Egypt. Once you create a gargantuan, voracious state apparatus, it must be fed. Is it a surprise that slavery became part of its diet? In a less totalitarian state, perhaps slavery wouldn't have been as necessary or as feasible. *This digression has been brought to you by the American Enterprise Institute.*

CHAPTERS 42–46

But that's the last bad word I'll have to say about Joseph. On to Joseph's reconciliation with his family, which is a four-chapter rush, and the first fully persuasive story in Genesis. Unlike a lot of the other stories, it always makes sense: the plot is clear; the characters behave in complicated, recognizably human ways; and it's hugely suspenseful.

A summary: Facing famine in Canaan, Jacob dispatches all his sons except his beloved Benjamin to Egypt to buy grain. They call on the vizier, Joseph, to beg for help. They don't recognize Joseph, but he recognizes them. Testing his brothers, he calls them spies and demands that one stay as a hostage until they return with their youngest brother. Inexplicably—since they don't recognize him—the brothers realize that this is the payback for their cruelty to Joseph: "Alas, we are being punished on account of our brother, because we looked on at his anguish, yet paid no heed as he pleaded with us." Joseph overhears them and *weeps* (1) privately. They depart with grain, and Joseph takes Simeon as his hostage. At home, Jacob refuses to let Benjamin return to Egypt, even after Reuben offers Jacob his own two sons as a sacrifice if Benjamin is hurt. (You need a flowchart to follow it: One son, Reuben, offering two grandsons so he can take another son, Benjamin, back to ransom yet another son, Simeon, all at the behest of still another, missing son, Joseph.) Finally, the famine is so severe that Jacob agrees to dispatch Benjamin to Egypt. When Joseph sees his younger brother, he again *weeps* (2) privately. He sells the brothers more grain, but plants a silver goblet in Benjamin's sack. Then he sends his servants to search the brothers and arrest them for theft. He demands that whoever stole the cup serve as his slave. When it turns up in Benjamin's bag, the brothers prostrate themselves before Joseph (as in his dream). Judah pleads eloquently for Joseph to spare Benjamin, saying that enslaving him would kill their father. Judah implores Joseph to take him as a slave instead. Finally Joseph, "who could no longer control himself," reveals himself to his brothers. Joseph *weeps* (3) again. "His sobs were so loud that the Egyptians [in other rooms] could hear." Then Joseph forgives them sweetly and wholly.

He sends the brothers back to Jacob, but not before throwing his arms around Benjamin and *weeping* (4) one more time. Jacob and all his sons and their families—seventy people in all, not counting wives or daughters, as, of course, the Bible doesn't—move to Egypt. Joseph meets them along the way, embraces his father, and *weeps* (5) "on his neck a good while." Then they settle in Egypt with Pharaoh's blessing and prosper.

The beauty in this story, beyond its basic happy ending—brothers redeemed, father at peace, etc.—is the heart of Joseph. Even as he tricks his brothers and makes them suffer, he is anguished. His tears signify goodness rather than weakness. He forgives his brothers for the terrible wrong they did him, because he knows his enslavement was all part of God's plan.

Do not be distressed or reproach yourselves that you sold me hither;
it was to save life that God sent me ahead of you. . . . God has sent

*me ahead of you to ensure your survival on earth, and to save your
lives in an extraordinary deliverance. So it was not you who sent
me here, but God.*

For me, Joseph is the most persuasive argument in Genesis for faith.
His consistent belief in the Lord, even through slavery and prison, car-
ries him forward. This faith doesn't merely make him great and powerful. It also makes him good. It makes him able to weep, and weep,
and weep some more, and forgive.

I also favor Joseph because he doesn't require any divine intervention. No miracles occur in the making of this patriarch. It's a story of
human achievement. Joseph does right, perhaps because he believes in
God—or perhaps because he is an inherently good man. God sends
Joseph symbolic dreams, but He never talks directly to Joseph, as He
did to Abraham, Isaac, and Jacob. Joseph's faith is our modern kind, a
faith in the unseen. Joseph is in the same position that we—assuming
you are as vision-free as I am—find ourselves in, trying to live faith-
fully with God in the background.

CHAPTERS 48–50

Jacob can't stop his old tricks. On his deathbed in Egypt, he decides to
adopt Joseph's sons Ephraim and Manasseh as his own. Jacob intentionally places his right hand on the younger son, Ephraim; and his
left hand on the older son, Manasseh. Joseph tries to switch the hands—
"Not so, Father . . . for the other is the first-born; place your right
hand upon his head." But Jacob refuses. He says Ephraim deserves the
greater, right-handed blessing, because Ephraim will be the greater
man. Even in death, Jacob has to wheedle and play favorites.

I happen to reach this passage shortly after Hanna and I decide to
start holding a family Shabbat dinner. I don't know if we are doing this
because I'm reading the Bible, or because it seems like a nice ritual,
or because Hanna found a good recipe for challah, but whatever the
reason we are trying to keep a regular date with our Shabbat candles
on Friday night. To be honest, it's all mumbo jumbo to me—lighting

candles, drinking wine, blessing bread, accompanied by incomprehensible Hebrew prayers—pleasant rituals, but meaningless. But when I read about the blessing of Ephraim and Manasseh, it clicks for me. On Shabbat, one of my duties is to bless our children. I put my hand on my Jacob's head (usually my *left* hand, since I am left-handed), and recite the prayer, which—I suddenly notice—is for God to make Jacob like Ephraim and Manasseh.

Till now, I didn't know who Ephraim and Manasseh were, or why I should bless my son in their name. But here it is, right in Genesis. I am following Jacob's own instructions: "By you shall Israel invoke blessings, saying: God make you like Ephraim and Manasseh." It's unsettling, in a good way, to find that the very words I am speaking to my son are those that my fathers and forefathers have been speaking to their sons on Friday night for 3,000 years. For almost the first time in my life, I feel a sense of continuity with my ancestors. I understand that I am heir to an ancient tradition, and am responsible for preserving it.

Yet even in this lovely tradition, the Bible compels ambivalence. In speaking the biblical blessing of Ephraim and Manasseh, I'm honoring the scheming of Jacob. And that's not the only thing troubling me as I finish Genesis. I began reading Genesis as a do-nothing Jew who believed in God. But as I have been reading, I find myself turning into the opposite, practicing my Judaism but doubting in God. The God of Genesis is capricious, unreasonable, and cruel: why should I want to believe in Him? It's a strange internal battle, and I don't know which side is going to win.

Jacob summons his sons to his deathbed for their blessing. We learn he has been paying very close attention. He strips Reuben of the rank of firstborn, because Reuben slept with Jacob's concubine—an incident that Jacob never mentioned when it happened. "For when you mounted your father's bed, you brought disgrace!" The next two sons, Simeon and Levi, were the murderers of Shechem's family—an incident Jacob made little of at the time. But now, he casts them out, condemning their tribes to subservience and weakness: "Cursed be their anger so fierce, and their wrath so relentless." The fourth son,

Judah—the stand-up guy who offered himself as a slave in Benjamin's place—is called the "lion" by Jacob and blessed with authority over the others. The other brothers are dealt with more cursorily, but there are lots of great animal metaphors: Dan is a "serpent by the road." Issachar is a "strong-boned ass." Benjamin is a "ravenous wolf." It's pretty obvious that these paternal blessings are a way of explaining the status of each of the tribes at the time Genesis was written. Because the tribe of Judah was supreme in Israel, Jacob's blessing elevates Judah. The tribes of Simeon and Levi were a mess, so Genesis explains this with Jacob's curse. Jacob and Joseph die, and that's the end of Genesis.

The Book of Exodus

Let My Complaining, Whining, No-Goodnik People Go!

In which the Israelites multiply in Egypt; Pharaoh enslaves them and then orders the slaughter of all firstborn Israelite boys; his own daughter saves one such boy, Moses, who flees Egypt after killing an Egyptian; God brings Moses to a burning bush, and orders him and his brother, Aaron, to free the Israelites; Pharaoh rebuffs Moses's demands, so God sends ten plagues, including the slaying of Egyptian firstborn males; finally the Israelites are allowed to leave and cross the Red Sea while Moses holds back the water; Pharaoh's army pursues them but drowns; God feeds the Israelites manna in the desert; they walk to Mount Sinai, where God issues laws and the Ten Commandments to Moses; the Israelites make a golden calf, which infuriates God; the Israelites build a tabernacle to carry the holy ark containing God's laws.

CHAPTER I

Jacob's descendants have multiplied and prospered in Egypt, "and the land [is] filled with them." The new pharaoh is alarmed at the population explosion and has "oppressed them with forced labor." Oddly, my translation never describes the Israelites as "slaves." Hmm. Maybe it's a peculiarity of the translation. Or maybe not. The Israelites do perform forced labor for Pharaoh, and they have Egyptian taskmasters who have "ruthlessly imposed" on them. But they don't seem to be owned by Egyptians. There appear to be limits on their maltreatment: they are compelled to supply labor, but there's no mention of their being deprived of property or banned from other work. None of this minimizes their suffering. I'm just struck by the absence of that word "slave," which is thrown about so casually everywhere else in the Bible (and which we repeat endlessly at the Passover seder: "We were slaves in Egypt . . .").

The Israelites keep multiplying, so Pharaoh orders Hebrew midwives to kill all boys born to Hebrew women. It doesn't work: two heroic midwives—Shifra and Puah—disregard the order. (These two are nearly the only working women in the whole Bible—at least the only working women who aren't prostitutes.) Increasingly panicked, Pharaoh demands that all newborn Hebrew boys be thrown into the Nile. Bad move. God is keen on tit for tat: in the Bible, when you do a wrong the very same wrong is often visited on you later. Joseph's brothers sell him into slavery in Egypt, and their descendants end up in bondage (or whatever) to Pharaoh. Pharaoh tries to kill the Hebrew firstborns, but in a few chapters, it will be the Egyptian firstborns who die. It's divine retribution, or, to use a catchier modern term, karma.

CHAPTER 2

I don't know where the Disneyfied idea about Moses, Prince of Egypt, comes from, but it certainly isn't in the Bible. Exodus has only the sketchiest details about Young Moses. The baby is floated down the Nile in a wicker basket and is rescued by Pharaoh's daughter. The princess then pays Moses's own mother to raise him. That's it. The story jumps immediately from the baby's rescue to Moses as an adult. There's not a word about Moses as an Egyptian prince. Pharaoh's daughter is not mentioned again, much less described as his mother. Moses never races a chariot, Heston-like, with Pharaoh's sons, or woos the almond-eyed princess Nefertiti, or marshals the Egyptian army, or competes for the double crown. Is Prince Moses just a modern confection, manufactured to lend some glamour to the story of Exodus?

Unlike greedy young Abraham, boring young Isaac, deceitful young Jacob, and proud young Joseph, Moses is born ready to do God's work. From the beginning, he stands up for justice and the little guy. His first recorded act (not including being plucked from the river) is murdering an Egyptian who was beating a Hebrew worker. Fleeing Egypt to escape Pharaoh's retribution, Moses continues crusading for justice. As soon as he arrives in Midian, he routs some obnoxious shepherds who are preventing a young woman from watering her flocks. Then he marries her. Her name is Zipporah, which clears up a family mystery. My Israeli father-in-law, who has a terrible memory for names, calls all men Moishe (Moses) and all women Zipporah. I always thought they were just common Israeli nicknames. Now I get the biblical joke.

Meanwhile, back in Egypt, the Israelites' "cry for help from the bondage rose up to God. God heard their moaning, and God remembered His covenant. . . . God looked upon the Israelites, and God took notice of them."

Well, thanks, Lord, but what took you so long? What were you doing during our four bad centuries on the Nile delta? At the beginning of Genesis, God was a hands-on Sovereign of the Universe—fashioning man from dirt, wandering through Eden in search of Adam, sniffing thoughtfully at Noah's burnt offerings, dropping by Abraham's tent to discuss Sodom and Gomorrah. But as Genesis progressed, He was increasingly an absent father. He never appeared to Joseph, and now He has left the Israelites sweating in Thebes for hundreds of years. I know He's a busy deity, what with all those galaxies to manage, but how come He didn't have time to check up on His Chosen People for twenty generations?

CHAPTERS 3–4

Now that God has finally decided to pay attention, He really pays attention. He throws up a burning bush to stop Moses in his tracks, then calls out to him, "Moses, Moses." Moses answers, "Here I am."

(This exchange—the repeated name, followed by "Here I am"—exactly duplicates the conversation between Abraham and God when the Lord stopped the sacrifice of Isaac.)

The episode of the burning bush is both high drama and low comedy. On the one hand, it is a profound encounter between a man and his maker. At the same time, it feels like nothing so much as a discussion between an enthusiastic father and his extremely sullen teenage son. God tries so hard with Moses, and Moses just brushes Him off. The Lord begins with a straightforward attempt to persuade Moses to help Him. He outlines the whole big story for Moses: *My people are suffering, I have heard them, I am going to rescue them and bring them to a land "flowing with milk and honey."* Then He says, rather gently, that He wants to send Moses to negotiate the Israelites' release. But—the gall of this young prophet!—Moses resists, "Who am I that I should go to Pharaoh?"

So God gets a little more insistent: "I will be with you." This isn't good enough for the lawyerly Moses, who now wonders what he should tell the Israelites about who sent him. "They ask me, 'What is His name?' What shall I say to them?" God, moving into thunder-and-lightning mode, declares, "Ehyeh-Asher-Ehyeh," which is usually translated, Popeye-like, as "I am that I am." Clearly getting peeved at Moses's hesitation, God repeats the whole exhortation, even more emphatically, "I have declared: I will take you out of the misery of Egypt to . . . a land flowing with milk and honey," etc.

But does this satisfy Moses? Of course not. He complains: "What if they do not believe me and do not listen to me?" So God tries the David Blaine method, turning Moses's rod into a snake and causing white scales to appear and disappear on Moses's hand. Moses, changing tactics, now moans that he can't go because he's a poor speaker, "slow of speech and slow of tongue." If any other human being bedeviled him so, God would have given him a smiting and found a substitute, but He merely rebukes Moses: "Who gives a man speech? . . . Is it not I, the Lord?" This still doesn't deter the vexatious prophet. (If he lived today, this is the point when Moses would be showing God two doctors' notes diagnosing chronic fatigue syndrome.) Moses groans, "Please, O Lord, make someone else Your agent." After all this whining and rebuffing, the Lord has had enough: He finally becomes "angry with Moses," and Moses agrees to do his bidding.

But here's the key point: Moses gets what he wants. At Moses's urging, God appoints Moses's brother, Aaron, to speak for him. Moses's back talk actually endears him to the Lord, just as Abraham's sass about Sodom and Gomorrah impressed Him. The Lord has no use for lumpish yes-men. His truest favorites so far—Abraham and Moses, as well as Jacob and Joseph—don't back down from Him. At the bush, Moses is incredibly, maddeningly frustrating. But he also asks all the right questions about his mission; he plans for every contingency; and he negotiates a better deal for himself. That's the kind of prophet I want on my team.

Back to Egypt: Aaron and Moses pay a visit to Pharaoh, and at first request merely that he allow the Israelites a few days off for a camp meeting in the wilderness. When the negotiations falter, Moses and Aaron increase their demands, eventually insisting that Pharaoh liberate the Israelites. As Pharaoh resists, Moses begins inflicting plagues on the Egyptians.

Curiously, the most compelling characters in the drama of the plagues are not Moses, Aaron, or Pharaoh, but Pharaoh's anonymous sorcerers. I am fascinated by these guys. We are introduced to them when Moses and Aaron first visit Pharaoh. To impress Pharaoh, Aaron throws down his rod and it turns into a snake. The cocky sorcerers toss down their rods, which turn into snakes, too. But then Aaron's snake gobbles theirs up. God 1, Sorcerers 0.

The sorcerers, of course, don't learn their lesson. Aaron and Moses begin delivering plagues, and the sorcerers keep thinking they can trump God. When Moses and Aaron turn the Nile to blood, the sorcerers do "the same with their spells." Aaron and Moses cover Egypt with frogs. The sorcerers do "the same with their spells." Moses and Aaron bring lice. But the sorcerers, their powers waning, can't conjure up lice. (That's really lame. Even I could conjure up lice: I would just drop by my daughter's first-grade classroom and rub a few heads.) A couple of plagues later, the sorcerers' defeat is total. Moses afflicts the

Egyptians with boils. The sorcerers, summoned to work their counter-magic, don't even show up: they can't, because they're covered with boils. The increasing feebleness of their dark arts makes for great black comedy—and hilariously effective testimony for God's power. The sorcerers are the gangster's dumb sidekicks, they're Hitler's generals, they're the cringing flunkies who do every tyrant's dirty work, and it's wonderful to see them meet the deserved misfortune of flunkies everywhere.

Except for the trouncing of the sorcerers, however, the plagues don't speak well for God. In fact, this is the most disturbing story in the Bible so far—even more troubling than the Flood. The ten plagues basically go like this. Moses and Aaron unleash a plague. Pharaoh promises to let the Israelites go if God will lift the plague. The plague ceases, and Pharaoh immediately reneges, so that another plague is unleashed. The mystery, of course, is: why does Pharaoh renege? Exodus tells us the answer: he reneges because God has "stiffened his heart."

Why would God keep hardening Pharaoh's heart so that He can inflict yet another monstrous plague? Why would God prolong the Egyptians' suffering? God tells us why. Listen carefully:

> For I have hardened his heart . . . in order that I may display these My signs among them, and that you may recount in the hearing of your sons and your sons' sons how I made a mockery of the Egyptians and how I displayed My signs among them—in order that you may know I am the Lord.

In other words, God is causing the plagues *so that we can tell stories about the plagues.* He's torturing the Egyptians so that we will worship Him. What kind of insecure and cruel God murders children so that His followers will obey Him, and will tell stories about Him? This is the behavior of a serial killer. (Also, how about that euphemism "displayed My signs"? You call them "signs"; I call them "plagues.") Yes, Pharaoh is a monster, and the Egyptians are brutal taskmasters. They deserve to be punished. But what's upsetting is that God takes delight in their suffering. He even performs the last and worst plague—the slaying of the firstborn—Himself. He wants the plagues to persist and worsen, so that we will tell stories about them. And lo and behold, 3,500 years later, that's exactly what we do every Passover.

CHAPTER 14

How stupid is Pharaoh? Egypt has been pummeled by frogs, vermin, lice, cattle disease, hail, and other plagues; it has lost all its firstborn males (the plague that finally leads to freedom for the Israelites); its gods are manifestly impotent against the wrath of our God. But that doesn't deter the idiotic monarch from pursuing the Israelites across the Red Sea.

(I just used my Bible to smash a bug on my desk. That's bad, isn't it?)

The crossing of the Red Sea was the Torah passage I recited at my bar mitzvah, back in 1983, so once upon a time I could even read this story in Hebrew. All I can remember now is that my bar mitzvah speech concerned the geographical debate over the actual location of the Red Sea. I studied maps showing potential crossing routes, and felt very proud at my daring choice of subject. (Twenty-five years later, I feel slightly dopey, since most scholars now agree that there was no exodus from Egypt, because the Israelites were never there.)

As I was poring over the maps, my thirteen-year-old self missed the real drama of this chapter: God's ongoing desire to exalt Himself through murder. Before the Egyptians are drowned in the sea, God tells Moses exactly what He is going to do. Moses will part the sea with his rod, and the Israelites will walk through. Then God will "stiffen the hearts" of the Egyptians so that they pursue, and God will drown them. God says, "I will gain glory through Pharaoh and all his warriors, his chariots and his horsemen." Or, to put it more truthfully: "I will gain glory through *killing* Pharaoh and all his warriors, his chariots and his horsemen." The moral problem isn't that God drowns the Egyptians. The Egyptians are wicked, and war is ugly. The problem is that God enjoys it.

CHAPTERS 15–17

A woman! There's a woman! For the first time in ages a living, breathing female appears. Moses's sister "Miriam the prophetess" leads the celebratory singing and dancing when the Israelites cross the sea. Thank goodness for a woman who's not trying to cuckold her husband, defraud her son, or scam the king; a woman who's not merely a wife to be mentioned in passing or a daughter tacked onto the end of a long list of sons.

Moses leads the Israelites into the wilderness. It's day one of their forty-year trek, and yet they're already complaining that they're thirsty and the only available water is bitter. We're a grumbling people, aren't we? Freedom after 430 years of captivity, and nothing to do but grouse. When the Egyptian army pursued them, the Israelites griped that they would rather have stayed slaves in Egypt than die by the sea. Now they're fussing that they're thirsty. God gives Moses a piece of wood that cleans up the water—the world's first Brita filter. Then the Lord reminds them that they're His Chosen People, and if they follow His laws and behave, they will be free of all the diseases that plagued the Egyptians. This is a resonant moment: His people suffering, God helps them, and lets them know that He will always be there for them.

But does that stop the Israelites from bellyaching? Nope. Just a few verses later they're complaining of hunger and chastising Moses for taking them out of Egypt, where at least they had plenty to eat. Again, God delivers, supplying manna to feed them, and even a double portion on Friday so they don't need to collect on the Sabbath. When a few of the Israelites try to gather manna on Saturday anyway, God explodes at Moses: "How long will you men refuse to obey My commandments and My teachings?"

But the Lord keeps delivering the manna. This gets at the central drama of Exodus. God, who hasn't hesitated to rub out other doubters, idolaters, and sinners (Sodomites, Lot's wife, Pharaoh, etc.), is patient with the Israelites, and tolerant of their distrust. Over and over, God tries to persuade His obstinate, suspicious, doubting Chosen People to put their faith in Him. Over and over they disappoint Him, but He tries again. God's understanding of human weakness and His persistent hope that we can overcome it are a powerful argument for faith.

CHAPTER 18

A fantastic chapter masquerading as a boring one. Moses's father-in-law Jethro watches Moses at work and sees that he wastes all day settling petty disputes. (He's the Jimmy Carter of prophets.) Appalled by the drain on Moses's time and energy, Jethro sits Moses down and tells him he can't do everything by himself. Jethro advises that he must deal only with the big things—issuing laws and ruling on the largest disputes. All minor matters should be resolved by magistrates selected by Moses. These judges, Jethro advises, should be capable, God-fearing, and incorruptible. Jethro proposes several layers of judges: some to preside over small groups of people, and others for groups of thousands. Jethro, in short, designs the first judicial system, and it's a superb one. It's largely independent; it's well-organized; it has clear lines of authority and even an appellate system. Is it any wonder that Jews are the world's great lawyers?

CHAPTER 20

The Ten Commandments. Or at least I think it's the Ten Commandments. I came up with nine, ten, and eleven commandments, depending on how I counted the first few verses. Does "You shall not make yourself a sculptured image. . . . You shall not bow down to them or serve them" count as one commandment (no graven images) or two? And are those instructions themselves merely a subset of the First Commandment "You shall have no other gods besides Me"? By counting the combination of no "sculptured image" and no bowing down as a single commandment and counting "no other gods" as a separate one, I managed to get ten.

Forgive me for being 3,000 years late in noticing this, but the commandments, the last six in particular (honor your parents, don't murder, don't commit adultery, don't steal, don't bear false witness, don't covet) pretty much cover the basic rules for a functioning society. What is more striking is what the commandments are *not*. In the popular mind, the Ten Commandments are a guide for moral living, rules that teach us how to be good. But they don't. They teach nothing about morality. The commandments are designed for keeping *order*. They concern how we act toward each other so that society functions. They don't try to create goodness. Except for "Remember the Sabbath" and "Honor thy father and mother," they don't tell us what we should do; they tell us only what we *mustn't* do.

I'm confused by the first two commandments, because they appear to acknowledge the existence of other gods. "You shall have no other gods besides Me" and "You shall not bow down to them or serve them." For a book that supposedly invented monotheism, the Bible sure has a lot of other gods. Did the Israelites believe that Baal & Co. were genuine supernatural beings but were second-raters and charlatans compared with the Lord? Or did they think these other gods were just figments, delusions imagined by the stupid Philistines and Amalekites? To ask it another way: Were the Israelites polytheists who believed their God trumped all the others? Or were they monotheists who thought all the other gods were imaginary? Exodus is not clear on this, but as I read the book, especially the commandments, they seem to be polytheists who thought they had picked the top god.

In a way, you might say that the book of Exodus is the story of how the Israelites discovered monotheism. After a 430-year breakup, God and His people are finally back together. They've committed to each other. They've moved in together: God is literally traveling with them. It's like a marriage. They have finally agreed to stop seeing other people (or gods) and be faithful to just one.

When He's commanding against idolatry, God says: "For I the Lord your God am an impassioned God"—other translations have the more vivid "jealous God"—"visiting the guilt of the parents upon the children, upon the third and upon the fourth generations of those who reject Me, but showing kindness to the thousandth generation of those who love Me and keep My commandments." Let's ignore the paradox of this, i.e., if I keep the commandments but my children don't, shouldn't they be protected by that thousandth-generation rule? What I am struck by is God visiting the guilt of the parents on the children. It's obvious why God would threaten it: there is no better way to discourage straying from the fold than instilling the fear that such straying will destroy your own children. Even so, this seems pretty unfair. I had always thought that we all get our own clean slate, a life that we can make or ruin on our own. It's alarming to think that we may not, that God is holding my sins against Jacob and Noa, and my parents' sins against me. (I wonder if my parents kept any false gods at home that they never told me about. I hope not.)

CHAPTERS 21–22

The fun part of the Bible skids to a halt, and the Lord gets down to the dreary business of governing. It's like that scene at the end of *The Candidate*, when Robert Redford, having finally won the election, says, "What do we do now?" Freed after 430 years, the Israelites have their "What do we do now?" moment. Up to this point, the Bible has been a cracking good adventure story, a Judean Robert Ludlum. Now it turns into a how-to manual. This isn't to say there aren't great tales to come—there's that golden calf—but I suspect they'll be more sporadic. This also isn't to say that the rest of Exodus is boring. It isn't. But it's a different kind of read.

The Ten Commandments are God's constitution—concise, magnificent, beautifully written, but a bit stronger on the ideals than the practicalities. So now God follows up with the detailed laws and regulations needed to enforce the commandments in daily life. Thou shalt not kill—that's pretty clear. But what happens if someone does kill? What if someone kills accidentally? What if someone kills a cow? Or a fetus? You see how this can get pretty complicated pretty quickly.

So, how does the Lord begin? With slavery, of course—verse after verse about how long a Hebrew slave must serve his master, who owns a slave's wife and children, what happens to a girl whose father sells her into slavery, and so forth. I know, I know: our modern ideas about slavery don't apply. This was an ancient, tribal culture; slavery didn't mean the same thing back then; the Israelites were practically abolitionists by the standards of the time; etc. Even so, isn't it disheartening that slavery is so central to God and His people that His laws address it first?

Once we finish with slavery, it becomes clear that God is a hanging judge. His punishment for intentional killing is death. Punishment for kidnapping: death. Punishment for idolatry: death. Punishment for striking a parent: death. Punishment for insulting a parent: death. (Hmm. Not sure I agree with that one—though it would cut down on the temper tantrums.) Punishment for bestiality: death. On the other hand, if you seduce a virgin, you only have to pay off her family. I don't understand how modern liberal Catholics, Jews, and Protestants can use the Bible to justify their opposition to capital punishment. If there is one thing God truly believes in, it's a good old firing squad.

These laws reveal more about the daily lives and concerns of our ancestors than the plot-heavy biblical stories. The laws depict the Israelites as obsessed with property rights and particularly focused on the health of their livestock, on which their economic prosperity depended. ("If someone's ox hurts the ox of another, so that it dies, then they shall sell the live ox and divide the price of it; and the dead animal they shall also divide.") The specificity of the rules also indicates a very law-abiding, and thus orderly, society—one in which law insulated people against arbitrary power.

Exodus 21, verse 22 is a law with some tricky modern implications. If a man pushes a pregnant woman and she miscarries, but is not otherwise hurt, then the offender only pays a fine to the victim's husband. So according to Exodus, killing this fetus is merely a property crime requiring only financial compensation, *not* a murder. If you're pro-choice, this might seem to prove that the Bible considers abortion a categorically different kind of deed from murder. But of course it's not that simple: pro-life and pro-choice groups roundly disagree about how to translate the verse. Pro-choicers read it in the way I just described. Pro-lifers insist that it's referring not to "miscarriage" (the word in my translation), but to a premature birth in which the infant survives.

CHAPTER 23

The chapter opens with probably the best paragraph I've ever read about justice:

> *You must not carry false rumors; you shall not join hands with the guilty to act as a malicious witness: You shall neither side with the mighty to do wrong—you shall not give perverse testimony in a dispute so as to pervert it in favor of the mighty—nor shall you show deference to a poor man in a dispute.*

Judges should sew this passage into their robes.

Later in the chapter, after a bunch of ceremonial laws, comes this: "You shall not boil a kid in its mother's milk." Every Jew who has been denied the ineffable joy of the cheeseburger should gaze upon this sentence and weep. As any observant Jew will tell you, modern Jews are not biblical Jews; we are rabbinic Jews. In other words, modern Jewish practice is based on the rabbis' traditional interpretations of scripture, rather than the actual words of the Bible. The law says only: *No boiling a baby goat in its own mother's milk.* But after centuries of rabbinic debate and the Rube Goldberg mechanism of Jewish legal interpretation, this little acorn has grown into a giant oak of dietary restrictions: separate meat and dairy restaurants, multiple sets of household china, elaborate (and ferociously argued) rules about how long a child has to wait to have an ice cream cone after having eaten a hot dog (Hebrew National, of course). I understand how relying on rabbinic interpretation rather than the literal words of the scripture can insulate us from draconian biblical laws, but it does seem silly in this case. God is concerned only about baby goats. Why should this mean that little Sammy can't eat a steak-and-cheese sandwich?

CHAPTER 24

The events in the Bible that are most shocking are often not miracles or high drama—floods, plagues, incest—but moments of everyday ritual. Here's one that jarred me. After writing down God's laws and reading them to the Israelites, Moses decides to reinforce the statutes with a sacrifice. The Israelites kill some bulls, and then Moses takes the animal blood and flings it onto the people, declaring, "This is the blood of the covenant that the Lord now makes with you concerning all these commands." Because the Bible is populated with characters who sometimes behave as we would, it's easy to forget that they had a primitive, tribal, nomadic culture. This is about as old school as it gets—the prophet showering his flock with bull's blood to guarantee God's promise.

Moses ends up spending forty days on Mount Sinai receiving the laws from God. Noah had forty days of rain. The Israelites wander forty years in the desert. (And doesn't Jesus pass forty days in the wilderness?) What's with forty? I understand seven as a magical number. Seven is small. Seven is indivisible. Seven days to make the world and rest. Seven times around Jericho till the walls fell. Seven brides for seven brothers. But forty has neither the mystical solidity of a prime number nor the satisfactory roundness of a number like 100. Forty is middle-aged. Forty is just—clumsy.

CHAPTERS 25–31

God: the first interior decorator. He issues incredibly detailed instructions about how to build His tabernacle. He has opinions about everything from the almond-blossom-shaped cups on the gold lamp stand to the silver sockets in each of the tabernacle's planks to the exact posture of the cherubim on the ark's cover: "The cherubim shall have their wings spread out above, shielding the cover with their wings. They shall confront each other." At one point God even brings out samples of lamps for Moses to examine, telling his prophet: "Follow the patterns for them that are being shown you on the mountain." He's a pretty mean fashion designer too: in a chapter devoted to the high priest's costume, God pays as much attention to the stitching as any contestant on *Project Runway*. Listen to how He describes the embroidery on a single garment: "A golden bell and a pomegranate, a golden bell and a pomegranate, all around the hem of the robe." The divine aesthetic presents us with a profound theological question: if God takes fashion and interior design so seriously, why are all synagogues so incredibly ugly? Discuss.

As I slog through these chapters about tabernacle design, I find myself asking: what's the point? Cain and Abel rated just a few verses. Why does it take twice as long merely to describe the clasps on the tabernacle's cloth sides? I assume there are a couple of reasons for this. The first is that the author of Exodus, like any good reporter, wrote what he knew. He presumably saw the tabernacle, or some descendant of it, and could write about it with exactitude. The second is that building and preserving the tabernacle were the most important tasks in the world for the Israelites. The tabernacle was literally where God visited them. As God tells Moses: "For there I will meet with you, and there I will speak with you, and there I will meet with the Israelites, and it shall be sanctified by my presence. . . . I will abide among the Israelites, and I will be their God."

I would be lying if I didn't admit that these chapters are coma-inducingly dull—like a very long, ill-written furniture assembly manual. But they also have a practical consequence for the Israelites that the story of Cain and Abel didn't. There was no more important job for them than getting that tabernacle right, making sure it was perfect so that God kept "abiding" among them. These chapters were how they stored the knowledge of the tabernacle for their heirs—for us.

CHAPTER 32

Moses is still up on Mount Sinai, transcribing God's architectural tips. Meanwhile, back at camp, the Israelites are getting restless. Tired of waiting for Moses, they demand that Aaron "make us a god." Aaron, displaying all the willpower of feckless brothers everywhere, immediately agrees and casts a golden calf for them. The Israelites bow down to it and declare, "This is your god, O Israel, who brought you out of the land of Egypt." Aaron builds an altar to the calf and declares a festival for feasting and dancing. Moses descends from the mountain, sees the party, and explodes. He shatters the stone tablets of God's laws. Then he burns the calf, grinds the ashes into powder, tosses the powder into water, and makes the Israelites drink the rank liquid. (This is a neat reversal of Moses's aquatic rescues earlier in Exodus, when he turned bitter water sweet.) Moses begins to chastise his brother, but Aaron, typically spineless, shrugs the blame off on the masses: "Let not my lord be enraged. You know that this people is bent on evil." Moses, possibly realizing that any more discussion with such a worm is pointless, doesn't press Aaron further. (The episode of the golden calf reminds me powerfully of the scene in *The Godfather* when worthless brother Fredo Corleone lays on the champagne and hookers for Michael in Las Vegas. Michael, who's in town to make a deal, sends the party away and rebukes his older brother. Aaron is the Fredo of Judea.)

Moses is furious with his people, but he also knows he must protect them from God, who's in a "kill 'em all, let Me sort 'em out" mood. God announces that He's going to destroy His "stiffnecked people" because of the calf. Moses gets wily. He cannily exploits the Lord's distaste for the Egyptians, telling God, "Let not the Egyptians say, 'It was with evil intent that He delivered them, only to kill them off in the mountains and annihilate them from the face of the earth.' Turn from Your blazing anger, and renounce the plan to punish Your people." Moses persuades the Lord to hold His fire. To appease Him, Moses has the Levites, the only tribe that remained loyal during the debacle of the calf, execute 3,000 idolaters, "brother, neighbor, and kin." (But what happens to Moses's own brother, the ringleader? Nothing. Aaron doesn't even get his wrist slapped.)

So the Israelites are saved again by God's mercy. Still, I can't help thinking that the *political* lesson of the golden calf is deeply disturbing. The story suggests that without an authoritarian leader like Moses, the Israelites will easily abandon God. Without a prophet and a dictator, our faith will fail.

CHAPTER 33

God keeps seething about the golden calf. He won't appear among the Israelites, because He knows He wouldn't be able to control His rage: "If I were to go in your midst for one moment, I would destroy you." To humble the Israelites more, God orders them to strip off their "finery." They must remain dressed simply for the rest of their desert exile, as a penance. This reminds me of an interesting divide in religious practice. In some religions, you honor God by dressing as sumptuously as you can for him. (See: rococo papal outfits or the florid church hats worn by African-American women.) In other religions, you honor God by dressing down. (See the nearly naked Hindu sadhus or monks in hair shirts.) Being either gaudy or humble seems to work fine. What hasn't caught on with the godly class—at least not till the rise of the mega-church—is business casual. Has a Franciscan ever gone to Mass in Dockers? Would you trust a rabbi in an Izod?

A funny, sweet incident occurs late in Exodus 33. As usual, Moses is begging God to be merciful to the wretched Israelites. God isn't interested. Instead, He changes the subject. Ignoring Moses's entreaties for the Israelites, God distracts the prophet by saying He wants to grant Moses's wish that he be allowed to see God. God says He can't let Moses see His face, because "man may not see Me and live." God has Moses stand in a rock crevice. God then carefully arranges Himself so Moses can see only His back. Or, to put it another way, God moons Moses.

CHAPTER 34

Moses climbs Sinai again to collect a pair of stone tablets to replace the ones he smashed at the golden-calf orgy. While he's up there, God comes to him and proclaims of Himself: "The Lord! The Lord! A God compassionate and gracious, slow to anger, abounding in kindness and faithfulness." Now, I don't want to quibble here, but does this sound like the God we've been reading about? Would you describe the God of Genesis and Exodus as *gracious*? As *abounding in kindness and faithfulness*? As *slow to anger*? After all, He flies off the handle before the Flood, is fairly merciless to Sodom and Gomorrah, and hardly abounds in kindness toward the Egyptians. He leaves the Israelites in bondage for 430 years, and has to be restrained by Moses from wiping out His Chosen People after they worship the golden calf. He's got lots of wonderful qualities—He's tough, clever, excitable, awesome, and forgiving—but not the ones He ascribes to Himself.

At this point, the Bible issues its first proscription against inter-marriage. God warns the Israelites against making friends with the Amorites and Canaanites they are about to conquer. If the Israelites let their boys marry these heathen girls, "their daughters will lust after their gods, and will cause your sons to lust after their gods." Jews today are still profoundly anxious about intermarriage, and for exactly the reason expressed in Exodus: *If you marry a shiksa, you'll fall for her false god.* But doesn't this fear of intermarriage suggest that God lacks confidence in Himself? After all, He has just gotten done telling us how great He is. He has given us the world's best laws, some fantastic holidays, and even a few good songs (though not as many as the Christians have, I admit). So, why is God so fearful that intermarriage would pull Israelites away from Him? Given God's greatness, wouldn't intermarriage do the opposite and attract more people to Him?

We've been duped! We've been fed a bogus Ten Commandments! On his two *new* tablets, Moses records "the terms of the covenant, the Ten Commandments." The chapter lists these commandments, and they have *nothing* to do with the familiar "Thou shalt nots" from Exodus 20. The laws in Exodus 20 were never called the "Ten Com-mandments," but these new laws are. The new ten include only two of the earlier commandments (keep the Sabbath; no false idols). The other eight commandments are such things as observing Passover (number three), bringing the first fruits of the harvest to the taberna-cle (number nine), never appearing before God empty-handed (number five), not boiling a kid in its mother's milk (number ten). These are technical or procedural commandments, the Judean equivalent of not wearing white shoes after Labor Day. They are much, much less gripping than the ten "Thou shalt nots." That is probably why these "Ten Commandments" were shunted aside and replaced with the much catchier laws of Exodus 20.

CHAPTERS 35–39

When you need to build a tabernacle, whom do you call? Bezalel, of course. Again and again, Moses talks up this guy, whom God endowed "with a divine spirit of skill, ability, and knowledge in every kind of craft." Bezalel and his sidekick Oholiab get more mentions in Exodus than anyone but Moses and Aaron. They're only subcontractors, but God loves them. (Keep that in mind during your next renovation.) And they deserve His love. Bezalel builds nearly the entire tabernacle himself. He designs it. He constructs it. He does the fine metalwork. He mixes up the anointing oil and prepares the incense. It's *Extreme Makeover, Tabernacle Edition*, and he's Ty Pennington—the architect, engineer, carpenter, perfumer, sculptor, blacksmith, jeweler, and goldsmith.

CHAPTER 40

God names feckless Aaron as his high priest and declares that Aaron's descendants will be an "everlasting priesthood throughout the ages." Couldn't the Israelites do better? First of all, Aaron—Mr. Golden Calf—is probably the most incompetent and faithless man among them. If God had picked anyone at random—*You, Uriah in the tribe of Asher, come over here and put on this sacral vestment*—He would have been more likely to find a suitable priest. And even if Aaron were the holiest man in the Sinai desert, the inherited priesthood would still be a bad idea. Up until now, God has been big on competence: smart Jacob steals an inheritance; wily Joseph talks his way to power; Moses, who's nobody's son, rises to become a prophet. So it's disheartening that a God who clearly believes in meritocracy over bloodlines suddenly establishes a priestly caste.

This brings us to the end of Exodus. The Israelites are out of Egypt. They're equipped with their basic framework of laws. They're armed with God's promise of land and conquest. And they're back in God's favor after a whole lot of heresy and complaint. What's left to accomplish?

THREE

The Book of Leviticus

Lovers and Lepers

In which God issues laws about animal sacrifices, lepers, sex, lepers, food, lepers, justice, and lepers; He does a little smiting, too.

Some of my friends doubted that my Bible reading would last past Exodus. *Oh, it's all thrills and giggles when you're dealing with the ten plagues and the Tower of Babel—but wait till you get to Leviticus!* They mentioned Leviticus in the same hushed, terrified way that mariners mutter, "Bermuda Triangle," or Hollywood executives whisper, "*Ishtar*." Leviticus, I was warned, makes even learned pastors weep with boredom, and turns promising young Talmudic scholars into babbling *US Weekly* subscribers. What would it do to an amateur like me?

So it was with trepidation and a large cup of coffee that I opened Leviticus. I'm happy to report that it's nowhere near as awful as advertised.

CHAPTERS 1–7

In his *History of the Decline and Fall of the Roman Empire*, Edward Gibbon wrote—with anti-Semitism, but respectful anti-Semitism—that

Judaism was defined by its "peculiar distinction of days, of meat, and a variety of trivial though burdensome observances." Trivial and burdensome—that's Leviticus!

We begin with the "Complete Guide to Animal Sacrifice." This section is perfectly useless for modern Christians and Jews, since Jews stopped sacrificing animals when the Temple was destroyed 2,000 years ago, and Christians never sacrificed them. But we're stuck with seven chapters about sacrifices, so let's make the best of them. If, by some *Connecticut Yankee*–type miracle, you ever find yourself in the Sinai desert, standing outside the "tent of meeting," here are some Emily Post–style tips for sacrifice etiquette. Offer an animal that's without blemish—God hates a scar. Don't be alarmed when the priests fling the animal's blood all over the altar. If it's a bird (ideally a turtle-dove), the priest will "pinch off its head" and tear it open by the wings. If you're bringing a grain offering, expect the priests to eat most of it themselves. That's their "most holy portion."

When should you sacrifice an animal? Well, just about anytime is fine: when a priest does wrong, a chieftain does wrong; or the whole community does wrong; when you've given birth, or finished your period, or touched a corpse; etc.

CHAPTERS 8–10

Here's an episode they probably skip at your church. God, who's been uncharacteristically quiet for the first chapters of Leviticus, returns with a vengeance. Moses ordains Aaron as priest—the ordination requires dabbing blood on "the ridge of Aaron's right ear," on his right thumb, and on his right big toe. Soon afterward, Aaron's sons Nadab and Abihu, who are also priests, offer incense to the Lord. But rather than the prescribed incense, they give God "alien fire." *Boom!* God incinerates them on the spot. More like a drug lord than a prophet, Moses tells Aaron his sons got what they deserved, and orders some cousins to drag the bodies away and drop them outside the camp. All they did was burn the wrong incense! Is the Lord really that petty? But maybe there's an important lesson here: The rituals that seem so picayune and random really matter. A few verses later, God lectures Aaron: "You must distinguish between the sacred and the profane, between the impure and the pure; and you must teach the Israelites all the law which the Lord has imparted to them through Moses." In other words, God seems to be saying that the deaths were not the merciless act of a vindictive deity. They were a warning to mind the details.

CHAPTER 11

Leviticus moves on to dietary laws. Unlike the sacrificial rules, these are restrictions that observant Jews still follow today. Forbidden to eat: a lot! Off limits are animals that don't chew their cud or don't have true hooves, sea creatures without fins and scales, most insects, "great lizards of every variety," pelicans, owls, bats, and more. As a pork-loving Jew, I notice two words especially. God says that the pig, because it doesn't chew the cud, is "impure." Understood. But *then* the Lord describes lots and lots of other animals—including lobster, shrimp, ostrich, and most insects—as "abominations." "Abomination" is a much stronger word than "impure." Does this imply that bacon, pork chops, pulled pork, and ham are less bad than lobster? Can it really be that eating pork is a minor dietary offense, the kashruth equivalent of a parking ticket? God, I hope so!

One of the longest dietary passages concerns which insects we can eat. This raises an obvious point: the ancient Israelites ate insects! (For the record, the Lord bans all bugs except locusts, crickets, and grasshoppers.)

Do these laws make sense? Does the Lord have a dietary plan? He's generally opposed to grossness and wriggliness: Everything that crawls or "has many legs" is forbidden. We can't eat any animals with paws. But I actually don't see a coherent scheme. Why are pigs bad but goats good? Why are camels bad but cows good? Why are herons bad but hens good? Am I missing something? Is there a logic to the dietary laws? Or are they rooted in so many diverse sources (what animals were around, how the Israelites could distinguish themselves from neighboring tribes, etc.) that it's folly to look for a guiding philosophy?

One dietary law does make perfect sense to me. God repeatedly promises dire consequences for people who eat blood. You mustn't go vampire because "the life of all flesh is its blood." That's why meat must be drained of blood before it may be eaten. I know—the bloodletting doesn't make any difference to the animal that's being consumed; it's just as dead no matter how it's slaughtered. Even so, draining the blood is a powerful metaphor. When you bleed an animal, you are somehow allowing the animal's life force to escape—that's why they call it "lifeblood." We are even ordered to honor the animal's sacrifice by burying the blood. Not that my qualms have ever stopped me from ordering my steak bloody rare.

CHAPTER 12

If a woman gives birth to a boy, she's "impure" for a week. If she gives birth to a girl, she's impure for two weeks.

CHAPTER 13

The lepers are coming! The lepers are coming! This is a mind-bendingly confusing chapter about how skin diseases make you impure. Unless you're a dermatologist, Leviticus 13 is nearly impossible to get through. I did my best. You try a bit.

> *When a person has on the skin of his body a swelling, a rash, or a discoloration, and it develops into a scaly affection on the skin of his body, it shall be reported to Aaron the priest or to one of his sons, the priests. The priest shall examine the affection on the skin of his body: if the hair in the affected patch has turned white and the affection appears to be deeper than the skin of his body, it is a leprous affection; when the priest sees it, he shall pronounce him impure. But if it is a white discoloration on the skin of his body which does not appear to be deeper than the skin and the hair in it*

has not turned white, the priest shall isolate the affected person for seven days.

The author has an obsession with leprosy. Again and again, he describes a skin problem in pustular detail, then concludes solemnly: "It is leprosy." In one of those biblical passages that sound more like *The Life of Brian* than like God's holy word, Leviticus orders that a leper be expelled from the camp, his clothes torn, and his head uncovered. Then "he shall cover over his upper lip, and he shall call out, 'Impure! Impure!'" The Israelites thought *everything* was leprosy. God help the poor teenager with a few zits. This anxiety about leprosy: Was it just paranoid primitive ignorance, or a foresighted public health precaution? The priests are instructed to quarantine those with skin diseases. Perhaps this is the first recorded example of a public health campaign.

Leviticus interrupts its warnings to reassure men that, yes, it's OK to be bald. "If a man loses the hair of his head and becomes bald, he is pure." And it gets better! God also approves of male-pattern baldness. "If he loses the hair on the front part of his head and becomes bald at the forehead, he is pure." So throw out that Rogaine. God loves a cue ball.

At the end of the chapter, Leviticus wanders way off into Weirdistan, prescribing what to do when you have an infection in your clothes. Such garment ailments, according to Leviticus, should be treated exactly the same way as skin diseases. So if your shirt suddenly develops an "eruptive affection," then the priest must be called to examine it, quarantine it, and diagnose it. Are your Levi's suffering from a "malignant eruption"? Has your favorite silk blouse ever been afflicted with the dread "streaky green or red" illness? I have no idea what this passage is talking about. Is there some deadly apparel plague that Burberry and the Gap have successfully hushed up?

CHAPTER 14

Leviticus isn't done with bizarre epidemics. Now it's houses that are getting sick, infected by "greenish or reddish streaks" on the walls. Unlike the clothing plague, this kind of sick-building syndrome makes sense to modern readers, at least those of us who've ever dealt with mold. (I caught the green streaks once—my upstairs neighbor's toilet had sprung a leak.) The priest is called to treat the wall pestilence, the house is quarantined, and if the malady spreads to other walls, *Amityville*-style, the house is torn down.

This section also prescribes the purification ritual for a healed leper. The former leper must shave off all his body hair—twice. More proof that God favors the bald.

CHAPTER 15

On to sex. As with food and skin, Leviticus demands a constant battle against impurity. For example, if a man ejaculates, he must bathe, and he remains impure for the rest of the day. Incidentally, this law suggests that the Bible tolerates masturbation, since the ejaculation described is one that *doesn't* occur during intercourse.

A menstruating woman? Impure, of course—for seven days. As with all the impure folks Leviticus describes, it's not merely that she herself is impure: anyone who even grazes her is contaminated, anything she sits on is impure, her bedsheets are impure, etc. If you merely touch a chair she sat on, you have to scrub your clothes and take a bath—and you still remain impure for the rest of the day. Judging by Leviticus, life was nothing but baths and laundry. How would these directives go over today? In his hilarious 2007 book, *The Year of Living Biblically: One Man's Humble Quest to Follow the Bible as Literally as Possible*, A. J. Jacobs carried a portable stool with him everywhere—so that he would never have to sit where a menstruating woman had been.

CHAPTER 16

I never knew that a "scapegoat" was a real goat. Did you? This fact appears in an extremely odd, yet poignant, passage. After Aaron purifies the tabernacle, he lays his hands on a goat's head, and confesses all the Israelites' sins to it—thus "putting them on the head of the goat."

Then he exiles the goat to the wilderness, ridding the Israelites of their iniquities. Poor goat.

CHAPTER 18

Hey—all you folks who say Leviticus is boring? You're nuts. It's riveting!

For example, Leviticus 18 is crammed with incendiary sex laws. The first group of laws concern "uncovering the nakedness" of women. You must not uncover female relatives. Also forbidden to uncover: any mother-daughter combination, any menstruating woman, and thy neighbor's wife. I don't know exactly what "uncover the nakedness" means. I suppose it means "have sex with," but why would Leviticus use a euphemism when the book is otherwise so explicit? These prohibitions are directed only at men. There's no parallel passage forbidding women from uncovering the nakedness of, say, their brother.

All this uncovering nakedness is a warmup for the hottest law of all, the number one all-time favorite, top-of-the-pops Bible verse for social conservatives, Leviticus 18:22:

> *Do not lie with a male as one lies with a woman; it is an abhorrence.*

A lot of ink, and probably some blood, has been spilled over the meaning of this verse. I can't count the number of times I've heard religious conservatives cite it in their condemnation of homosexuality. On the other hand, I once listened to my rabbi hold forth for twenty minutes about why the word "abhorrence" actually has a much milder meaning than, well, "abhorrence." (Other translations use the word "abomination," which doesn't much help my rabbi's case.) Despite his impassioned argument, I don't think supporters of gay rights are going to get very far by trying to deny the Bible's opposition to homosexuality. There is no *Brokeback Mount Sinai*. In this verse about abhorrence, plus a similar verse in Leviticus 20 mandating death for gay sex between men, plus the destruction of Sodom, the Bible is pretty clear about male homosexuality. (Lesbian sex isn't mentioned in the Bible.) So how can Bible-loving supporters of gay rights rebut Leviticus 18:22? The strongest counterattack, I suspect, is to point out all the other things the Bible is equally clear about. It imposes the death penalty for gay sex, yes—but also for cursing your parents and for violating the Sabbath. It imposes exile for sex with a menstruating woman. And so on. Supporters of gay rights can turn the Bible back on the social conservatives: why do they fixate on abhorrent gay sex but not on abhorrent menstrual sex, or cursing one's parents, or the Sabbath violating? Dare them to take *all* of God's laws so seriously.

In a fascinating aside, God tells why He's so worried about sexual misbehavior. It's not at all the explanation I expected. He says that the Israelites must follow sexual laws in order to *keep the land pure*. The reason the Israelites are allowed to expel the Canaanites from the Promised Land is that the enemy violated these moral laws, and the land punished them: "Thus the land became defiled; and I called it to account for its iniquity, and the land spewed out its inhabitants. . . . So let not the land spew you out for defiling it, as it spewed out the nation that came before you." According to the Lord, the *land* is alive—the land itself can be purified or defiled, the land can rise against the people. An Orthodox friend of mine often talks to me about his mystical connection with Israel, and I have always (inwardly) pooh-poohed it as ruthless conservative nationalism pretending to be religious romanticism. But I take back my pooh-poohing. Until this passage, I never fully understood that when God makes His covenant with Israel, He is actually making a three-legged deal: He makes a covenant with His people, *for His land*. Maybe that's why so much of Genesis is about real estate. Maybe that's why, for many faithful Jews, being Jewish in America, Canada, or France is not being wholly Jewish at all: they are cut off from the land that is our covenant with God. We're not His Chosen People anywhere. We're His Chosen People on His Holy Land. And that's why the land must be pure.

CHAPTER 19

Leviticus 19 is glorious, a catalog of laws that's even more impressive, in its own way, than the Ten Commandments. No one can argue with the Ten Commandments—who favors murder?—but they're pretty vague. The laws in Leviticus 19 are beautiful for their mix of pragmatism and justice. Let me quote the middle of the chapter at length; it's so good:

> *You shall not pick your vineyard bare, or gather the fallen fruit of your vineyard; you shall leave them for the poor and the stranger: I the Lord am your God.*
>
> *You shall not steal; you shall not deal deceitfully or falsely with one another. You shall not swear falsely by My name, profaning the name of your God: I am the Lord.*
>
> *You shall not defraud your fellow. You shall not commit robbery. The wages of a laborer shall not remain with you until morning.*
>
> *You shall not insult the deaf, or place a stumbling block before the blind. You shall fear your God: I am the Lord.*
>
> *You shall not render an unfair decision; do not favor the poor or show deference to the rich; judge your kinsman fairly. Do not deal basely with your countrymen. Do not profit by the blood of your fellow: I am the Lord.*
>
> *You shall not hate your kinsfolk in your heart. Reprove your kinsman but incur no guilt because of him. You shall not take vengeance or bear a grudge against your countrymen. Love your fellow as yourself: I am the Lord.*
>
> *You shall observe My laws.*

Top that, Congress! In just a few sentences, the Torah speaks up for justice, charity, workers' rights, and the disabled; it condemns financial crimes, gossip, and war profiteering; and it offers perhaps the most perfect one-sentence directive on human behavior: "Love your fellow as yourself." (Ever wonder where Jesus got "Love thy neighbor"? Wonder no more.)

I particularly adore the percussive repetition of "I am the Lord." It's the key to the whole chapter. Why? Start with an obvious point: these are *not* laws that people want to follow. The employer *wants* to hold the wages overnight. The farmer *wants* to pick up fallen fruit. The victim *wants* to take vengeance. So why should they follow these laws? In a tribal society, a society without a constitution, a Supreme Court, or a history of common law, how do you justify laws like these? How do you enforce them? There's a lot of modern conservative legal scholarship about "natural law," which, as I crudely understand it, is that idea that there is a basic underlying legal code, largely derived from the Bible, that is independent of the Constitution and the Declaration of Independence—laws just like these. But, as this litany suggests, even biblical law is not natural at all. Law can exist only if there is power to enforce it (the police, the courts). "I am the Lord" is a statement of faith, but even more a statement of *force*. For the Israelites, what upheld these laws? The knowledge that the Lord—the God of Sodom and Gomorrah, the God of the ten plagues, the Really Supreme Smiting Court, was there to enforce them. "I am the Lord. You shall observe My laws."

Hmm, I just noticed a contradiction. How can I reconcile this praise of the laws in Leviticus 19 with what I wrote a few paragraphs ago about the antigay law in Leviticus 18? A minute ago I was bemoaning that law and looking for ways for gays to subvert it. Here I'm praising other Levitical laws. But Leviticus isn't consistent—why do I have to be? The laws in Leviticus are a mix of the sublime and the ridiculous—and the repellent. Just after the incredible "I am the Lord" passage, for example, come bizarre laws against mixing fabrics and crossbreeding animals. These laws, in turn, are followed by wonderful statutes about respecting the elderly, being kind to strangers, and doing business with honest weights and measures. And those, in turn, are followed by draconian laws imposing death for idolatry, adultery, incest, homosexuality, and bestiality.

Where do I get off deciding that certain Levitical laws are glorious and universal, true 3,000 years ago and true today (*You shall not render an unfair decision; do not favor the poor or show deference to the rich*), whereas others are archaic and should be tossed away (*Do not lie with a male as one lies with a woman; it is an abhorrence.*)? Fundamentalists solve this problem by accepting all the laws as true. But the rest of us must pick and choose. Unless you're willing to live in a Taliban-esque world of moral absolutism, in which adulterers and homosexuals are dragged from their beds and murdered, you have to take some laws and chuck others. We talk about the Bible as if there is only one. But if there's anything I've learned from these months with the Good Book, it's that we all have our own Bible. We linger on the passages we love and blot out, or argue with, or skim the verses that repel us. My Bible, I suppose, has a very long Leviticus 19, and a very short Leviticus 18.

CHAPTER 20

My Bible probably has a short Leviticus 20, too. This chapter is like *Law and Order: SVU*—in which the Lord specifies punishment for sex crimes. The sentence that appears most often is "They shall be put to death." Execution is the price for sex between adulterer and adulteress, man and stepmother, man and daughter-in-law, man and man, man and beast, or woman and beast. A threesome of man, woman, and her mother is singled out as especially heinous: the punishment is not just death but death by burning. God allows a few tender mercies: marrying a sister is punished only by excommunication; sex with a menstruating woman incurs only banishment; and sex with an aunt or sister-in-law merely guarantees that the culprits will die childless.

CHAPTER 21

Out with the Martin Luther King Jr. God of Leviticus 19, who spoke up so movingly for the blind and deaf. In with the Martha Stewart God—a finicky Lord who's peeved by human frailty and offended by illness. God's fussiness shows up when He issues His rules for the priesthood: no one who's blind, a hunchback, or a dwarf; or who has scurvy, a broken leg, a boil-scar, one leg longer than the other, or crushed testes can join God's squad. "Having a defect . . . he shall not profane these places sacred to Me."

CHAPTER 25

Every seven years, we're required to give the land a Sabbath, a rest from planting. God promises to deliver bumper harvests in year six so that no one goes hungry. And every fifty years, there's a jubilee year, which is another year with no planting and is the time when land is returned to its original owner. As I read it, farmland couldn't be sold permanently; it could only be leased until the next jubilee year, when the original owner could redeem it. Good intentions, bad public policy. I don't need to tell any of my readers who own real estate what folly this must have been. Such half-century leaseholds would have discouraged land improvements, prevented economies of scale, kept property in the hands of lazy owners, and suppressed entrepreneurship.

Like most first-time readers of the Bible, I've been stunned by the amount of slavery in the Good Book. The second half of Leviticus 25 is particularly shocking. At first it sounds quite tolerant, because it specifies all the ways in which indentured Israelites must be well treated. You can hold them only until the jubilee year: they can never become property. "You shall not rule over [them] ruthlessly; you shall fear your God." This is all very apples and honey.

But note whom the passage is *not* talking about: all the non-Israelite slaves. They, by contrast, become property "for all time." Leviticus says you may not treat Israelite slaves "ruthlessly." But what does that imply about non-Israelite slaves? Want to be ruthless? Be ruthless!

Ironically, a nice riff about equality in law comes right before the passage on slavery: "You shall have one standard for stranger and citizen alike." Great stuff! Of course Leviticus doesn't really mean it. Every so often the Bible nods toward a universal brotherhood of man. These are the "kumbaya" verses that are quoted by modern politicians and civil rights activists. But they are aberrations. Most of the time, the Bible conceives of a tribal world, a world of a Chosen Us, and a nearly subhuman Them—an Us who can never be slaves, but a Them who can be exploited ruthlessly, a Them who are property, a Them whose firstborn can be smitten.

CHAPTER 26

The first two verses of Leviticus 26 are: *Don't make idols, and keep the Sabbath.* If I could boil down the Bible so far into two sentences, they would be: Don't make idols. Keep the Sabbath. I haven't kept a tally, but I'd bet that the Bible has already issued this pair of laws at least fifteen times. By contrast, "Thou shalt not kill" rates only half a dozen reminders.

Why do idols and the Sabbath dominate the Torah? Let me hazard a guess. A key purpose of the Bible was to distinguish the Israelites from those around them, to make them feel different from the nearby peoples who worshipped Baal or Molech. But the most obvious big laws—don't kill, steal, covet, etc.—are nearly universal. Even those loathsome Molechites probably had laws against stealing. The laws that the Bible keeps noodging us about, by contrast, are those that *separate* Israelites from their neighbors: No idols, a seventh-day Sabbath, no eating blood, etc. Not killing doesn't make you different from a Molechite, but not working on Saturdays does. The *unusual* rules are the ones Israelites must observe if they're going to remain a distinct, independent people. They are the laws that keep Israelites from becoming Molechites.

What happens when Jews don't observe those unusual laws? Just look around you. Or just look at *me*. Those unusual laws go unobserved by American Jews like me, and the result is that we are largely indistinguishable from American Christians and atheists. We and the atheists and the Christians keep the same big laws—we're not killing people or dishonoring our parents or coveting—but since we ignore the defining Jewish laws about the Sabbath or eating bacon, our identity blurs. And that, I assume, is why the Torah keeps bothering us about them.

OK, back to Leviticus 26, which is among the finest bits of writing in the Bible. It's divided in two parts. In the first, the Lord tells the

Israelites what glories await them if they obey His laws. They'll get rain for crops, bumper harvests, easy victory in war. In the second part, God warns what will happen if they disobey Him. This bifurcation enables us to weigh precisely how much God values love and fear. His rewards for good behavior take up eleven verses. His punishments for bad behavior go on for twenty-seven verses. God cursorily promises milk and honey. But he waxes enthusiastic about suffering. Let's sample just a few lines. This must be the most menacing speech ever recorded:

> *If you reject My laws and spurn My rules . . . I will wreak misery upon you . . . you shall sow your seed to no purpose, for your enemies shall eat it. . . . I will break your proud glory. I will make your skies like iron and your earth like copper. . . . I will go on smiting you sevenfold for your sins. I will loose wild beasts against you, and they shall bereave you of your children . . . though you eat, you shall not be satisfied . . . your land shall become a desolation and your cities a ruin.*

It's a bunny boiler! The threats are incredibly scary but also a little bit funny. It's a shaggy dog story of divine vengeance. Just as you think it's finally about to end, God suddenly remembers another comeuppance ("the land of your enemies shall consume you") and flies off the handle again.

CHAPTER 27

If the author of Leviticus had an editor, the book would end with the thunderclap of Chapter 26. Instead it finishes with a whimper: this extra Chapter 27, about taxation and tithing. We are ordered to tithe one-tenth of our harvest and animals to the Lord. Is this law still in force? Are Jews still supposed to obey it? If so, here's yet another way I'm falling short. But how am I supposed to tithe one-tenth of two cats?

FOUR

The Book of Numbers

The Source of All Jewish Comedy

In which the Israelites take a census, complain a lot, send spies to the Promised Land, and annoy God so much with their griping that He condemns them to forty years in the desert; Moses quashes two rebellions, then is himelf banned from entering the Promised Land; a prophet named Balaam rides his donkey and refuses to help the Israelites' enemies; the Israelites enrage God by "whoring" with Moabite women, prompting Moses to order a mass slaughter of enemy women and children.

CHAPTERS 1–4

They weren't kidding when they called this book Numbers. It starts with a tribe-by-tribe census. Demographers will be enthralled to learn that there are a total of 603,550 Israelite men. Hmm. This is exactly the same number of men counted in the first census, taken a year earlier and mentioned in Exodus. That's fishy, don't you think? Women, of course, aren't counted at all.

CHAPTER 5

Another Monty Python–style episode. If a husband suspects his wife of adultery, he takes her to the tabernacle. A priest casts a spell upon holy water, then makes her drink it. If nothing happens to her, she's innocent. But if her belly distends "and her thigh shall sag," she's an adulteress.

CHAPTER 7

Numbers 7, in which tribal chiefs deliver their offerings to the tabernacle, reminds me of a question that's been bugging me ever since I came across the sublime name Zillah in Genesis. (She was the wife of Lamech.) Why do parents limit themselves to just a few biblical names (Isaac, Ezekiel, Samuel, Rebecca, etc.), and ignore so many other marvelous ones? This chapter alone has Eliab, Zurishaddai, Eliasaph, Gamaliel, Ochran, Gideoni, and Ahira. Wouldn't life be better with fewer Davids and Pauls and more Ahiras and Zurishaddais?

CHAPTER 8

God's abhorrence of body hair continues. In Leviticus He praised bald men and ordered healed lepers to depilate. Now He mandates that His tabernacle servants purify themselves by shaving off all their body hair. (And on the eighth day, the Lord created the Abercrombie and Fitch catalog.) A couple of days after reading this verse, I happen to watch *United 93*, in which the 9/11 hijackers are shown shaving their body hair before the suicide mission. In Islam, shaving body hair is a martyr's purification ritual, perhaps rooted in Koranic instruction. It is an eerie parallel to this instruction in Numbers, and a sickening reminder of the way ancient rituals can be turned to modern evil.

CHAPTERS 9–11

After a book and a half of rules, the desert drama finally resumes. The Israelites set off again toward the Promised Land. Naturally they start griping. After just three days of walking, the Israelites are already "complaining bitterly." Fed up with their whining, the Lord sends a ravaging fire into their camp. Moses prays, and the fire dies. The people soon start moaning again, this time about the food: "Nothing but this manna," they grumble. "If only we had meat to eat!" Like a mean babysitter, God tries an old trick: "You want chocolate? I'll give you so much chocolate you'll puke." He says, "The Lord will give you meat and you shall eat. You shall eat not one day, not two, not even five days or ten or twenty, but a whole month, until it comes out of your nostrils and becomes loathsome for you." God sends a flock of kamikaze quail, who crash to their deaths around the camp, forming piles several feet deep. As the Israelites gorge on the birds—"the meat was still between their teeth, not yet chewed," as Numbers puts it, vividly—the Lord afflicts them with a plague, and the greediest die.

CHAPTER 12

A fascinating episode of racism, with God and Moses on the right side (sort of). The jealous siblings Miriam and Aaron are grumbling against Moses because he married "a Cushite woman." My Bible says that "Cushite" means she's from Nubia or Ethiopia—African rather than Semitic. Aaron and Miriam insinuate that they deserve to be prophets on a par with the unsuitably married Moses. God hears their bellyaching, and summons all three siblings to the tabernacle for a powwow. He fires both barrels at Aaron and Miriam. How dare they compare themselves to their brother? Moses, He tells them, is nothing like their pathetic selves. "My servant Moses; he is trusted throughout My household." ("Trusted throughout My household"—I love that phrase.) Moses gets to talk to God "mouth to mouth. . . . He beholds the likeness of the Lord." The Lord leaves the tent in a huff (or perhaps in a puff, since He appeared as a cloud).

As He departs, Miriam's skin is eaten away with "snow-white scales." This is a delicious irony: having criticized the black wife, she turns agonizingly white, not unlike Michael Jackson. Moses intercedes on her behalf, imploring God to heal her. God answers that she'll have to wait: "If her father spat in her face, would she not bear her shame for seven days?" So Miriam is expelled from camp for a week until her white sores disappear.

The Cushite episode speaks well for the Lord's attitude about race, but not for his attitude toward gender. It's heartening that God doesn't tolerate the grousing about Moses's African wife. On the other hand, he punishes only Miriam for her rebelliousness. Weak-willed, traitorous Aaron, who learned nothing from his disloyalty during the episode of the golden calf, walks away unscathed.

CHAPTERS 13–14

Preparing to conquer the Promised Land, Moses dispatches a dozen spies, including Joshua, to reconnoiter Canaan. Is the soil rich or poor? Are the inhabitants strong or weak? Are the cities mighty or feeble? The scouts spend forty days in Canaan and return with an evenhanded report. The land *is* flowing with milk and honey, but the cities are fortified. When the spy Caleb says that the Israelites can certainly conquer the land, the other spies (except Joshua) recant their story. They turn on Caleb and began spreading lies: Canaan is actually filled with giants—bloodthirsty "Nephilim," the offspring of human women who married angels.

The Israelites immediately quail. "If only we had died in the land of Egypt . . . or if only we might die in this wilderness. Why is the Lord taking us to that land to fall by the sword?"

What's with the histrionic fatalism of the Israelites? Whenever Moses or his people run into even the slightest trouble, they wail the 1500 BC equivalent of, "Kill me now!" or "I wish I were dead!" (In Numbers 11, for example, Moses cries to the Lord, "If you would deal thus with me, kill me rather, I beg you.") I hope my fellow Jews won't take offense, but it seems to me that this is a distinctively Jewish form of complaint. "Kill me now" is a foundation of modern Jewish humor—the mother who sticks her head in the oven when her son drops out of medical school or dates a Christian girl, for example; or the entire oeuvre of Woody Allen. I suspect the Torah is the source of this exaggerated fatalism. What began as genuine, if melodramatic, anguish in Exodus and Numbers has, over thousands of years, and by millions of irreverent yeshiva boys, been tweaked into comedy.

Anyway, back to the Israelites, who are now weeping and demanding to return to Egypt. Joshua and Caleb yell at the Israelites to pull themselves together, insisting that they'll easily conquer Canaan if they just obey the Lord. Listen carefully to how Joshua and Caleb describe the inhabitants of Canaan, the people who possess the land the Israelites want to seize: "Have no fear then of the people of the country, for they are our prey." Prey—that's a breathtaking and sinister word! Again we're reminded that the Bible is *not* aspiring to be a book for everyone. It is *not* preaching universal truth for all men. This is the work of a single tribe at war with everyone around it.

The inconstancy of the Israelites again peeves the Lord, who threatens once more to abandon His covenant. Moses talks Him out of it, reminding Him that He is "slow to anger and abiding in kindness; forgiving iniquity and transgression." Now, as I've discussed, this is a deeply inaccurate description of the Lord, who is quick to anger and short on kindness, but the flattery works. God agrees not to kill off the Israelites, though He doesn't let them walk free, either. He says that none of the Israelites who came out of Egypt will be allowed to enter the Promised Land. They must all wander the desert for forty years (forty again). This is one ruthless deity: "Your carcasses shall drop in this wilderness. . . . Thus you shall know what it means to thwart me." God spares brave Caleb and Joshua—they alone will survive to enter the Promised Land.

Who deserves our sympathy during this terrible episode? The Lord is impatient and remorseless with His Chosen People. But can you blame Him? The Israelites are impossible: faithless, childish, and cowardly.

But can you blame *them*? One lesson of America's recent wars is that people who've been oppressed for generations are not immediately ready for rational self-government. They have habits of violence and intolerance that can't be shrugged off in a moment. The Israelites were in bondage for 430 years: it's unreasonable to demand that they immediately govern themselves and trust in God. God abandoned them for twenty generations, yet now He expects absolute loyalty after just a few months of wandering. So I sympathize with the Israelites' fears. They need, perhaps, a gentler God. But for the same reason, it's very hard to argue with God's forty-year plan. Just as it took a generation for Korea and Germany to shake off their war trauma, so the Israelites need a generation in the wilderness. The freed slaves are too timid and unstable to conquer the Promised Land. The testing of the desert journey—the self-sufficiency it requires of the young Israelites—will harden them for conquest. So God is being cruel but practical, ruthless for a purpose.

CHAPTER 16

An astonishing rebellion against Moses. A Levite named Korah and a few sidekicks denounce Moses for hoarding God's love. The rebels declare: "For all the community are holy, all of them, and the Lord is in their midst. Why then do you raise yourself above the Lord's congregation?" Moses challenges the rebels to a divine duel. Korah and his 250 followers are to show up (at dawn, of course) and the Lord will choose who is truly holy. The next morning, they gather outside the tabernacle—not just the 250 rebels, but all the Israelites, who now support Korah against Moses. This is a very bad decision. Again, the Israelites face the prospect of becoming seriously un-Chosen. The Lord cautions Moses and Aaron, "Stand back from the community that I may annihilate them in an instant." But Moses once more intervenes to save them, rebuking God exactly as Abraham did about Sodom: "When one man sins, will You be wrathful to the whole community?" God agrees (again) not to kill everyone but orders the Israelites to move away from the tents of Korah and two other rebel leaders.

Moses then explains to the Israelites how he'll prove that the Lord speaks through him alone. He tells them, "By this you shall know it was the Lord who sent me to do all these things. . . . If [the rebel leaders] die as all men do, if their lot be the common fate of all man-kind, it was not the Lord who sent me. But if the Lord brings about something unheard-of, so that the ground opens its mouth and swal-lows them up . . . you shall know these men spurned the Lord." And lo and behold, the ground "burst[s] asunder" and the earth swallows up Korah, his fellow leaders, and all their wives and children. The other 250 rebels are engulfed by fire.

Despite his defeat, Korah raised a critical question: Why should the few priests and prophets monopolize God? What's so great about Moses that he should control access to the divine? In the 3,500 years since, many religions have come down on Korah's side, deciding that God belongs to the masses, not to an anointed elite. (See Martin Luther, for example.) But the Bible disagrees. It rules emphatically—smitingly—for Moses, for the few rather than the many.

I have neglected to mention the most interesting word in the chap-ter: Sheol. Moses says that when the earth swallows the rebels, they will fall into Sheol. I cheated and looked at the commentary, which says that Sheol is the "netherworld, the abode of the dead." This chal-lenges one of my strongest held (and favorite) beliefs about Judaism—that we have no afterlife. Ignoring the hereafter, I always thought, makes Judaism and Jews more concerned with life on Earth. If there's no salvation, you'd better make the most of the present. But Sheol knocks all this down. Does this mean that Jews have a heaven and a hell? Can we get saved, too? And damned? How important is Sheol to our theology, anyway?

CHAPTER 17

The Israelites still haven't learned their lesson. The very day after Korah's execution, they complain about it. As you can imagine, God is not pleased. As in a summer rerun, the Lord tells Moses and Aaron to stand aside so He can annihilate the Israelites—this time with a plague. Moses and Aaron soothe the Lord by burning incense, but not before 14,700 Israelites are killed.

Let us pause here to discuss an obvious puzzle in the text. Time and again, according to the Bible, the Israelites have witnessed the Lord do something utterly miraculous that ought to end their doubts about Him, yet time and again the Israelites keep kvetching. They beg for food: He supplies them with manna. They need water: Moses brings it forth from a rock. They must cross the Red Sea: He pushes the ocean back. Over and over and over again, He presents evidence of His absolute power. Just one day before, He had caused the rebels to be swallowed by the earth and consumed by fire. Isn't that pretty convincing evidence of His absolute power? I don't know about you, but had I been an ancient Israelite and witnessed such awesome doings, I would have been a fervent Torah-thumper. Yet the Israelites remain faithless and fickle.

This leads me to the following line of inquiry. If you're still dubious after witnessing all that has been described in the Torah, either:

(1) You are a faithless, cynical skeptic.

or:

(2) You didn't actually witness the events that you are supposed to have witnessed.

Both of these explanations are problematic for anyone who believes that the Bible is literally true. If the Israelites are so faithless that even the most obvious miracles won't convince them, then they're truly hopeless, and stupid. The second explanation seems to be the common-sense account of the Israelites' behavior, but it's troublesome, too. If the described miracles never occurred, then the Bible is made up, and that would be an even bigger mess for a believer.

CHAPTER 20

This chapter was my brother's bar mitzvah portion. (June 1980. I wore dorky glasses. John had a Jew-fro.)

Moses's sister, Miriam, who hasn't spoken a word since God afflicted her skin, dies and is buried in a single sentence. It doesn't take a radical feminist to see unfairness in God's treatment of Moses's brother and sister. Miriam is plagued, banished, shunned, and ignored. Weak-willed

Aaron, three times a traitor, is rehabilitated—speaking still to God and advising Moses.

Again the Israelites are parched and they wish they were dead. God instructs Moses and Aaron to assemble the Israelites in front of a rock, and then "order the rock to yield its water." Instead of talking to the rock as instructed, Moses strikes it twice with his staff. Water pours forth anyway; the Israelites are mollified.

The Lord is furious because the brothers hit rather than spoke to the rock. Because they didn't trust in Him, the Lord rules that they too must die before they reach the Promised Land. This seems awfully harsh. First of all, in previous droughts (back in Exodus), God instructed Moses to strike rocks to release water. Isn't it possible that Moses simply made a mistake this time? And even if the striking was intentional, hasn't Moses earned the right to be a little bit frustrated? God, after all, flies into a towering rage whenever the Israelites whine or cross Him. Moses, by contrast, has been a paragon of patience, enduring the most outrageous behavior of the Israelites (and of God) with tolerance and wisdom. Yet when Moses displays even the tiniest bit of pique and whacks the rock, God issues a death sentence. It's terribly unfair to His greatest servant.

See you never, Aaron! Soon after this episode, the feckless brother dies—stripped naked on the top of Mount Hor. I'll miss Aaron—he really gives you someone to root against—but I'm sure the Israelites are going to do better without his sorry, no-account self.

CHAPTER 21

The Israelites are bellyaching again, this time about the manna. ("We have come to loathe this miserable food.") The Lord, as always, responds unpleasantly to their complaints, unleashing a plague of vipers against them. (*Snakes on a Plain?*) The terrified Israelites apologize. At God's advice, Moses fashions a serpent out of copper and attaches it to a flagpole. Any victim of snakebite who looks at the statue is immediately healed.

I'm pretty impressed by the variety of God's afflictions. So far, the Lord has inflicted on the wandering Israelites skin diseases, food poisoning, sundry plagues, several fires, an earthquake, and now snakes. It's like a *Saw* movie.

CHAPTERS 22–24

A long, bizarre episode about the Moabite king Balak, the seer Balaam, and Balaam's donkey. The story goes like this. King Balak, fearing the Israelite army, asks Balaam to curse the Israelites. Though not an Israelite himself, Balaam consults with God, who orders him not to help Balak: "You must not curse that people, for they are blessed." So Balaam refuses Balak. But the king won't take no for an answer. Balaam consults God again, who tells him to visit Balak but to obey only the Lord's orders.

At this point, the story is interrupted by one of the most curious incidents in the Bible so far. God is seemingly irked at Balaam for accepting Balak's invitation—even though God Himself told Balaam to accept it, but hey, that's Yahweh for you—and blocks Balaam's way with an invisible angel. Balaam keeps urging his ass forward, but the angel won't let the animal pass. Balaam beats the ass, who proceeds to open her mouth and protest, "What have I done to you that you have beaten me?" The Lord reveals the angel to Balaam, who apologizes (though not to the ass).

Say what you will about the Bible's reliability, about its improbable events and unbelievable miracles, but the Good Book does not— unlike Greek and Roman mythology, many fairy tales, and most religions—traffic in talking animals. Balaam's ass and the snake in the Garden of Eden are the only exceptions I can think of. I have no clever explanation for this absence of chatty camels and sassy roosters, but it certainly makes the Bible a more persuasive book. I suppose the Bible suspends its usual prohibition against talking beasts because Balaam's ass is an effective way to teach us about the invisible powers of God. Balaam can't see the angel, and so he assumes nothing is there. He can't imagine that the ass could be a thinking, feeling creature, and so he beats her cruelly. The ass's voice and the revelation of the angel remind him of the endless and impossible powers of God. And indeed, the story ends with Balaam fully on God's team. Instead of helping Balak, Balaam praises Israel and predicts Moab's defeat.

God is very appealing in the story of Balaam, and I think I've figured out why. It's the first Bible story told from the point of view of Israel's enemies. Since the Garden of Eden, we have heard only from our side—from Isaac, not Ishmael; from Jacob, not Esau; from the Israelites, not the Egyptians. History is written by the victors. (Imagine the story of Exodus if it were told by Pharaoh. In fact, don't imagine it; write it as a novel. And give me a ten percent royalty for the idea.) But this episode is seen through the eyes of Balak, who's an enemy of Israel, and of Balaam, who, although not exactly an enemy, is not a friend. Oddly, the result is a story that makes God look much better than He does when He's among the Israelites. With His Chosen People, God is bullying, capricious, and cruel. He doesn't listen. He's impatient. But with Balaam, God shelves the whole Almighty Avenger shtick. Instead, He cajoles the skeptical Balaam and wins him over to the Israelites' side. It is here, *away* from His Chosen People, that God is the subtle, wise, and persuasive deity we know and love.

CHAPTER 25

The Lord has made it abundantly clear that He dislikes sexual misbehavior, loathes intermarriage, and despises idolatry. What happens when you combine all three of His favorite sins? Gentle chiding? Sweet persuasion? I don't think so. Let's watch.

The Israelite men go "whoring" with Moabite women and start to worship the Moabite god Baal as well. This drives the Lord into a rage. Rather than proposing to wipe out all of Israel—His usual response to idolatry and lawbreaking—He limits himself to ordering that the ringleaders be publicly impaled. Before this can happen, however, an Israelite man and a Midianite woman happen to stroll by the tabernacle. Aaron's grandson Phinehas sees the mixed couple and immediately spears them to death. In modern America, this would be a hate crime. But God delights in the killing. He appoints Phinehas and his descendants as His priests "for all time," and He orders Moses to take fierce revenge on the Midianites. (Given that all the loose *Moabite* women and only one stray Midianite girl were tempting the Israelites, it hardly seems fair to go after the Midianites. But the Lord's ways are mysterious.)

Not mentioned during this episode is that Moses's wife Zipporah is a Midianite. This is another example of God's allowing one law for Moses but imposing a much stricter one on His people. To be fair to the Lord, Moses married Zipporah before the Israelites were freed from Egypt, before they'd established a national identity, before God had issued all His laws. Here in the desert, decades later, the Israelites are in a death struggle with neighboring tribes. Only one tribe, and one God, can win. Viewed from this angle, God's prohibition against intermarriage isn't so vindictive. The Israelites are winning the war on the battlefield, but if they start picking up the local floozies and bowing to the local idols, they risk losing everything.

CHAPTER 27

One of my favorite chapters, for a very personal reason. It begins by describing the plight of five sisters whose father, Zelophehad, has just died. He had no son, so the daughters are his only heirs. They petition Moses to be allowed to inherit his holding in the Promised Land. Moses appeals to the Lord, who rules that their cause "is just." They can have the land. Furthermore, the Lord says, this is not just a single case; it's precedent: from now on, if a man dies without sons, his daughters inherit his property. Feminists like this story, because it's the first major endorsement of women's rights in the Bible. Legal scholars also study it: they call the petition by Zelophehad's daughters the world's first lawsuit.

But that's not why I love it. Four of Zelophehad's daughters have names that sound in English like off-brand pharmaceuticals: Mahlah, Hoglah, Tirzah, and Milcah. But the fifth daughter is named Noa. (This is *not* the same name as Noah the ark builder's, whose name is

actually pronounced "No-ach" in Hebrew. Noa is pronounced "No-ah.")
Noa is a very popular Israeli girl's name—there's a famous Israeli
pop singer called Noa. It means a lot to me because it is my daughter's name. Unlike Jacob, whose nasty tendencies have made me
sorry I've given my son his name, Noa is a straight-up Bible heroine.
I hope my own Noa grows up to have as much moxie as her ances-
tress (though I'd rather that I didn't have to die for her to get a
chance to shine).

Noa's story isn't the only incident in the chapter with important
modern consequences. God instructs the dying Moses that it's time for
him to distribute his authority to his heirs. So Moses lays hands on
Eleazar, son of Aaron, and invests him with priestly authority. And he
lays hands on Joshua, and orders him to govern the Israelites. This is a
profound moment, because it is the *first separation of church and state.*
Religious authority goes to the priest Eleazar, secular authority to the
warrior Joshua. Neither is supreme, and they are independent of each
other. This is remarkably canny of Moses and the Lord. Speaking for
God *and* ruling the Israelites was often too much for Moses. Whenever
he went off up Mount Sinai in the service of the spiritual, his unruly
people would rebel and make trouble. And when he focused too much
on the daily needs of the Israelites—as when he supplied them with
water by striking the rock—he would neglect God's instructions.
Splitting the authority allows the undistracted Joshua to carry out the
gritty, down-to-earth work of conquering the Promised Land. Meanwhile, Eleazar can make sure to mind the Lord's p's and q's.

So Numbers 27 is a liberal's paradise: the first lawsuit, the first
women's rights, the separation of church and state. Throw in a few
pro-choice sentences, and ACLU members would be brandishing cop-
ies of the book of Numbers instead of the Constitution.

CHAPTER 31

The most hideous war crime in a Bible filled with them. As with the
story of Dinah, sexual misbehavior spurs the ugliest vengeance. At
the start of Numbers 31, God tells Moses he must complete one more

task before he dies: taking vengeance against the Midianites for the mixed coupling back in Numbers 25. Moses dispatches his army, which quickly kills the five Midianite kings and slaughters the Midianite men. The Israelites capture the Midianite women and children and march them back to camp. Moses is furious that his generals spared the Midianite women. Moses orders his troops to execute all the Midianite boys and all the Midianite females except for the virgins. This is a sick, grotesquely disproportionate atrocity, collective punishment of a most repellent sort—and all to take revenge for one bad date between an Israelite and a Midianite girl. Numbers, living up to its name, informs us that 32,000 virgin females survive the mass execution (and are then enslaved, incidentally). By my rough estimate, this means the Israelites killed more than 60,000 captive, defenseless women and boys.

Let's pause for a second to consider Moses's rage at the Midianites. For most of the last three books, Moses has been begging God to show mercy. But God is on the sidelines during the slaughter of the Midianites: it is Moses himself who demands the killing. Where does his new anger come from? Perhaps it's the fury of a frustrated old man who's been barred from his Promised Land. Or perhaps it's the homicidal megalomania that descends on so many dictators who hold power too long.

Moses himself seems to acknowledge that this massacre of innocents goes too far. He orders his death squads to stay outside the camp after they finish their butchery. They need a week away from the tabernacle to purify themselves. The Bible never mentions such a quarantine for Israelite soldiers after other battles. But, as Moses recognizes, these killings are not war; they are murder, and they defile his people.

CHAPTER 33

Numbers 33 lists every place the Israelites have camped during their forty years in the wilderness. It's dull as dishwater to read, but it serves a fascinating purpose. At the end of the list, God issues orders to the Israelites: cross into Canaan, smash the idols, dispossess all the inhabitants, and take the land for yourselves. Had the chapter skipped the travelogue and begun with God's fearsome instructions, it would seem brutal. The forty-year-itinerary—the weary, heartbreaking journey—reminds the Israelites of their suffering and justifies conquest. Why is it all right to sack and destroy another civilization? Because of what the Israelites endured, that's why. The forty-year accounting says: you've earned it.

CHAPTER 36

The last chapter in Numbers, and my favorite character, Noa, appears for an encore. Some of Noa's tribal elders are worried that if she and her sisters marry outside their tribe of Manasseh, their land will pass out of the tribe's control. This wouldn't be fair, the elders tell Moses. He agrees—land may not pass from one tribe to another. So Moses orders Noa and her sisters to marry men from their own tribe. I don't know what my tribe is (Washingtonians? journalists?), but to my own Noa I make this promise: you can marry whomever you want, sweetie.

FIVE

The Book of Deuteronomy

The Bible's Fifth Beatle

In which Moses harangues the Israelites, issues some new laws, and dies.

I have no idea what I'm going find in Deuteronomy. Before I started reading the Bible, I had at least a vague sense of the first four books. I knew that Genesis was Adam, Abraham, etc. Exodus was ten plagues, Ten Commandments, and so forth. Leviticus was laws. Numbers, I figured, was about numbers. But Deuteronomy is obscure—the Millard Fillmore of the Bible, the Torah's fifth Beatle. As far as I can remember, I've never read a word of Deuteronomy, never heard anyone recite Deuteronomy at the synagogue, never seen *Deuteronomy: The Movie*, never been to a Deuteronomy-themed costume party.

CHAPTER I

It turns out Deuteronomy consists of several rambling, Fidel Castro–length speeches by the dying Moses to his people. Think of it as the Moses farewell tour. Here in the opening chapter, the prophet recaps the wilderness years—name-checking various stops on the schlep, recalling a few of the bigger laws, and rebuking the Israelites for the myriad complaints and betrayals that got them banned from the Promised Land for four decades.

I'm most struck by one of Moses's asides. While describing how he chose tribal chiefs, he mentions the Lord's promise (originally in Genesis, but repeated several times) to make the Israelites as "numerous as the stars in the sky. May the Lord, the God of your fathers, increase your numbers a thousandfold."

Mission not accomplished. Today the worldwide Jewish population stands at about 13 million. According to the censuses in Numbers, there were approximately 600,000 adult male Israelites, so the total Israelite population would have been about 2 million. In other words, Jewish population has multiplied only sevenfold—not a thousandfold—in the last 3,500 years. Total global population, by contrast, has increased 150-fold during the same time. Even assuming that the Torah exaggerated the number of Israelites by a factor of ten, the Jewish population has still increased only seventyfold—less than half as much as the world's population.

By some measures, of course, the Israelites have been a smashing success: how many worshippers of Baal remain today, or Amorites or Hittites or Canaanites? The Israelites survived, and that's more than their enemies did. It's also true that, if we measure by power, accomplishments, and wealth, Jews are phenomenally successful. Their global influence has certainly grown a thousandfold. But that's not what the Torah was counting. By the biblical standard, we're failing. Jews are a demographic down arrow, an ever smaller part of the global community. (Current Jewish population growth is close to zero.) Have we failed God, or has He failed us? Or, to ask the question differently: given that it began before Christianity, Islam, and Buddhism (and at the same time as Hinduism), why is Judaism such a tiny stream?

When I mention this demographic failure to some Christians, they insist that they should be included in the count of the Israelites, since

they consider themselves heirs to God's covenant. If they are, the goal
of increasing a thousandfold has been achieved.

CHAPTERS 2–3

Back in Numbers, the spies embellished their scouting report from
Canaan with stories of terrifying giants. Now Moses observes that the
lands of the Ammonites and Moabites used to be ruled by giants and
gloats over the Israelites' conquest of King Og of Bashan, the last surviving giant. Og's iron bed, Moses reports, is thirteen feet long. Why
were the Israelites so anxious about giants? Had they discovered huge
fossils that they couldn't explain?

CHAPTER 4

Considering that Jews took monotheism to the top of the charts, the
Bible has so far been surprisingly weak on the concept. But now we get
the full-throated endorsement of one and only one god that we've been
waiting for. At the start of Deuteronomy 4, Moses suggests the existence of rival gods, asking his people if any other tribe "has a god so
close at hand as is the Lord our God" or if other tribes have ever
"heard the voice of a god speaking out of a fire, as you have, and survived." Both questions tacitly accept polytheism while nudging the
Israelites toward thinking that their God is special. But as the chapter
progresses, the other gods shrivel. Moses mocks idolatry, sneering
that the idolaters' handmade gods "cannot see or hear or eat or smell."
By the chapter's conclusion, Moses has ascended to full-on monotheism:
"It has been clearly demonstrated to you that the Lord alone is God,
there is none beside Him. . . . The Lord alone is God in heaven above
and on earth below, there is no other." That's pretty clear.

CHAPTER 5

In general Deuteronomy seems intent on trying to clean up the messes of the first four books. In the preceding chapter, it vetoed polytheism. Now Deuteronomy 5 resolves the mystery of the two Ten Commandments. As you recall, Exodus 20 lists the ten familiar "thou shalt nots" but does *not* describe those laws as the "Ten Commandments." Instead, that name is given to a different decalogue issued in Exodus 34, a dreary set of procedures and rituals.

Deuteronomy resolves the conflict by rewriting history. Moses reissues the "thou shalt nots" of Exodus 20, and declares them to be the Ten Commandments issued on Mount Sinai.

From a theological and ethical perspective, there's no question that these Ten Commandments are superior to the dull Exodus 34 rules. But I am still puzzled by the ambiguity. In Exodus it is pretty clear that the laws of Chapter 34 *are* the Ten Commandments. I wonder if the disagreement between Exodus and Deuteronomy reflects a conflict between two competing visions of Judaism. Could it be that there were priests and leaders, including the author of Exodus, who believed that the laws of Chapter 34—which outline essential ritual obligations, after all—were indeed the most important rules? And could it be that Deuteronomy—a later book—is attempting to refute that interpretation, and to claim that the grander, more elegant, universal "thou shalt nots" represent the true heart of God's teaching? Even so, it's a little creepy and Orwellian. *The commandments in Chapter 34? What commandments? You must be imagining things.* I'm struck, once again, at how often the Bible shows its seams. My childish notion was that the Bible was a singularity, a unified whole, but the more I read it, the more I see it wrestling with itself.

CHAPTER 6

I was wrong. I *have* heard Deuteronomy in the synagogue before. In fact, I've heard Deuteronomy *every time* I've ever been to synagogue. That's because, as I discovered today, the Shema—the most famous of all Jewish prayers—comes from Deuteronomy 6. It begins: "Hear, O Israel, the Lord is our God, the Lord is one." Again Deuteronomy preaches the absolute monotheism the earlier books only nod at.

The Shema, which orders us to love God with all our heart and mind, is followed by rip-their-guts-out curses from God and Moses. That's how the whole book goes: gorgeous invocations of faith alternate with lightning bolts. It's like a biblical good-cop, bad-cop routine. At any given moment, it's not clear if we're supposed to love God or fear Him, so we'd better do both.

Just a few paragraphs after the Shema, there's another passage I've heard many times before—the instructions for what to tell your children when they ask about the Exodus from Egypt. Jews recite these verses every year during the Passover seder. "Then you shall say to your children, 'We were Pharaoh's slaves in Egypt, but the Lord brought us out of Egypt with a mighty hand . . .'"

I don't think it's an accident that so much of the ritual language in Judaism comes from Deuteronomy. (There are several other examples, which I'm skipping.) Deuteronomy seems intentionally written as a CliffsNotes for Judaism, clarifying and simplifying the murky first books. Most scholars agree that the author of Deuteronomy is not the same as the author or authors of the four preceding books, and it's obvious on the page. The first books are a jumble of stories, rituals, and laws. They are choppy, episodic, scatterbrained, self-contradictory—and lots of fun. But Deuteronomy is a lawyer's book, as tightly organized as a Supreme Court brief. It makes the clearest possible arguments, ties off loose ends, and elides problems. There are no sloppy asides, no incoherent stories with talking asses, no inconsistent patriarchs. Deuteronomy attempts to knit the chaos of the first four books, that random array of laws and stories, into a single coherent theology. Deuteronomy means "second law" in Greek, and that may be its name because it's a second try at the same material—this time stripped to the bone, with all the ambiguities cut out. I understand why no one teaches Deuteronomy to little kids. In taking out all the inconsistencies, Deuteronomy also removes all the people and all the stories. There's no one to root for in Deuteronomy.

CHAPTER 8

Another line from Deuteronomy that everyone knows: "Man does not live by bread alone."

CHAPTERS 9–10

Moses sounds like a new man in Deuteronomy, and I don't much like him. The kindness and humility he displayed in the other books have vanished and have been replaced by saliva-spraying resentment. He rails against the Israelites for their defiance and inconstancy. What's the reason for Moses's insults? I can think of two. First, they're a natural human reaction to his situation: he's dying, he's disappointed, and he's jealous of the Israelites who will cross into the Promised Land, so he's laying into them. Second, it's a canny way to keep the Israelites motivated. Think of their position. God has told them they're going to conquer Canaan with ease. They're finally leaving the blasted desert for a land flowing with milk and honey, where life will be easy, the figs juicy, and the olive oil virginal. They've got their great laws, their four-star general Joshua, their ark, their commandments. They're feeling pretty smug. *Of course* they think they deserve the Promised Land. Moses is vilifying them in order to dent that complacency. If they get cocky, they'll lose their edge. They'll go soft. They'll fall for other gods.

For perhaps the 387th time in Deuteronomy, Moses lays into the idolaters. It's the usual speech—blessings for the faithful, certain death for the heretics—but then it takes a sharp turn. Moses suddenly starts talking about what to do if "your brother . . . or your son or daughter, or the wife of your bosom, or your closest friend" urges you to worship a rival god. Moses leaves no ambiguity: "Show him no pity or compassion . . . but take his life. Let your hand be the first against him to put him to death."

In the popular imagination, the Bible is the most conservative of all books. But passages like this one are a reminder of the Good Book's radical morality. According to Deuteronomy, fidelity to God is so much more important than family that it's better to murder your friend or wife or child than to tolerate his or her faithlessness. I don't think this is what people mean when they talk about the Bible's "traditional family values."

CHAPTER 20

A sublime passage. Before battle, the priests walk through the army's ranks, asking if any soldier has a house he has built but not consecrated, a vineyard he has planted but not harvested, or a woman he has paid a bride price for but not married. Anyone who does is sent home, so that, in case he is killed in battle, another man won't occupy his house, or harvest his crops, or marry his girl. It's a heart-stopping moment, at once sweet and dark. It's lovely in the way it recognizes that young men must get the chance to live, to taste the joy of life, before the state demands that they die for it. A little later, Deuteronomy insists that a newly married man be given a year at home with his wife—"to gladden" her, as Robert Alter's translation sweetly puts it—before he has to join the army.

Unfortunately, the remainder of Deuteronomy 20 is pure sulfur. Moses establishes the rules for conquest. A city must be offered the chance to surrender to the Israelite army. If it does, all its citizens will be spared, but enslaved. If the city fights, then all its men will be executed when the battle ends and all the women and children will be taken as booty. But—and what a but this is!—these forgiving rules apply only outside the Promised Land. Within the Promised Land, it doesn't matter if a city surrenders: "you shall not let a soul remain alive." God's law is genocide.

And environmentalists, check this out: you should kill all the babies, murder the girls and boys, put the women to the sword, but you can't touch a leaf on a tree. Yup, it's God's direct order: no cutting down the trees in the enemy's orchards. And this is a *moral* rather than utilitarian instruction. It has nothing to do with preserving the tree for your own future harvest. Rather, chopping down trees is forbidden because the trees can't make the choice to flee. But isn't this a weird sort of morality, which says that trees should be spared because they have no choice about where they're rooted, but every baby must be murdered?

CHAPTER 21

There's a *CSI: Judea* moment at the start of Deuteronomy 21: if you find a dead body in the countryside and the killer is unknown, the elders of nearby towns must measure the distance from the corpse to their village. The elders of the closest town then have to find a heifer—and not just any heifer, but one that has never worked—break its neck, and wash their hands over its body while declaring, "Our hands did not shed this blood." This absolves the town's guilt for the unsolved murder. This ritual is at once Dada and oddly appealing. The contamination from a murdered, unclaimed body is so profound that it requires a superconcentrated dose of absolution, the triple cocktail of animal sacrifice *and* ritual hand-washing *and* prayer.

Whoa, Nelly! Here's a law that must give biblical literalists connip-tions. If you have a disobedient son, then you can take him to the elders of the town and proclaim,

> *"This son of ours is disloyal and defiant; he does not heed us. He is a glutton and a drunkard." Thereupon the men of his town shall stone him to death. Thus you will sweep out evil from your midst.*

When I bugged her about it, my rabbi advised me that we're not to take the son-killing law literally. That may be so. I've certainly never seen anyone's son getting stoned—stoned in *that* way, I mean. Even so, the more I read of Deuteronomy, the more it disturbs me. The first four books of the Bible are full of immoral behavior, divine fickleness, and savage laws, but all balanced by extraordinary stories of decency and courage, the wisdom of Moses, the underlying love of God, and some of the most beautiful words you will ever read about protecting the poor, weak, and innocent. But Deuteronomy is cold. The warmth and humanity have drained away, leaving nothing but icy laws and a vengeful prophet.

CHAPTER 22

The law about killing a son is followed very quickly by one about killing a daughter. If a man marries a woman and then claims she's not a virgin, there are two possible outcomes, both ugly. First, her father can prove her virginity by displaying the bloody sheet. "Here is the evidence of my daughter's virginity." In that case, the falsely accusing husband is fined and flogged. But if the charge can't be refuted, the wife is brought to her father's house and stoned to death.

Cross-dressing—a huge no-no. Women must not wear men's clothing, and men must not wear women's clothing. It's "abhorrent."

CHAPTER 24

Can we apply Bible stories to modern American politics? Let's try. Governor Mitch Daniels of Indiana, a staunch Republican and a committed Christian, married his wife, Cheri, in 1978, and they had four daughters. They divorced in 1994. She remarried but soon divorced her second husband. Then Mitch and Cheri remarried. A heartwarming love story, right? A testament to the power of marriage and family? Not according to Deuteronomy 24. If a husband and wife divorce, and she remarries and then divorces again, her first husband may not remarry her, "since she has been defiled—for that would be abhorrent to the Lord." Governor Daniels, any thoughts?

The biblical fixation on female purity always puzzles me, and this is a particularly baffling instance of it. If female chastity is what matters, doesn't the "defilement" occur when the woman marries her second husband? If you're going to condemn her looseness, wouldn't the second marriage be the event that troubles you? Why should the remarriage to the first husband be so offensive?

CHAPTER 25

Levirate marriage is that between a man and his dead brother's widow. (Remember it from the story of Onan in Genesis?) But if the man *refuses* to marry his brother's widow, she "shall go up to him in the presence of the elders, pull the sandal off his foot, spit in his face, and make this declaration: Thus shall be done to the man who will not build up his brother's house!" The brother's house will then be known as "the family of the unsandaled one."

CHAPTER 26

This is a very boring chapter.

CHAPTER 27

First came the Ten Commandments. Now here are the Twelve Curses. I had never heard of this wonderful dozen—have you? Moses tells the Israelites that after they cross into the Promised Land they must assemble at various mountains while the priests proclaim twelve curses. The curses are magnificent: "Cursed be he who insults his father or mother. . . . Cursed be he who misdirects a blind person. . . . Cursed be he who lies with his father's wife. . . . Cursed be he who accepts a bribe in the case of the murder of an innocent person," etc. These curses cover less ground than the commandments—they mostly relate to sex crimes and unethical behavior, with very little about God or obedience—but they're very exciting.

CHAPTER 28

I thought Moses was rough when he cussed out the Israelites in Leviticus 26, but those threats were amateur hour compared with the bottle-and-a-half-of-tequila, waving-a-loaded-pistol threats Moses makes here at the climax of Deuteronomy.

As in Leviticus, Moses begins by reminding the Israelites of the glories that await them if they obey the Lord: "Blessed shall you be in the city and blessed shall you be in the country. . . . You will always be at the top and never at the bottom." Moses quickly drops the happy talk and moves on to imprecations. He begins calmly enough, with simple reversals of the blessings—"Cursed shall you be in the city"—but he soon becomes much more graphic and histrionic. Imagine being trapped in a stalled elevator with the world's most unpleasant insult comic—not just Jackie Mason, but a divinely inspired Jackie Mason—and you will have some sense of what the next fifty-four verses are like. Let me pick out just a few lines at random.

> *You shall become a horror to all the kingdoms of the earth. Your carcasses shall become food for all the birds of the sky. . . .*
>
> *The Lord will strike you with the Egyptian inflammation, with hemorrhoids, boil-scars, and itch, from which you shall never recover. . . .*
>
> *You shall not prosper in your ventures, but shall be constantly abused and robbed. . . .*
>
> *If you pay the bride-price for a wife, another man shall enjoy her. . . .*
>
> *You shall be in terror, night and day, with no assurance of survival. In the morning you shall say, "If only it were evening!"; and in the evening you shall say, "If only it were morning!"—because of what your heart shall dread and your eyes shall see. . . .*
>
> *She who is most tender and dainty among you . . . the afterbirth that issues from between her legs and the babies she bears; she shall eat them secretly, because of utter want.*

Holy hemorrhoids! Eating the afterbirth! I don't think I've ever read anything as scary. I'm not easily spooked, but I actually start sweating while I'm reading this.

It's terrifying to contemplate a world without God. But it's almost more terrifying to contemplate a world with a God who issues such threats. If this is what our loving God would do to us, well, God help us.

CHAPTER 29

Moses gathers all the Israelites for a *final* final speech, telling them
that now is the moment they seal their covenant with God before
crossing into the Promised Land. I'm confused about this covenant
business. God made a bunch of binding covenants with Abraham,
Isaac, and Jacob, all of which He applied to their descendants. He
also made covenants with the Israelites when—forgive me if I forget
one or two occasions—they left Egypt, received the commandments
at Mount Sinai, and were spared after transgressing in the wilderness. Now they're signing yet another agreement, just as they're about
to cross into Canaan. How many dratted covenants does one divin-
ity need, especially since they all say virtually the same thing? Isn't
the whole point of a binding covenant that it's *binding*—that it lasts
forever and doesn't need to be renegotiated every few chapters?

CHAPTER 30

For most of the preceding three and a half books of the Bible, Moses
has been battering us with thousands of rules, hundreds of warnings,
dozens of legal anecdotes. But now, frustrated and near death, he boils
all of God's teaching down to a single sentence. As he builds up to it,
he sounds very much like a high school football coach giving a half-
time pep talk to his losing team: It is "not too baffling for you. . . . It
is not in the heavens, that you should say, 'Who among us can go up to
the heavens and get it for us and impart it to us?' . . . No, the thing is
very close to you, in your mouth and in your heart." Look, it's simple,
people! It's a choice between "love and prosperity" and "death and
adversity." All you need is

> to love the Lord your God, to walk in His ways, and to keep His
> commandments, His laws, and His rules, that you may thrive and
> increase, and that the Lord your God may bless you.

That's it. That's all we have to do. I can imagine the Israelites muttering: *Now he tells us! Why couldn't he have said this before all those rules about lepers?*

CHAPTER 33

Moses says good-bye to the Israelites and blesses each of the tribes. This scene mirrors the end of Genesis, when the dying Jacob blesses each of his sons. The Mosaic blessings are very similar to Jacob's, from the ripe animal metaphors—Dan is a "lion's whelp" and Joseph a "firstling bull"—to the explanations for the geographical location and economic interests of the tribes (e.g., Asher is said to bathe his foot in olive oil because the land where Asher settles is rich in olives).

Among other things, this parallelism ratifies Moses's place in the pantheon with Jacob. Unlike patriarchs Abraham, Isaac, and Jacob, he is not the literal, biological father of the Israelites. Yet Moses is more interesting, powerful, and good than they were. It's Moses who shaped the Israelites into a nation, led them to the Promised Land, and gave them their laws—the three acts that still define Jews today.

Here's a deathbed scene to remember. After the Ten Commandments, countless intercessions with God to beg for mercy, and the most eloquent proclamations of justice the world has ever known, these are Moses's very last words: "Your enemies shall come cringing before you, and you shall tread on their backs." That's the way to go, Moses—kicking them when they're down! Then God's greatest prophet climbs Mount Nebo and dies.

The Book of Joshua

Why So Many Bible Hookers?

In which Joshua and the Israelites cross the Jordan River, invade the Promised Land, conquer Jericho, and slaughter lots of Canaanites.

CHAPTER I

After the death of Moses, Joshua consolidates his power, telling tribal leaders that the invasion of the Promised Land begins in three days.

Joshua also talks to God, who orders him to read the "book of the law" that Moses prepared—the very Torah we've just finished reading. He tells Joshua: "You shall meditate on it day and night, so that you may be careful to act in accordance with all that is written in it. For then you shall make your way prosperous, and then you shall be successful." This instruction marks the beginning of biblical scholarship. Let 3,500 years of argument begin.

CHAPTER 2

Joshua dispatches two spies to Jericho, where they take shelter in the house of the prostitute Rahab. When the king of Jericho catches wind of the spies and confronts Rahab, she hides them on her roof. The danger passes, and she explains to the spies why she's helping them. She says she has heard of the Lord's mighty deeds—the Red Sea crossing, the defeat of King Og, etc.—and that these triumphs made the Canaanites' hearts "melt" with terror. She begs the Israelites to spare her and her family when they conquer Jericho. The spies promise to protect her, and escape back to Joshua.

Back in Exodus, you may remember, God prolonged the ten plagues because He wanted the Israelites to tell stories about His might. The Israelites kept recording God's triumphs—composing poems and writing down tales that spotlight His greatness. A key purpose of these stories must have been to terrify God's enemies. That psychological warfare is paying off. Thanks to the stories of God's awesomeness, the battle for Canaan is half won. The Canaanites already know they're going to lose. As Rahab says, "There was no courage left in any of us because of you."

On to bawdier matters. Joshua 2 raises a pressing question: What's with all the prostitutes? There's scarcely an unmarried woman in the Bible who isn't a prostitute, or treated like one. Tamar turns a trick with her father-in-law Judah. The Moabite women whore themselves to the Israelites. The Midianite harlot is murdered by Phinehas. The loose behavior of Jacob's daughter, Dinah, sparks mass slaughter. And now Rahab. No wonder they call prostitution the oldest profession—it's the only profession that biblical women seem to have.

I have a rudimentary theory about this. In many tribal cultures, women have been essentially banished from the public sphere in order to control their virtue. We see this today in strict Islamic cultures, where women aren't even allowed to speak to men other than their husbands and relatives. Throughout the Bible, the Israelites have been obsessed with controlling the sexual behavior of their girls and women. That's why there are so many laws about female purity, sexual misbehavior, and intermarriage. Presumably because of these sexual constraints, the Israelite women seem to have played no role in public life. Except for Moses's sister, Miriam (and, in passing, Noa and her sisters), there hasn't been one woman since Exodus who's had any public presence. Perhaps we keep hearing about prostitutes because all the other women were locked up in the kitchen.

CHAPTERS 3–4

All 2 million Israelites must cross the Jordan River to enter the Promised Land. One man from each tribe stands in the middle of the river. The river stops, all the water piles up in a wall on the upstream side, and the Israelites and the ark cross on dry land. Those of you who have been to Israel are scoffing: *Big deal! The Jordan "river" is about as deep as my bathtub, and not much wider.* The book specifies that the crossing was at flood stage, when the river is somewhat more intimidating. Even so, this is highly unimpressive. More important, why do a kiddie-pool rip-off of the Red Sea crossing? The parallelism reminds us that God has again allowed us to cross into a new world. From the Red Sea crossing came the giving of the laws, the rise of Moses, and the transformation of Israel into a great nation. From the Jordan River crossing will come the conquest of the Promised Land and the fulfillment of God's covenant.

CHAPTER 5

As soon as the Israelites have crossed the Jordan, God orders Joshua to "make flint knives and circumcise the Israelites." Apparently circumcisions were suspended during the wilderness years. (I'm guessing they were canceled owing to a shortage of bagels and lox.) Anyway, Joshua and his aides proceed to circumcise all the Israelite men—that's a cool million of them. And these aren't kids, either; they're grown men. Ouch! The Lord is delighted and says the mass surgery has "rolled away the disgrace of Egypt." The Israelites name the spot where they're camped the "Hill of the Foreskins." (Now that's a place

I don't want to visit next time I'm in Israel. Can you imagine going there with kids? *Jacob, don't pick that up! No, Rachel, you can't keep that "ring" you found.*)

The Israelites eat their last meal of manna. Imagine the rejoicing.

CHAPTER 6

According to the song:

> *Joshua fought the battle of Jericho, Jericho, Jericho*
> *Joshua fought the battle of Jericho*
> *And the walls came tumbling down.*

But Joshua didn't fight the battle of Jericho, because there was no battle of Jericho. Joshua has the Israelites circle the city once a day for six days. On the seventh day, they circle Jericho seven times, with seven priests blowing seven rams' horns. At the end of the final circuit, Jericho's walls collapse in a heap. The Israelites charge and sack the city without a fight, killing every living thing—all the people and animals—except the prostitute Rahab and her family.

CHAPTER 7

Now that Jericho's down, I figured the rest of the conquest would be easy. But it stalls. The Israelites dispatch an undersized army to the next city, Ai. Ai repels the 3,000 Israelites, and kills thirty-six of them. The hearts of the Israelites "melted and turned to water"— a phrase that the book of Joshua has used several times already, but only to describe a routed enemy. A devastated Joshua tears his clothes in mourning, and tries to figure out what went wrong. (Don't you wish our leaders took war as seriously?) Joshua wails to God: *Why did you bring us all the way to the Promised Land if you were just going to destroy us?* God, with thrilling directness, orders Joshua to be a man. "Stand up! Why have you fallen on your face?" God informs Joshua that they lost the battle because an Israelite stole devotional objects belonging to God. Joshua can redeem Israel only by rooting out and punishing the thief.

The rest of the chapter unfolds like Shirley Jackson's famous short story "The Lottery." (In fact, I wouldn't be surprised to learn that Jackson modeled "The Lottery" on Joshua.) Slowly, with an ominous, telescoping rhythm, Joshua seeks the criminal. He surveys all the tribes, and selects Judah. He examines every clan of Judah, and picks out the Zerahites. He quizzes every family in the clan, and settles on the Zabdis. He goes one by one through the Zabdi household, and finally fingers the young man Achan as the thief. Joshua's interrogation of Achan is gently, horribly devastating. Listen to Joshua's ingratiating, but arm-twisting, language:

> *"My son, give glory to the Lord God of Israel and make confession to Him. Tell me now what you have done; do not hide it from me."*

Achan instantly confesses to stealing silver, gold, and cloth, and tells Joshua where to find them. Joshua's men collect the loot, and offer it back to God. Good cop Joshua disappears, to be replaced by the ruthless avenger. Joshua tells Achan, with what sounds like a line from a Schwarzenegger movie: "Why did you bring trouble on us? The Lord is bringing trouble on you today." The Israelites stone Achan to death and then burn his body. They also incinerate his family, and heap all their bodies with stones. (Another nasty collective punishment.) What's troubling about this episode—or, if you're a very observant Jew, what may be compelling about it—is the notion that the fate of Israel hangs on the behavior of one person. The sin of a single insignificant man is enough to shatter God's covenant with Israel and stop the conquest of the Promised Land. The implication of the story is that when any of us steals, cheats, lies, kills, or commits adultery, we are not mere sinners or simple criminals. We are Achan, threatening to ruin our families, our tribe, our city, and our nation.

CHAPTER 9

Until Joshua, the Israelites' battles have all had an aura of inevitability. In earlier books, we knew that the Israelites were going to rout the enemy because God was leading them, or that they were going to be routed because they had displeased the Lord. The Bible ignored the human element—the general's strategy, the enemy's tactics, etc.—because the divine will was all that mattered. But in Joshua the outcome is uncertain, because God leaves the work up to His people. The result is a thrilling series of stories about strategy, deceit, and intimidation—lessons in biblical game theory. For example, when Joshua seeks revenge against Ai, he dupes the enemy army with a fake retreat, drawing it into a fatal ambush. Later, it's Joshua who's outfoxed. The Gibeonites—who are Joshua's next target—hear about Jericho and Ai, and they're understandably terrified. How can they save themselves from Joshua's exterminating army? The Gibeonites dress up in tattered clothing and appear at the Israelite camp, pretending to be ambassadors from a "very far country." They tell Joshua they've heard about the Israelites' grand victories and want to make a peace treaty. As evidence of their long journey, they display moldy bread, worn-out wineskins, and ragged clothes. Joshua falls for their deceit and "guarantees their lives" in a treaty. Three days later, the Israelites realize they've been scammed by the neighboring Gibeonites. They can't carry out the usual sack, murder, and obliteration, because they've sworn an oath to safeguard the Gibeonites. Joshua lets the Gibeonites live, but he indentures them as servants, assigning them to gather wood and draw water for their Israelite masters.

The moment when Joshua discovers that the Gibeonites have bamboozled him is astonishing, because it suggests that Joshua is extraordinarily obtuse. Joshua asks them, apparently in earnest, "Why did you deceive us, saying 'we are very far from you,' while in fact you are living among us?" To which the Gibeonites respond, sensibly: *Uh, because you exterminate your enemies!* Is Joshua serious when he asks this question? Is he so lacking in empathy that he doesn't understand why the Gibeonites would try to save their own skins?

CHAPTER 10

A grim business. Five Ammonite kings unite against the the Israelites. Joshua gets wind of their plans, marches his army all night, and surprises the enemy. The Israelites rout them in the field, and then God finishes them off, sending a brutal hailstorm that kills more Ammonites than the fighting did.

After the victory, the Israelites capture the five fleeing Ammonite kings. Joshua drags the monarchs before him and orders his generals, "Put your feet on the neck of these kings." As they stand on the kings' throats, Joshua tells his commanders, "Do not be afraid or dismayed: Be strong and courageous; for thus the Lord will do to all the enemies against whom you fight." Then, Joshua himself executes the kings and hangs their bodies in the trees. This episode is so proudly barbaric that it's painful to read. It's clear that we readers are supposed to take the Israelites' side here—they're conquering the Promised Land, they're God's Chosen People, the Ammonites are vile idolaters, etc.—but I find the unapologetic savagery unbearable.

This probably reveals a profound weakness in me, but I imagined myself—in the way one always imagines oneself inside a book—not as one of my own ancestors, the victorious Israelite generals, but as a heathen king with a boot on my neck, moments from a brutal death.

Joshua and the Israelites have been doing nothing but killing in this book—killing by the thousands, killing women, killing children, killing animals—but it is the death of these five men, who aren't even innocents, that arouses the most revulsion. There's an obvious reason for this, one Stalin understood: "A single death is a tragedy, a million deaths is a statistic." All the other killings in Joshua are mass killings. This is the only time the book of Joshua gives us death in a tight close-up, and it's appalling.

The rest of the chapter is gruesome, but in the statistical way. Joshua sweeps from city to city across southern Canaan, sacking them one after another:

Joshua took Makkedah on that day, and struck it and its king with the edge of the sword; he utterly destroyed every person in it; he left no one remaining. . . . Then Joshua passed on . . . to Libnah. . . . He struck it with the edge of the sword, and every person in it; he left no one remaining in it. . . .

To Lacshish. . . . He took it on the second day, and struck it with the edge of the sword, and every person in it. . . .

Gezer. . . . Joshua struck him and his people, leaving him no survivors. . . .

To Eglon. . . . [They] struck it with the edge of the sword, and every person in it he utterly destroyed that day.

I don't know how anyone could read this book without despair. Joshua is a genocidal brute, and God is unfathomably cruel. It doesn't matter that God has promised this land to Israel: no god can justify such smug, wanton murder.

Unfortunately, this is not the kind of moral problem that can be solved by saying: well, it's OK because it never really happened. It's bad whether it's real or made-up. If the book *is* true, and the Israelites did conquer genocidally, why was God so unfathomably cruel? And if the book isn't true and the conquest didn't happen like this, why did the Israelites tell these stories so enthusiastically? Why were they so proud of even fictional brutality?

CHAPTERS 13–19

Though the Israelites seem to have killed everyone around, they actually haven't managed to conquer the entire Promised Land. There's a lot of unannexed territory, particularly in the plains, where the enemy is armed with fearsome metal chariots. But Joshua's getting old, and everyone seems sick of fighting, so the war winds down and the distribution of land begins. Joshua divides all the land of Israel among the tribes—there are seven chapters of property records.

CHAPTER 22

Here's a fascinating, tense moment. With the Promised Land under control, Joshua allows the tribes of Gad, Reuben, and Manasseh to cross back to the eastern side of the Jordan, where they will settle. Back on the east side, the three tribes build a huge altar. The tribes in the Promised Land hear about this altar. Because the only permitted altar is the one in the tabernacle, they suspect that the three trans-Jordan tribes have abandoned Yahweh for Baal or some other false god. The tribes in the Promised Land prepare for a holy war to crush the idolators. They dispatch Phinehas—the hotheaded priest who murdered the Midianite harlot—to rebuke the tribes that built the altar. The leaders of Reuben, Gad, and Manasseh inform him that there has been a terrible misunderstanding. They didn't build the altar for real sacrifices. It's just for show. It's a "copy" of the real altar. Because they're on the far side of the Jordan, away from the ark and tabernacle, they want to make sure that their kids remember the Lord. This stand-in altar will remind their children to love God. The other tribes accept the explanation and stand down. They even thank the altar builders for their attention to God.

This is a very important moment for Judaism, and perhaps for all religions, because it marks the end of Judaism as a faith bounded by place. From now on, it can go anywhere. All religions, I suspect, begin with a central sacred place or object, but can grow only when they accept a stand-in for the holy of holies, when they allow the semisacred to take the place of the sacred. The crucifix in churches is an example, and so is the ark in all synagogues. The moment when a religion creates its first copy is, in some sense, the moment when it starts being a religion. Until now, God has literally been with *all* the Israelites. He travels with them in the tabernacle. He lives with them. Now that the tribes are scattering across Israel, they face the problem of how to keep God with them everywhere. On the west side of the Jordan, they will abide near the tabernacle and thus hold onto their direct connection to God. But the trans-Jordan tribes need to create a substitute for that tabernacle (just as all Jews had to create a substitute after the Temple was destroyed 2,000 years ago). This altar by the riverside marks the birth of Judaism as a worldwide religion: from now on, the Israelites can travel away from the tabernacle, because they can create a copy. They can take God wherever they go. And so can we.

CHAPTER 24

Sometimes, the most fascinating parts of the Bible are the bits that have been left out. Remember the story of Dinah, which caused me to start reading the Bible? The final verses of Joshua remind us of that story, but listen to what they *don't* say. Joshua dies at age 110 and is buried. The bones of Joseph, which have been carried all the way from Egypt, are also buried in the Promised Land "in the portion of ground that Jacob had bought from the children of Hamor, the father of Shechem, for 100 pieces of money." What isn't mentioned is that Jacob bought the land from the children of Hamor before Jacob's sons tricked and murdered them.

SEVEN

The Book of Judges

The Meathead and the Left-Handed Assassin

In which the Israelites are repeatedly conquered after reverting to idolatry, then saved by fighting judges such as Deborah, Gideon, Jephthah, and Samson; Delilah gives Samson a haircut; and the Bible's most revolting sex crime is committed.

The first thing I'm noticing about the book of Judges is that there don't appear to be any actual judges in it. The people who are called "judges" are actually generals, left-handed assassins, female guerrillas, polygamist warriors, fratricidal maniacs, and holy child-killers. No judging seems to occur in Judges—unless your idea of justice is *Judge Dredd*. But if you want good stories, this is the book to read. It's a shot of adrenaline.

To save us all time later, let me summarize Judges in two sentences: The Israelites revert to wicked idolatry and are conquered by neighboring tribes. A great warrior emerges to rout the enemy; the Israelites prosper until he dies, at which point they backtrack to paganism. Wash. Rinse. Repeat.

CHAPTERS 1–3

The orderly society established by Joshua dissolves into Hobbesian chaos. The Israelites split into squabbling tribes and are beset by Philistines, Jebusites, Canaanites, and various other menacing ites. They sign peace treaties with the enemy to end the fighting, but this infuriates God. An angel visits to denounce the Israelites for making the treaties, which violate God's direct orders to spurn the enemy. The Lord declares He will no longer help them against the Canaanites. They're on their own.

Even so, God occasionally delivers a fighting judge. The first memorable one is Ehud, the left-handed avenger (the only left-wing judge in Judges, as far as I can tell). After King Eglon of Moab defeats the faithless Israelites, Ehud pays him a visit, with the pretext of bringing tribute. Hiding a sword under his clothes, Ehud announces: "I have a secret message for you, O king." Eglon agrees to see him alone—in the bathroom. When they're closeted together, Ehud says—and I love this line, which was written by a man with a wicked sense of humor, a biblical Quentin Tarantino—"I have a message from God for you." Then he stabs the king in the belly, so hard that the "dung comes out." Ehud escapes and leads the Israelites to victory over the Moabites. As a left-hander, I find this story particularly inspiring.

CHAPTER 4

At every bar mitzvah, the birthday boy reads two passages in Hebrew. One passage is taken from the Torah (the first five books of the Bible) and one from the haftarah, which consists of selections from the rest of the Jewish Bible, such as Judges or Prophets. (Let me note, red-faced, that I was about twenty-nine years old before I realized that "haftarah" was not "half-Torah." I thought "half" signified that it was less important than the Torah.) As I mentioned, at my bar mitzvah my portion of the Torah was the best the Bible has to offer: the crossing of the Red Sea. I had forgotten until now that my haftarah portion was also pretty spectacular: Judges 4, a story that has inspired assassins and nutcase serial killers for 3,000 years.

We begin the chapter with the Israelites groaning as usual under the rule of enemy tyrants, in this case Jabin and his general Sisera, whose 900 iron chariots were the M1 Abrams tanks of their day. But they don't scare the Israelite prophetess Deborah, who persuades Barak to raise a 10,000-man army to confront Sisera. (Deborah is a proto–Joan of Arc figure.) 'Fraidy-cat Barak won't go to fight unless Deborah accompanies him. At Deborah's urging, Barak begins the battle at just the right moment and routs Sisera's force.

General Sisera flees the battlefield, and arrives at the tent of Heber the Kenite. Heber's wife Jael greets Sisera and offers him hospitality: "My lord, turn aside to me; have no fear." (A nice thing about Judges 4 is that it has not one but two heroines: neither Deborah nor Jael is a prostitute, and both are awesome role models because of their courage and their skillful manipulation of weak men.) Sucker that he is, Sisera accepts Jael's invitation and enters her tent. He asks her for a sip of water. She gives him a drink of milk instead. Jael covers the exhausted general with a blanket and he falls asleep. Then she picks up a tent peg, tiptoes over to him, and hammers it through his skull, "until it went down into the ground." Barak stops by the tent in pursuit of Sisera, and Jael invites him in: "I will show you the man whom you are seeking."

The episode of Jael and Sisera is a perfect short story, as heart-stopping as anything Poe ever wrote. First, let's admire how transgressive it is: Jael shreds the essential law of hospitality that defines tribal and Middle Eastern societies. She opens her home to Sisera, nourishes him, and puts him to sleep in her tent—all so she can assassinate him in the most brutal way possible. Its literary greatness comes from its slow buildup, the quiet accretion of details to heighten the tension. There's Jael's mysterious, beckoning invitation: "turn aside to me." Is it sexual? There's that moment of rest and safety when Sisera enters the tent, a sigh of relief that turns out to be a trap. Then there's the turn of the story: He asks for water, and she serves milk. If this were a horror movie, the piano would now start plinking ominously in the high register. Why does she give him milk? Is she toying with him? We know it means she's not exactly the subservient hostess she's pretending to be; we know that something is awry, but we don't know what it is. (It's the first recorded case of lactose intolerance.) The unease subsides because she offers a motherly good night and gently covers him with a blanket. Then the assassination itself is utterly shocking: a quiet, domestic moment suddenly transformed into a Freddy Kreuger gore fest. Read the murderous sentence and revel in its bloody genius:

> But *Jael wife of Heber took a tent peg, and took a hammer in her hand, and went softly to him and drove the peg into his temple, until it went down into the ground—he was lying fast asleep from weariness—and he died.*

A hammer to the head—that's exactly what this story is.

CHAPTERS 6–8

Bad times, so God calls a new judge. The Lord's angel appears to a lowly farm boy, Gideon, and announces, "The Lord is with you, you mighty warrior." Demonstrating refreshing skepticism (and clearheadedness), Gideon responds: "But sir, if the Lord is with us, why then has all this happened to us? And where are all his wonderful deeds?" Good questions, young man. The angel doesn't really answer but instead orders Gideon to deliver the Israelites from the Midianites. Again, the skeptic pipes up: "But sir, how can I deliver Israel? My clan is the weakest in Mannasseh, and I am the least in my family." The angel, getting impatient, tells him he will succeed. But Gideon refuses to act unless God supplies more proof. The angel ignites Gideon's offering of meat and cakes, and this fiery evidence finally persuades Gideon that he's dealing with the divine.

At last, a Bible hero I can groove with! The Bible has been knocking down its heroes one after another: Isaac, Jacob, Joshua, and others are not the paragons I remembered. But Gideon is another matter. He's the Bible's first empiricist, with a wry doubt that seems distinctly modern. Not since Moses has anyone dared to toy with God as Gideon does, and even Moses didn't have the brazenness of Gideon. He's the very model of the skeptic—dubious, but rational. He's the kind of man I'd like to be.

Gideon becomes a hellacious warrior for God. He tears down the altars to Baal. He sounds his trumpet, summoning allies to join him. (So *that's* Gideon's trumpet!) Before he leads the army into battle, he again tests God. (The test involves wool and morning dew and isn't worth explaining.) God passes the exam, but our demanding judge still isn't satisfied. He asks the Lord for yet more proof that He will aid Israel. Again, God performs a miracle.

Gideon amasses a 32,000-man army, but the Lord says he doesn't need that many soldiers to defeat the Midianites. So Gideon asks anyone who's fearful to go home. That leaves him with 10,000 men. Sounding like Donald Rumsfeld before the invasion of Iraq, God tells Gideon he still has too many troops. The Lord has Gideon bring all the men to the river to drink. Gideon discharges every soldier who laps water with his head down, like a dog—such a man presumably wouldn't be alert in battle. That leaves Gideon with just 300 fighters.

But 300 was plenty for the Spartans at Thermopylae, and it's surely enough for God's Chosen against the Midianite horde. That night, Gideon sneaks his 300 into the Midianite camp, where they all blow trumpets and shout, "For the Lord and for Gideon." Then, they turn the Midianites into hamburger.

Let me rescind some of my enthusiasm for Gideon. He's one angry man. A couple of Israelite villages refuse to provision Gideon's army, because he hasn't yet captured two Midianite kings. Gideon vows revenge. In due course he captures the enemy kings—Gideon always gets his men—then plans a sadistic reprisal against the defiant towns. He captures a young man from one of villages, and interrogates him till he gives up the names of seventy-seven village officials and elders. Gideon seizes the seventy-seven and has them trampled to death underneath thorns and briers. Good Lord! Doesn't this sound like something that would have happened in rural Poland in 1943?

The Israelites beg Gideon to be their king, but he refuses, saying the Lord will rule them. This rejection of the crown seems to be a terrible mistake. If there's any lesson in Judges, it's that people need to be ruled. Israel keeps reverting to idolatry because it lacks a powerful central authority. The occasional martial hero (Gideon, Ehud, Barak) can rout the enemy in the field, and create a brief respite between subjugations. But the good times don't last, because there's no central government to organize the army, secure borders, and enforce laws. Religions are always leery of government, fearing that secular rulers will claim powers that ought to belong to God. But Judges is brutal evidence that the absence of government is much worse than government. This book of the Bible is, in some sense, a vindication of Dick Cheney's worldview. Activist "judges" *are* the problem. They've left the Promised Land a mess. What Israel needs is a strong executive.

One happy coda to the Gideon story: As I was finishing *Good Book*, Hanna gave birth to our third child. We named him Gideon.

CHAPTER 9

Gideon sires seventy sons. After his death, one of them, Abimelech, decides he alone should rule. The original gangbanger, he hires a militia of riffraff—"worthless and reckless fellows"—and massacres all his brothers but one. The lone surviving brother, Jotham, warns the Israelites not to let the fratricidal Abimelech become their king. Jotham's warning takes the form of a lovely fable about how the trees chose a monarch. As far as I can remember, Jotham's tale is the first parable in the Bible. Until now, the Good Book has been pretty literal-minded: When someone acts wrongly, God calls out his misbehavior, then smites him. When God has a law, He issues it, and doesn't wrap it in a metaphor. Jotham's parable is a preview of what's to come with the prophets and Jesus.

But I guess the Israelites found parables as hard to understand as we do today, because they ignore Jotham's caution and crown Abimelech king anyway. He is probably the worst monarch ever born. His capital, Shechem—the same star-crossed town wiped out in the story of

Dinah—eventually turns against him. Abimelech slays the Shechem militiamen who rebel against him, incinerates 1,000 Shechemites taking refuge in the temple tower, razes the city, and sows the land with salt. But he gets his just deserts. As he besieges the next town, a woman drops a millstone on his head. Abimelech begs his servant to stab him to death: "Finish me off, that they may not say of me, 'A woman killed him!'" But of course, that's what we remember: that a woman killed him. There's a great finishing touch to the Abimelech saga: "When the men of Israel saw that Abimelech was dead, everyone went home." *Everyone went home*—what a sublime, casual farewell to a horrifying story.

CHAPTER 10

Two forgettable judges: Tola and Jair. Jair has thirty sons who rode on thirty "burros" and owned thirty "boroughs"—apparently a stilted English rendering of a Hebrew pun. For all its depravity, Judges is easily the funniest biblical book so far, full of potty humor and sharp wit.

CHAPTER 11

If you have children, you might want to skip this chapter. It's a horror. Jephthah, the son of a yet another prostitute, flees from his brutal brothers and becomes a crime boss. He's the first Jewish mobster, the original Bugsy Siegel. But when the Ammonites invade Israel, the elders beg Jephthah to organize the defense. Jephthah agrees. He soon finds himself debating the Ammonite king. The Ammonite demands the return of land conquered by the Israelites. Jephthah counters that the Israelites won the land fair and square in battle, have occupied it for 300 years, and have been ordered by the Lord Himself to keep it. Jephthah tells the king, "Do you not hold what Chemosh your God gives you to possess? So we will hold on to everything that the Lord our God has given us to possess."

And there, my friends, you have practically the entire history of Israel, of the Middle East, and of planet Earth, in two short sentences.

Your God says it's yours. Our God says it's ours. Meet you at nine AM on the battlefield.

At this point, the story turns black. Jephthah makes a vow to God—a foolish vow, a pointless vow, but a vow nonetheless—that if God helps him defeat the Ammonites, he will give as a burnt offering whatever awaits at his door when he returns home from battle. The Israelites rout the enemy (of course), Jephthah returns home, and—you know how this ends. In a moment so ghastly it must have been ripped off by the Greek tragedians (and Hollywood):

> *When Jephthah arrived at his home in Mizpah, there was his daughter coming out to meet him, with timbrel and dance. She was an only child; he had no other son or daughter. On seeing her, he rent his clothes and said, "Alas daughter! You have brought me low; you have become my troubler! For I have uttered a vow to the Lord and I cannot retract."*

It gets worse. The daughter agrees. With perfect filial piety and faith, she volunteers for the sacrifice. In the most excruciating passage, she asks only that she be allowed to go off with her friends to mourn her virginity. "She and her companions went and bewailed her maidenhood upon the hills. After two months' time, she returned to her father, and he did to her as he had vowed. She had never known a man."

Argh. It's clear that the author of Judges recognizes the horror of the story, because the final verse of the chapter notes that Israelite maidens spend four days every year "chanting dirges" for Jephthah's daughter. But make no mistake: Jephthah is heroic for honoring his commitment to God. He's almost the only man in Judges who does what he promises to do, who doesn't complain or doubt. His holy rigidity is glorious.

But this leaves us with a dreadful question: what kind of God is so inflexible that he demands child sacrifice rather than cancel a foolish oath? When Abraham brought Isaac to the mountain, God sent the ram and stopped the murder. This time, He sends no ram. He condemns the child to the pyre instead. God tested Abraham's fidelity, and then spared the innocent boy. In Judges, God tests Jephthah's fidelity, but lets the innocent girl die. Why? What's changed, my Lord? Remember, in Deuteronomy and Numbers, the greatest crime of the Israelites' enemies—and the key reason they must be driven from the Promised Land—is that they sacrifice their own children to their gods. Yet here God's greatest warrior does the same, and the Lord seems unbothered. Perhaps the lesson of this horror is that in a disordered nation like Israel during the era of Judges, where people are only intermittently faithful, terrible things will keep happening.

Whatever the reason, Judges has left me bewildered. It's an awful book. I don't mean that it's boring: on the contrary, it's a great read. But it's morally repellent, perhaps even more disturbing than Joshua because it's much more graphic. In fact, it is so troubling to read that you have to wonder what the point of it is. Why are we asked to churn through this carnival of gore, immorality, fratricide, infanticide, and regicide, especially since God's redemptive love is mostly absent? And wouldn't it be more persuasive if the worst things happened to *faithless* Israelites, rather than to innocents and true believers such as Jephthah's daughter?

Perhaps the main difficulty is what I would call the "cheerleading problem." Who are we supposed to root for? Are we supposed to rejoice that the left-handed assassin Ehud has gutted fat King Eglon, or spare a moment to mourn the degrading circumstances of Eglon's death? Or consider the triumphal Song of Deborah in Judges 5, which commemorates the slaying of Sisera. The song makes brutal fun of Sisera's mother, who's waiting for her son to return from war. Sure, Sisera's mom may be the enemy, but it's grotesque to mock her suffering. Only a sadist could enjoy the sanguinary glee of Judges. But the book is here for a reason, so what is it?

In *Before Abraham Was*, professors Arthur Quinn and Isaac Kikawada of the University of California, Berkeley, write that Judges:

> *can be seen as a moral test for its readers. Those who are like the sinning Israelites will simply enjoy the story of Deborah as a victory of "us" over "them"—and will be indifferent to the truth or to the sentiments of common humanity, as long as this indifference*

is to "our" advantage. Those, in contrast, who do see the ironies, see the parallel between the mother of Sisera and the daughter of Jephthah, the treachery of Jael and that of Delilah, will find Judges an excruciating experience, a wrenching call to humility and repentance.

CHAPTERS 13–16

Has there ever been a more depressing story about the relationship between men and women than the tale of Samson? Its two conclusions are:

(1) Women are deceptive and heartless.
(2) Men are too stupid and sex-crazed to realize this.

An angel appears to a barren woman to tell her she will bear a son who will deliver Israel from the Philistines. The angel warns that she must never cut his hair, because he will be a "nazarite" dedicated to God. The woman passes this news on to her husband, Manoah—as usual, the husband gets a name; the wife doesn't. His response is hilarious. He doesn't believe her. Instead of taking her word, he prays that the Lord will send the angel again to tell them "what we are to do concerning the boy who will be born." So even though the angel already told his wife what they are to do, Manoah insists on being told again. (I have a relative like this, who annoyingly insists that you repeat to him anything you already told his wife.) The angel does return, and reiterates to Manoah what he already told Manoah's better half. In due course a son is born, and they name him Samson.

Visiting a nearby town, young Samson sees a Philistine girl and falls in love with her. Manoah and his wife then become the first Jewish parents in history to complain, *You couldn't find a nice Jewish girl?* Truly. They say, "Is there not a woman among your kin, or among all our people, that you must go to take a wife from the uncircumcised Philistines?" But their son just has a thing for pagan chicks. Samson insists that dad arrange a marriage with the Philistine babe.

The Samson I met in Sunday school was brave, innocent, and holy.

The real Samson, I'm dismayed to learn, is anything but. Samson is the original meathead—born 3,400 years too early to be a hockey goon, or the fraternity rush chairman. On the way to his wedding, Samson tears a young lion apart with his bare hands. Later he eats honey from the lion's carcass. At the wedding banquet, Samson bets the Philistine guests they can't solve his riddle, which is about the lion and the honey. The riddle stumps the Philistines for three days. Eventually they threaten Samson's bride, saying they'll kill her and her dad unless she coaxes the answer out of Samson. She nags and wheedles and cajoles her husband for four days. Samson, clearly not the sharpest sword in the scabbard, eventually tells her the answer. She immediately passes it on to the Philistines, who solve the riddle. This enrages Samson, who also seems to think the Philistines have slept with his wife. (He tells them: "[You] plowed with my heifer.") So the furious judge murders thirty other, apparently innocent, Philistine men. According to Judges, Samson kills them while he is possessed by the "spirit of the Lord"—a kind of holy 'roid rage. It's not at all clear why God would encourage such pointless murder.

Now it gets really complicated. Following the slaughter, his father-in-law gives away Samson's wife to Samson's best man, and offers Samson his wife's sister instead (echoes of Laban and Jacob). Samson, who must be off his meds, flips out at the wife swap. He catches 300 foxes, attaches torches to their tails, and releases them into the Philistines' fields, where they burn the crops down. (Like so many mass murderers, Samson gets off on torturing small animals. No word, PETA friends, on the fate of the foxes.) One bad turn deserves another: the Philistines retaliate by incinerating Samson's wife and father-in-law. Then Samson takes revenge by butchering a mess of Philistines. The Philistines give tit for tat by dispatching an army against Samson's land, Judah. To stop the war, Samson agrees to let Judah hand him over to the enemy, but the minute he's in Philistine custody, "the spirit of the Lord rush[es] on him," he breaks his shackles, grabs a donkey's jawbone, and massacres 1,000 Philistines with it. Is there a lesson in this escalating slaughter? I don't see one, except perhaps: don't tell riddles. That's what started the war.

And last we come to that sizzling hot temptress, the Mata Hari of the

Middle East, Delilah. Judges doesn't say Delilah is a Philistine, but given Samson's addiction to foreign sexpots, and given her eager cooperation with the Philistine elders, it's probable that she was. Samson falls hard for her. The Philistine bosses order her to discover the secret of his strength, so the Philistines can capture him. I always thought Samson revealed the truth about his hair to Delilah immediately. He doesn't, and that delay shows him to be even more of a sucker than I remembered.

Delilah asks him why he's so strong. Not trusting her, he tells her that if he's tied up with seven fresh bowstrings, he will become weak. She ties him up with seven fresh bowstrings—presumably while he's sleeping—and brings in Philistines to seize him. He, of course, snaps the bowstrings and drives off the attackers. At this point, any man who's not a complete moron or entirely whipped would dump the treacherous vixen. But not Samson, who appears to be the dumbest Jew in history. Instead, he again cuddles with Delilah. She again asks for the secret of his strength. He lies to her again. The Philistines try to capture him again, on the basis of the lie, and he defeats them again. This happens a third time, but still he doesn't leave her. Finally she—like his dead first wife—nags him so much that he gives up his secret.

We all know what happens next. A very bad haircut. The Philistines arrest him and gouge out his eyes. The Philistines—apparently not brainiacs either—allow him to grow his hair again, then bring him out to dance at a celebration of their god Dagon. Shaggy Samson calls on the Lord to return his strength. He pushes down the banquet hall, killing all 3,000 guests and himself. Even in death, he remains an unappealing figure. He's chosen by God, but he's entirely ungodly. He looks out only for himself. His campaign against the Philistines—which costs the lives of innocent Israelites and Philistines—has no holy or pragmatic purpose. He doesn't seek the good of Israel or the glory of the Lord; he seeks only private revenge.

CHAPTERS 19–21

Each time I think Judges can't get any more gruesome, it proves me wrong. Here's the story. A Levite man's concubine runs away from him. (Actually, the text is ambiguous about whether she is his concubine or his wife.) The Levite follows her to her father's house in Bethlehem and persuades her to reconcile. They begin their journey home. Late in the afternoon, they approach a non-Israelite city, but the Levite refuses to spend the night there. "We will not turn aside into a city of foreigners, who do not belong to the people of Israel." (Remember this decision!) So they go on to the Israelite town of Gibeah, where an old man offers them shelter. Like a terrified bit player in a horror movie, he warns them to avoid the town square. They bunk at the old man's house, but when night falls, the men of the town, a "perverse lot," pound on the door and demand that the Levite come out, "so that we may have intercourse with him." You remember the story now, right? This is what happened in Sodom, when the townsmen demanded to rape Lot's guests. In that case, God intervened and brimstoned everyone.

Not this time.

As in the story of Lot, the host tries to protect his guest, offering his own virgin daughter and the Levite's concubine to the mob instead. The mob refuses them. The Levite, desperate to save himself, grabs his concubine, and shoves her out the door to the mob. "They wantonly raped her, and abused her all through the night until the morning. And as the dawn began to break, they let her go." She collapses at the door of the house. In the morning, the Levite opens the door and finds her lying on the threshold. Does he offer an apology for sending her in his place? Does he offer her a word of comfort? Nope. He says, "Get up . . . we are going." She doesn't answer, so he tosses her on the back of the donkey and starts toward home. By the time they get home, she has died.

(Every now and then you hear about an eight-year-old who has memorized the whole Bible. It makes you think: parents let kids read *this*?)

And it gets even sicker. He cuts her body into a dozen pieces and sends them throughout Israel, demanding that the twelve tribes aid his revenge. "Has such a thing ever happened since the day that the Israelites came up from the land of Egypt?"

What is the point of this shocking reworking of the tale of Lot? In Lot, it was the wicked Sodomites who committed the crime. Here, God's own Chosen People are the rapists. (Had the Levite and the concubine stopped in that town of foreigners, they would have been safe.) In Genesis, God intervened to save Lot and his family from the mob. Here God is absent, presumably disgusted with the moral decay of His people. And the Levite himself, though a victim of the mob, is almost as wicked as they are: he's a coward who surrenders his woman to save himself, then cruelly neglects her after the gang rape.

An army of 400,000 Israelites demands that the tribe of Benjamin turn over the Gibeah rapists. The Benjaminites refuse, and after three days of bloody fighting, the town of Gibeah is eradicated, and all the Benjaminites except 600 men are dead. The other Israelites refuse to let their daughters marry any of the Benjaminite survivors, but they feel "compassion" for the men, because they don't want the tribe to go extinct. So how do the Israelites show their compassion? They besiege a nearby city, and slaughter all the residents except 400 virgin girls, whom they give to the Benjaminites. They're still 200 wives short. So the Israelites tell the unmarried Benjaminites to kidnap 200 more girls from the town of Shiloh.

And then the book ends, with a marvelous, hit-the-nail final verse: "In those days there was no King in Israel; all the people did what was right in their own eyes." This perfectly captures the pessimism of Judges. Men who abandon God—and reject earthly authority—will find themselves in a chaotic, frightful land, a place of hideous crime and persistent idolatry, a place where law is dead, and only personal vengeance remains.

EIGHT

The Book of 1 Samuel

The Bible's Bill Clinton

In which the prophet Samuel rules Israel and anoints Saul as the first king; Saul quickly loses God's confidence; Samuel decides that the young shepherd David will succeed him; David defeats the giant Goliath and becomes Saul's greatest general; the jealous Saul tries to kill David, who flees into exile; the Philistines defeat and kill Saul.

CHAPTERS 1–3

It's no wonder priests, ministers, and rabbis have spent so much time, during the last two millennia, discouraging regular folks from reading the Bible on their own. The Good Book makes most of its clerics look like sleazeballs. The first high priest was Aaron, the Fredo Corleone of the Sinai. Then Aaron's two priest sons dissed God so badly that He smote them. Here at the beginning of 1 Samuel—"First Samuel," as it's pronounced—we meet Eli, Israel's top priest, who also does the profession no favors. Sitting in the temple one day, he observes a visibly distressed woman, Hannah, praying for the Lord to give her a son, because she's barren. Eli sees her lips moving, but can't hear her speaking. Does he ask her what's wrong? Does he offer succor and counsel? Uh, no. He accosts Hannah angrily and says, "How long will you make a drunken spectacle of yourself? Put away your wine." What a welcoming man of God!

Rather then telling Eli to stick it where the Lord don't shine, Hannah apologetically insists that she's not drunk, but "pouring out my soul before the Lord." (A lovely description of prayer, don't you think?) Eli tells her that God will grant her plea for a son, and He does. Hannah dedicates little Samuel to God. She drops him off at the temple as soon as he's weaned; this seems a little rough on both mom and baby, if you ask me.

At the parting, Hannah sings a lovely poem of praise to the Lord. (A small sample: "He raises up the poor from the dust; He lifts the needy from the ash heap to make them sit with princes and inherit a seat of honor.") Here's a question. There are few women in the Bible, yet they sing many, even most, of the book's great songs: Miriam's celebration after the Red Sea crossing, the song of Deborah, and Hannah's hymn here, to name a few. Why would songs and poetry particularly belong to women? And, as a cultural matter, did women, who are otherwise so silent, really take public roles as singers and poets?

Eli and his priest sons raise Samuel and do just as lousy a job with the boy as you'd expect three men to do (*Three Priests and a Baby*). The sons are "scoundrels" who steal the animal sacrifices, eat the burnt offering, and sexually harass and seduce the temple's girl assistants. Eli, a feckless father, weakly chastises his sons, but doesn't stop their misbehavior. An angel tells Eli that his family will be tossed out of the priesthood; his sons will die on the same day; and a faithful new priest—Samuel, we realize—will take their place.

And, lo, it comes to pass. God begins talking to Samuel, and he soon becomes Israel's top prophet.

CHAPTERS 4–7

Raiders of the Lost Ark, the prequel. The Philistines rout the Israelite army, so the Israelites dispatch the ark of the covenant—the sacred box containing the Ten Commandments and other holy objects—to the battlefield in hopes of harnessing its divine power for victory. A curious thing happens: the ark fails the Israelites. (This contradicts everything Steven Spielberg taught me about the ark's absolute power. What kind of world do we live in, where you can't even trust Spielberg?) Initially terrified of the ark, the Philistines recover and outfight the quavering Israelites. They capture the ark and kill Eli's two sons, who were guarding it. When Eli hears of his son's deaths, he falls backward out of his chair, breaks his neck, and dies. Then Eli's daughter-in-law, who's in labor, hears of her husband's death and also dies, but not before giving birth to a son, Ichabod, whose name means, "The glory has departed from Israel." Now that's a kid with bad karma.

OK, back to *Raiders*. The jubilant Philistines place the captured ark in the temple of their god Dagon. In the morning they find the statue of Dagon facedown before the ark. They return Dagon's statue to its pedestal, but the next morning they find it on the ground again, this time with the head and arms chopped off. And the ark is just getting started with the poor Philistines. It then inflicts hemorrhoids on the people of Ashdod. (So Spielberg was also wrong about the ark causing your face to melt. It works its magic on your other end.) The Philistines move the ark to Gath, and sure enough, the Gathites soon have hemorrhoids, too. The ark goes to Ekron, and, yup, it's Preparation H time there as well. (The "H" stands for "holy.") With Ekronites dying, the Philistines are desperate to return the ark. Their priests advise sending it back with a "guilt offering" to appease God. What's the gift they come up with? Five gold mice and five gold hemorrhoids! What would a gold hemorrhoid even look like?

I'm apparently not the only one who wondered about the gold hemorrhoids. As I was finishing this chapter, *Biblical Archaeology Review* published an article speculating that the hemorrhoids were actually phalluses, and that the real affliction which struck the Philistines was not hemorrhoids but erectile dysfunction.

Samuel leads a religious revival in Israel, persuading his people to tear down their statues of Baal and return to the Lord. Thus inspired by God, the Israelites reconquer the Philistines. Let's pause for a second to note the profound difference between Samuel and the judges in

Judges. The judges fought battles and deposed enemy tyrants, but
rarely exhorted the Israelites to love and fear God. As a result, their
success was temporary. The Israelites backslid as soon as the judges
died. Samuel reminds the Israelites that they will thrive only insofar
as they obey God. Worldly success is always caused by faith. So Samuel, unlike the judges, is actually judging his people.

CHAPTER 8

Yet more bad men of the cloth: Samuel's sons follow him into the
priesthood, but they "took bribes and perverted justice." Again the
Bible is reminding us of the evils of inherited power. In Numbers, the
Lord made the priesthood hereditary. That was clearly a mistake. Every priest so far—Aaron, Eli, and now Samuel—has had wretched,
undeserving sons. The Bible is refreshingly meritocratic: again and
again it measures the worth of men by their deeds, not their bloodlines. Except for the original patriarchs, none of the great Jewish biblical stars has gotten a leg up through nepotism. Moses is a self-made
prophet. We know nothing of Joshua's parentage. Gideon is the youngest son in the weakest clan of the feeblest tribe. Samson came from
nothing; Samuel, too. One reason why Americans read the Bible more
enthusiastically than, say, Europeans may be that we are a deeply
meritocratic people, and the Bible affirms that equal opportunity is
God's plan, too.

Even so, the Israelites want a monarch. Weary of war and fearful
that Samuel's corrupt sons will succeed him, the Israelites beseech the
aging priest to anoint a king to rule them. Samuel bristles and gives a
brilliant, moving sermon against monarchy: "These will be the ways
of the king who will reign over you: He will take your sons and appoint them to his chariots. . . . [H]e will appoint for himself commanders of thousands and commanders of 50s, and some to plow his
ground, and to reap his harvest, and to make his implements of war
and the equipment of his chariots. He will take your daughters to be
perfumers and cooks and bakers. He will take the best of your fields
and vineyards and olive orchards and give them to his courtiers," etc.

It's very convincing, yet "the people refused to listen." They continue to demand a king. The Lord tells Samuel: *Go ahead, give them their king.*

Really, can you criticize them for wanting a monarch? We just finished a book, Judges, which is all about what happens when there is no leader—mass murder, gang rape, anarchy, and so forth. The Israelites had lived through that nightmare. Samuel's theoretical warnings against kingship fail against the lived misery of Judges. Kings may be corrupt and brutal, but the Israelites aren't stupid for choosing monarchy over anarchy. I would have done the same.

CHAPTERS 9–10

Samuel is keeping his eyes peeled for a suitable king. The Lord tells him that His favored candidate is about to visit. It turns out to be a young man named Saul, who has lost a donkey and wants Samuel to help divine its whereabouts. These two details perfectly sum up the character of the future king: Saul's the kind of person who loses the animal he's supposed to watch and then wastes the time of Israel's most powerful man in order to find it. He's at once incompetent, careless, and entitled. But Samuel only notices that Saul is the best-looking man in his tribe and the tallest Israelite around, and so he has him anointed king in a private ceremony.

Samuel convenes all the Israelites to crown the new king. When he announces his choice of Saul, the young man has vanished. A search party discovers him hiding in the luggage. A sympathetic reading of this episode is that Saul is a modest young man, showing proper humility in the face of God's extraordinary demand. A less forgiving reading is that he's not merely careless and incompetent but also deeply phobic. How many warning signs do you need? Even Samuel recognizes that Saul isn't qualified to rule. Rather, he merely observes that Saul is very tall: "There is none like him among all the people."

CHAPTER 12

Samuel gives his farewell address. It's a lovely sermon, a stark contrast to the wild threats issued by the dying Moses and Joshua. Samuel glumly accepts that the Israelites want a king but reminds them that their earthly monarch cannot hold a candle to the only ruler who matters. Rather than worrying about "useless things," Samuel exhorts, they should revere God. Samuel is unlike any biblical figure before him. Unlike the patriarchs, he does not appeal to economic self-interest by talking of covenants and the Promised Land. Unlike the judges, he does not seek mere military triumph. And unlike Moses, he is not concerned about codifying laws for an entire people. No, Samuel is focused on *individual* belief, the unshakable obligation of each Israelite to love and fear the Lord. More than anyone else in the Bible so far, Samuel speaks a modern language of faith. I'm adding him to my very short list of Bible heroes I could name a son after: Abraham, Joseph, Caleb, Samuel, and, of course, Gideon.

CHAPTER 13

King Saul starts a war with the Philistines. After Saul's son Jonathan routs an enemy garrison, the Philistines roll their 30,000 chariots against the Israelites. Big problem. Saul's forces flee into caves, and the king expects Samuel to rescue him. (Though Samuel has already given his farewell address, he keeps reappearing throughout the book.) Instead of waiting for Samuel's arrival, Saul makes the burnt offering himself. When Samuel shows up, he flies into a rage at Saul's apparent blasphemy. Saul has violated Israel's strict division of church and state. In handling the burnt offering, Saul usurped the cleric's job. This alarms Samuel because it undermines essential priestly authority. Saul, like a greedy president or King Henry VIII, is trying to undo the separation of powers. Samuel won't stand for it. He tells Saul his days as king are numbered: God will find a more obedient monarch, "a man after His own heart."

CHAPTER 15

The battle between Samuel and Saul escalates. Channeling the Lord, Samuel orders Saul to "utterly destroy" the Amalekites by killing all their men, women, children, and animals. Saul disobeys. He kills everyone except the king, and he spares the best livestock. The Lord and Samuel are furious that Saul has flouted God's direct order. (This puts modern readers in the bizarre position of siding with God and genocide against Saul's mercy.) Confronted by Samuel, Saul sputters that he kept the animals alive only so they could be sacrificed to the Lord. (Given Saul's lack of fidelity, this is almost certainly a lie.) Samuel rebukes the king: "Has the Lord as great delight in burnt offerings and sacrifices as in obedience to the voice of the Lord? Surely to obey is better than sacrifice, and to heed than the fat of lambs."

I'm not sure what to make of Samuel's conclusion that obedience trumps anything else, even good intentions. It's a very militaristic philosophy: you must obey orders, even when you think you have a better idea. Samuel again disavows Saul, then executes the Amalek king himself.

"And the Lord was sorry that He had made Saul king over Israel." I bet He was sorry. Just as the Israelites are discovering what a pain it is for them to have a king (especially a nut like Saul), God is discovering what a pain it is for *Him* to have a king. A king, after all, sets himself outside God's laws. A king doesn't think the rules apply to him. According to the Bible, there can be only one true king. That's very galling for the king on Earth, who will do everything he can to circumvent God's rule. In a sense, the face-off between Saul and Samuel anticipates the history of western civilization until 1900. God and his priests demand one thing; the king thinks he knows better; the sparks fly upward. Saul is a troubled soul and a rotten monarch, but I can't help sympathizing with him against Samuel. The priest is doing everything he can to topple the king and bring down the monarchy he despises. Why shouldn't Saul try to control his own kingdom?

CHAPTER 16

The Lord dispatches Samuel to Bethlehem to find a new king. Samuel ends up at the house of Jesse and Jesse's sons. Apparently having learned nothing from the fiasco with Saul, Samuel starts to choose Jesse's tall, handsome eldest son as the anointed one. God interrupts irritably and says, "Do not look on his appearance or on the height of his stature . . . for the Lord does not see as mortals see; they look on the outward appearance, but the Lord looks on the heart."

In many ancient myths and holy books, heroes are taller and stronger than ordinary men. But the Bible is full of regular guys. Tall Saul is the exception, the only champion of God chosen for his appearance. (And look how that turned out.) Otherwise, the Bible heroes are average Jobs—frail and cowardly Jacob (rather than manly Esau), stuttering Moses, little Gideon.

Samuel rejects Jesse's seven oldest sons. Then, as in the story of Cinderella, he asks if there is another sibling. The youngest, the shepherd David, is summoned from the fields. The Lord says he's the one, and Samuel anoints him. Let me partially retract the comments I made in the last paragraph. Right after the moving speech about how God doesn't pay attention to outward appearance, the Bible ogles David, who "had beautiful eyes, and was handsome."

As soon as David is anointed, the "spirit of the Lord departed" from Saul, and he starts being tormented by an "evil spirit." (Given his symptoms, it sounds as if he's suffering from something like schizophrenia, or possibly epilepsy, or perhaps a really nasty depression.) Saul is soothed only by music. By coincidence, Saul hears that David is great on the lyre and summons him to court. David quickly becomes Saul's favorite and calms him with songs whenever the madness descends. This tips us off to David's slyness. He's been anointed king by Samuel, yet he never reveals this to Saul. The whole episode is very *All About Eve.*

CHAPTER 17

David and Goliath—it's just as good as I remember. You know the story. The Philistines and Israelites prepare for war. When the armies assemble, the Philistines send out their champion, Goliath. He stands either nine and a half feet tall or six and a half feet tall, depending on which translation you believe. Let's make him nine and a half feet tall. "The shaft of his spear was like a weaver's beam, and his spear's head weighed 600 shekels." I don't know what that means, but it sounds scary. For forty days Goliath shouts challenges at the Israelites, and for forty days Saul can't find a willing champion. Meanwhile, Jesse sends young David to the battlefield with a care package of bread and cheese for his older brothers. David hears Goliath's challenge, and he's furious: "Who is this uncircumcised Philistine that he should defy the armies of the living God?" David's oldest brother, Eliab, chastises him for butting in on the affair. David doesn't back down, and he's brought to Saul.

Saul scoffs that David's too young and inexperienced to fight Goliath. David counters that he kills lions and bears while protecting his flock. Saul doesn't really have any other choice, since his men are cowards, so he names David as his champion. David tries on Saul's armor, but it's too cumbersome. He goes unprotected into battle, carrying only his slingshot. Naked before God, David embodies manly faith. He taunts the giant. "You come to me with sword and spear and javelin, but I come to you in the name of the Lord of hosts, the God of the armies of Israel, whom you have defied." You know the rest. One rock slung. One dead giant.

I must confess I'm pretty excited to be reading about my namesake. Throughout my childhood, I had a poster on my wall, showing a painting of David with the head of Goliath. (It was by Andrea del Castagno.) I then took it with me to college. Like the David in the painting, I was tall with curly brown hair, and I always identified with him. We were not much of a Bible household—my parents are the most secular of Jews—and David was the only figure in the Bible I ever thought about. As a little boy, I wanted to be brave like him. As a teenager I got an illicit thrill out of the story of Bathsheba. I wasn't sophisticated, but insofar as I had a biblical hero, it was David. Now that I am actually reading his story, I'm glad that he's living up to my childhood idealization.

CHAPTERS 18–19

"The soul of [Saul's son] Jonathan was bound to the soul of David, and Jonathan loved him as his own soul." Hmm. Does it mean what I think it means?

David rises to command Saul's army and leads the Israelites to one victory after another. Saul becomes envious when he hears the people singing, "Saul has killed his thousands, and David his ten thousands." Saul, by now quite loony, sets out to kill his young rival. He has as much success as the CIA had with Fidel Castro (and has almost as much imagination as the CIA). He heaves his spear at David but misses. Next, he tells David he can marry his daughter Michal if he brings Saul the foreskins of 100 Philistines. Saul expects David to die in the attempt. (This foreshadows David's own crime against Bathsheba's husband.) But the mission is no problem for David, who kills 200 Philistines—100 extra for good measure—and returns with the fleshy bits. Let's not dwell on what Saul did with the present.

Time for plan C. Saul tells Jonathan he wants to assassinate David. Jonathan warns David, then talks his dad out of the attempt, convincing him that David is innocent. Saul promises he won't try to kill David, and he really seems to mean it. But sure enough, the next time David and Saul are alone together, the king again flings his spear at David, who runs away. So Saul sends his guards to capture David, but his wife, Michal—Saul's own daughter, you remember—makes a mannequin of David out of the household idol and hides it in the bed while David escapes.

This episode of the idol in the bed is a fabulous reminder that the Bible has not only given us much of the language we speak—words, phrases, aphorisms—but also invented our very idea of what a story is. The dummy in the bed has reappeared thousands of times in books, in movies, on television, and in real life, for serious purposes (the prisoner breaking out of jail, the hero avoiding the murderer), and for comedy (the teenager sneaking out after curfew). It's a 3,000-year-old plot gimmick.

CHAPTER 20

David and Jonathan get ever more *Brokeback*. The two are thrown together repeatedly, as Jonathan keeps tipping David off about Saul's plans to kill him. Jonathan and David sneak off and swear their love for each other. Later, when David knows he has to flee Saul's court permanently, they rendezvous in a farm field, kiss, weep, and bid each other good-bye. Again I ask: does this mean what I think it means?

CHAPTERS 21–25

Having made his final break with Saul, David sets himself up as a guerrilla, a freedom fighter at the head of a 600-man militia. He's the George Washington of Judea. Meanwhile, Saul sinks ever deeper into paranoia. When he hears that some priests lent David a sword, he orders eighty-five of them murdered and then wipes out the city where they lived. One survivor escapes and finds David, who blames himself for the massacre.

You may bite my head off for saying this, but David reminds me powerfully of Bill Clinton (and not just because of their sexual appetites and their love of music). Like Clinton, David brilliantly combines two virtues and one vice. He truly loves God. He is profoundly warm and empathetic—he's continually feeling the pain of others. Yet he cannily exploits his understanding of human nature for his own advantage. He's always gaming people, measuring them, working them over to gain an edge (e.g., he adores Jonathan, yet flips him against his dad).

David's guerrilla army rescues an Israeli town from the Philistines. Rather than thanking David, Saul immediately besieges the town to trap David's army inside. David and his men escape to the wilderness. Saul pursues him, and in a brilliantly cinematic moment—you can imagine it filmed from above by helicopter—the two armies are on opposite sides of the same mountain, David marching right into Saul's trap. Suddenly, Saul is summoned away to repel a Philistine incursion. Saul returns with another huge force. David and his men take shelter in a cave. By coincidence, Saul ducks into the cave "to relieve himself." David's men urge him to kill the king while he's vulnerable, but instead, David sneaks up and clips a corner from Saul's cloak. When Saul leaves the cave, David follows him and confronts him with the torn piece. "See, my father, see the corner of your cloak in my hand; for by the fact that I cut off the corner of your cloak, and did not kill you, you may know for certain that there is no wrong or treason in my hands. I have not sinned against you, though you are hunting me to take my life."

Ever prone to histrionics, the mad king shouts and weeps. He forgives his protégé and apologizes hysterically. "You are more righteous than I; for you have repaid me good, whereas I have repaid you evil." Saul recognizes that David will indeed be king and begs him not to wipe out Saul's family when he takes the throne. Saul goes home and leaves David in peace. Saul has already promised forgiveness to David three times before this and has always reneged. I am betting this amnesty won't last, either. In Saul's defense, he's not calculating in his betrayals of David—he's just so deranged that he can't help himself.

CHAPTER 25

David's always working the angles. Nabal, a "surly and mean" tycoon, is married to the "clever and beautiful" Abigail. David sends ten of his men to ask Nabal for food. They tell Nabal that they could have stolen his livestock, but they didn't. In exchange for that restraint, they suggest, Nabal should feed David and his militia. Nabal brushes them off, saying, "Should I then take my bread and my water, and the meat that I slaughtered for my own shearers, and give them to men who come from I don't know where?" His rebuff enrages David, who immediately marches his army toward Nabal's farm. Abigail hears that they're coming and thinks fast. She collects huge quantities of provisions and waylays David's men before they reach Nabal. She flings herself at David's feet and begs him not to take vengeance, saying that if he kills Nabal, he will have a guilty conscience. David agrees, but takes all the food (200 fig cakes—yum!). Several days later, the Lord smites Nabal. David immediately marries Abigail.

A couple of things about this story:

(1) David is such a horndog that he picks up a widow at a funeral.

(2) The first time I read it, I enjoyed the meet-cute romance between David and Abigail and shared David's righteous indignation against the miserly Nabal. But when I read it again, I was appalled. David is a shakedown artist. Reexamine the facts of the story. David's men tell Nabal they didn't steal his animals—the obvious threat being: if you don't pay up, we *will* steal your animals. It's a protection racket. Nabal is absolutely right. He shouldn't have to feed David's army rather than his own men. David marching his army against Nabal is like a capo sending his hit man to break a deadbeat's knees. It's extortion. David walks away with all the food he can carry. And Nabal, the victim of this crime, is smitten for his troubles.

CHAPTER 26

David and his lieutenant Abishai sneak into Saul's camp at night and walk right up to the sleeping king. It's a repeat of David's encounter with the peeing Saul in the cave. Abishai begs to assassinate the king, but David—cannily thinking ahead to when he will wear the crown and malcontents will want to kill him—forbids it: "No one can lay hands on the Lord's anointed with impunity." Instead, David steals Saul's spear and water jar and tiptoes out of the camp. From a far hilltop, David then taunts Saul's commander Abner for not guarding Saul: "You deserve to die, because you did not keep watch over your lord the king."

Saul hears David's voice and calls out to him. David begs for peace. Saul immediately apologizes again and implores David to come back. Knowing just how fickle and deranged Saul is, David doesn't accept the invitation, but he does return the spear and water jar, and they part friends. Saul's farewell to David—which turns out to be the final words between them—is: "May you be blessed, my son David! You shall achieve, and you shall prevail." This is the benediction of a father to his heir: he blesses David and calls him his son. This further legitimizes David's claim to succeed him, right?

CHAPTER 27

David is sick of the hassle of living in Israel. (I know how he feels: Israelis can be *so* rude.) So, he defects to the Philistines. This is shocking. It's as if General MacArthur had moved to China in 1951. The Philistines are tyrannical, thuggish idolaters, chariots-of-mass-destruction-driving villains, and David has been doing little but murdering them for the past ten chapters—yet they're still better allies than David's own king. David and his 600 men become a bandit gang. They raid all the neighboring tribes except the Israelites, sack towns, slaughter women, and steal livestock. It's ugly.

Still, let's note what David does *not* do during his exile among the Philistines. He does not worship idols. He may not be particularly faithful during this period—his conversations with God certainly decrease in frequency—but he never abandons the Lord.

The Philistine king, Achish, decides to make war against Israel and tells David he must accompany the Philistines. David doesn't hesitate: he eagerly volunteers to serve as Achish's personal bodyguard and fight his own countrymen. But Achish's generals distrust David—they fear he'll switch sides during the battle—and they persuade the king to send him home.

CHAPTER 28

When King Achish invades Israel, Saul, who's more and more cuckoo, decides he needs to consult with Samuel. Since Samuel is now dead, this is a problem. Saul disguises himself and visits the Witch of Endor. He begs her to conjure the ghost of Samuel. This episode drives home, as if we could have forgotten it, the faithlessness of Saul. He has explicitly banned witchcraft, and the Lord made it abundantly clear in Leviticus that witchcraft is absolutely, utterly, completely forbidden, an automatic death-penalty offense—do not pass Go; do not collect 200 shekels. Yet Saul is so scornful of God that he consults the witch anyway. (And he's so spineless that he can't even make a decision about war strategy without ghostly advice.)

Samuel comes when summoned, but he's steamed. He reminds Saul that the Lord "has become your adversary." He also predicts that Saul and his sons will die the next day. This plunges Saul into despair, but after a nice steak dinner, he returns to the battlefield.

CHAPTER 30

A stupendous digression. David returns home to find that the Amalekites have sacked his town and kidnapped his wives. David and his men weep till they can weep no more. (Young men, take a lesson from David: He's a warrior, he plays the lyre—the guitar of its day—and he's not afraid of a good cry. Now do you understand why the chicks dig him?) David prays to God, who tells him to pursue the raiders. As he and his men chase the enemy, they encounter an Egyptian boy, the slave of one of the Amalekites. He is sick, so the Amalekites left him behind to die. David and his men feed and nurse the boy back to health. He leads them to the Amalekite camp, where they rescue David's wives and kill the raiders. The story hinges on the Egyptian slave boy. Here we have the tables of Exodus turned: instead of Egyptians with Israelite slaves, we have Israelites with an Egyptian slave. Do the Israelites maltreat him or set him to work, as the Egyptians did to them? No: they feed him, revive him, liberate him. It's a tribute to David's big heart (as well as his strategic brilliance, since he uses the boy to win the battle). The Bible is surprisingly short on acts of mercy, but this one glows on the page.

Let's also pause for a second to appreciate the structural brilliance of 1 Samuel. Here in its final chapters, the book jumps back and forth between David and Saul. It's a fantastic contrast. In David's chapters, we witness fidelity, mercy, and martial genius. In Saul's, we see degradation, idolatry, and incompetence. The crosscutting heightens the tension of the stories and prepares us for David's coming triumph.

CHAPTER 31

One final jump cut takes us back to Saul versus the Philistines. This battle is a rout. The Philistines kill Saul's sons, including David's favorite, Jonathan. Saul doesn't last much longer. Wounded by an arrow, he begs his servant to finish him off, "so that the uncircumcised may not run me through and make sport of me." The servant refuses, and Saul falls on his sword. The Philistines cut off his head and impale his body to a wall.

NINE

The Book of 2 Samuel

God's Favorite King

In which David is crowned king of Judah, then becomes ruler of all Israel when Saul's son is assassinated; he makes Jerusalem his capital and moves the ark there; he seduces Bathsheba, impregnates her, gets her husband, Uriah, killed in battle, and marries her; God punishes David by killing the baby, but they have another son, Solomon; David's son Amnon rapes his sister Tamar, so another of David's sons, Absalom, has Amnon killed; exiled for that crime, Absalom returns and deposes David, who eventually defeats his son; Absalom gets stuck in a tree by his hair and is killed by David's men.

CHAPTER I

Always a good weeper, David cries again about the death of Saul and Jonathan. It's genuine sorrow. David, let's remember, never touched a hair on Saul's head, even when Saul was trying to kill him. David's lament is gorgeous. It is the source of the phrase: "How the mighty are fallen." David reserves his deepest sadness for Jonathan, of course: "Your love was wonderful to me, more than the love of women."

CHAPTERS 2—3

David gets himself crowned in Hebron—but only as king of the southern territory of Judah. Saul's son Ishbaal still rules the other tribes of
Israel. You don't have to be a champion linguist to notice something
curious about Ishbaal's name. Why would the king of Israel be named
after Baal? Biblical scholars obsess over words that are based on the
names of gods. Such "theophoric" names help reveal the true history
of the text. As James Kugel points out in *How to Read the Bible* (a book
I read *after* I read the Bible), Israelite names are often based on the two
popular names of God in the Bible, "El" and "Yahweh." E*l*ijah, Beth*el*,
Isra*el*, and others are connected to El. Names such as *J*onathan and
*J*oab derive from Yahweh. So what about Ishbaal's name? It suggests
that at least some Israelites retained close ties to Baal, despite their
nominal monotheistic worship of Yahweh.

War erupts between the rival kings, with David getting the best of
it. David demands the return his first wife, Michal, who's in her
brother Ishbaal's custody. When David and Saul had their falling-out,
the king had remarried Michal to another man. In a heartbreaking
scene, Michal is sent back to David, with her new husband, Paltiel,
trailing behind her, sobbing.

Let's linger for a moment on this episode. David has an exquisite
ability to make husbands suffer. He got Nabal smitten by God and
married Nabal's widow, Abigail. Now he's leaving Paltiel heartbroken
to retrieve Michal, whom, as we'll learn in a few chapters, he doesn't
even like. And pretty soon, he'll get Bathsheba's husband killed so he
can marry her, too. It's the nature of sexually voracious men to humiliate cuckolded husbands and boyfriends. But David is the world
champion. His sexual pursuits leave men not merely embarrassed but
dead.

Ishbaal's top general, Abner, proposes to defect to David's side.
They meet for a secret dinner at which Abner vows to rally the other
tribes to David's side. David's general Joab is infuriated at Abner's
ascendance, because Abner murdered one of Joab's brothers. So Joab
tricks Abner into meeting with him, then stabs him to death. Abner's

assassination infuriates David, who asks God to make sure that Joab's male descendants will either (a) die violently; (b) go hungry; (c) catch leprosy; (d) have odious "discharges" (don't ask!); or (e) be effeminate (the actual words are "handle the spindle"—which means do women's work). Even so, David retains Joab as his top commander. The man knows how to kill.

CHAPTERS 5–6

Ishbaal is assassinated. David, who is thirty-seven years old, finally rules all of Israel. He quickly captures Jerusalem from the Jebusites and dubs it the City of David. Until now, Jerusalem has been the Sacramento or Memphis of the Promised Land, just another midsize town. Hebron, Bethel, and Shiloh have been far more important to biblical geography. But David turns Jerusalem into the holy metropolis. He settles there and has a grand palace built from cedar trees sent by the king of Tyre. He rapidly fathers eleven new kids by a variety of concubines and wives.

David decides to bring the ark to Jerusalem. He leads the expedition to fetch it, dancing and singing in front of the cart holding the ark. When the oxen jostle too much, the cart driver Uzzah steadies the ark with his hand. Bad, bad move. God smites him on the spot. David is furious about the Lord's retaliation against Uzzah, and he should be. That's an absurdly excessive punishment. My question for you, Lord: what if Uzzah hadn't steadied the ark, but instead let it fall to the ground? Would that have been better?

After the smiting of Uzzah, David is so terrified of the ark that he decides not to take it to Jerusalem after all. He parks it at the house of Obed-dom the Gittite. As soon as the ark arrives, everything goes right for Obed-dom. It's as though he hit the holy lottery. When David sees Obed-dom's good fortune, he rushes back to collect the ark and bring it to Jerusalem, dancing all the way. His wife Michal rebukes him as a "vulgar fellow" for cavorting in front of servant women. David snaps back that he was dancing for the Lord—the very Lord who chose him to be king instead of Michal's father, Saul. And he says that the maids who saw him dancing would actually "honor" him for his exuberance. It couldn't be any clearer: dancing and music delight God. This is very *Footloose*. Michal is viciously punished for her dance criticism: she's barren, presumably because David now refuses to sleep with her—even though he broke up her other marriage to reposses her. Question: how do Christian denominations and colleges that forbid dancing reconcile their position with God's obvious love of the cha-cha?

CHAPTER 7

This must be a chapter that's important to Christianity. God says that one of David's heirs "shall build a house for my name, and I will establish the throne of his kingdom forever. I will be a father to him, and he shall be a son to me. When he commits iniquity, I will punish him with a rod such as mortals use, with blows inflicted by human beings." Surely this starts to explain why Jesus claimed descent from David. Again and again, the Hebrew Bible gives us stories that will be repurposed in the New Testament. Perhaps that's because everything in the New Testament happened the way the book says it did, and Jesus really was descended from a king who ruled 1,000 years earlier. Or perhaps the authors of the New Testament wanted to link Christ to ancient messianic Jewish traditions, such as this verse.

CHAPTER 8

David's a fabulous king—with military victories abroad, and fantastic domestic policy at home. He "delivered justice and equity to all his people." *Equity*—that's an interesting word. So far, the Bible hasn't been much concerned with equity. The Good Book tends to celebrate the best men, most fearsome warriors, most godly prophets, and boldest kings. But this verse suggests that the Israelites cared about the little guy, too.

CHAPTER 9

Still missing his beloved, David searches for Jonathan's surviving relatives. He hears about Mephibosheth, a son of Jonathan who avoided fighting in the wars because he has crippled feet. David gives all of Saul's land to Mephibosheth and then summons him to live at court. David even insists that Mephibosheth eat with him every day. (Is this such a great reward? Would you really want to live at the house of a rich acquaintance, mooching his food and liquor, always having to thank him? It would be like *Entourage*, but without the girls or the Lamborghini.)

CHAPTERS 11–12

This is the moment we've been waiting for. All of 2 Samuel so far has been a roadblock on the path to these chapters, the tale of David and Bathsheba. Here's how the story begins:

> *It happened, late one afternoon, when David rose from his couch and was walking about on the roof of the king's house, that he saw from the roof a woman bathing; the woman was very beautiful.*

What a setup! A first paragraph couldn't be more provocative. A man spying on his neighbor! And she's in the bath! And she's hot! Forgive me for revealing a bit more about my adolescent reading habits than I should, but isn't this the world's first *Penthouse* letter? (What would the headline have been? "Afternoon Delight," of course.)

Her name is Bathsheba, and her husband is serving in David's army. David sends for her and immediately sleeps with her. Now comes a part of the story I don't remember from childhood, and it turns the episode from *Penthouse* to a Lifetime Channel Special Movie Event. Bathsheba announces: "I am pregnant." Oops. The zipless affair has suddenly gotten complicated. David recalls Uriah the Hittite back from the front and does everything but spike the guy's K-rations with Viagra to get him to sleep with Bathsheba, and thus become the putative father of David's kid. But Uriah, stubbornly religious, won't touch Bathsheba, because he has been ritually purified for war. David gets panicky and rolls out plan B. He dispatches Uriah to the front and orders General Joab to get him killed. Joab screws up, and lots of other soldiers die, too. David doesn't seem to mind, because his rival is out of the way. David marries Bathsheba as soon as her mourning ends.

God sends the prophet Nathan to rebuke David. Nathan tells David a parable about a rich man who, when visited by a guest, steals the one lamb owned by a poor neighbor in order to feed his visitor. Though David's a horndog, he has an innate sense of justice, and he recognizes that the rich man's behavior is grotesque—"the man who did this deserves to die!" But he doesn't realize that this story is about him till Nathan bellows: "That man is you!" Then, Nathan delivers God's punishment: God will kill David's son. David is genuinely remorseful, almost suicidal.

A son is born to Bathsheba, and he immediately falls deathly ill. David weeps, fasts, and pleads with God to spare the child, but on the seventh day the boy dies. This prompts one of the most extraordinary scenes in the Bible. If you ever want proof that the Bible is psychologically complex, that its characters are as rich and nuanced as any ever described, read the back half of 2 Samuel 12. When David learns the baby is dead, he briefly prays, then returns home, and promptly sits down for a big meal, his first in a week. His servants, both curious and shocked at his apparent callousness, ask him: "While the child was alive, you fasted and wept; but now the child is dead, you rise and take food!"

> *While the child was still alive, I fasted and wept, for I said, "Who knows? The Lord may have pity on me and the child may live." But now that he is dead; why should I fast? Can I bring him back again? I shall go to him, but he will never come back to me.*

Just imagine the traffic in David's brain at this moment. He's sorrowful at his son's death. He's gloomy because the Lord—for the first time—did not answer his prayers. He's feeling profound self-disgust at his own sin. But finally, above all else, he recognizes that he has to keep going. He must eat, he must remain strong, for he is still the *king*.

David consoles Bathsheba, then immediately sleeps with her. She conceives and gives birth to another son. They call him Solomon. The name means "replacement."

CHAPTERS 13–19

There hasn't been any incest for several books, so we're definitely due. David's eldest son, Amnon, falls in love with his gorgeous, virginal half-sister Tamar. (Wait a second! One of our previous victims of incest was also named Tamar. Note: Don't name daughter Tamar.) Amnon pulls the old pretend-to-be-sick-so-she-brings-you-chicken-soup trick. (Admit it: when you were in college, you tried it on that pretty sophomore! And it worked, didn't it?) Tamar shows up with the soup—cakes, actually—and Amnon says, "Come, lie with me, sister"—which, when you think about it, is just about the yuckiest pickup line imaginable. Tamar resists: "Don't do such a vile thing!" Apparently trying to buy time, she suggests that he hold off because their father, David, might actually let them get married. Amnon doesn't listen and rapes her.

What follows is even grimmer: "Then Amnon felt a very great loathing for her; indeed his loathing for her was even greater than the passion he had felt for her." He sends her away. She begs him not to, arguing that sending her away is even worse than the rape. Can someone explain this to me? Why would she want to stay with him after the rape? Does she think that (1) being sent away is awful because it stigmatizes her as a rape victim and thus as spoiled, unmarriageable, and a shame to her family, or (2) having raped her, he at least ought to marry her—a dismal outcome, but better than being discarded?

Enter the other villain of the piece, Tamar's full brother Absalom. He also seems to be curiously obsessed with her. There's no incest between them, but their relationship is definitely weird. From Tamar's behavior— the torn robe, the ashes she smears on her head, etc.—Absalom figures

out that Amnon has raped her. Absalom tells her to keep quiet. She holes
up in Absalom's house, "a desolate woman." We hear no more of Tamar
after this: having been raped, she might as well be dead.

King David learns about the incestuous rape but, because Amnon is
his firstborn, doesn't punish him. Absalom bides his time before taking revenge. After two years, Absalom invites Amnon to a sheepshear-
ing feast. While Amnon is drunk, Absalom has his servants murder
him. (Pretty cowardly not to strike the blow himself, don't you think?)
Absalom flees into exile.

After three years, David rescinds Absalom's banishment, but the
king still refuses to see his estranged son. After two more years of
sulking around, Absalom becomes frustrated. He tries to get Joab to
intercede for him, but Joab won't answer his messages. So Absalom
burns Joab's field to the ground—that's a nice way to send a
message—and Joab finally listens to him. With Joab's intercession,
David finally agrees to meet Absalom, and they kiss and make up.

Absalom is one of the most puzzling characters we've met so far.
He's full of resentments, and he bears grudges. He craves his dad's approval, yet having regained it, he immediately subverts David. Absalom stands outside the palace door and intercepts everyone coming to
David for justice. Absalom issues his own legal decisions instead, and
soon steals "the hearts of the people of Israel" from King David. Absalom has the patience of the truly cunning. Having waited two years to
seek revenge on Amnon and three years for his banishment to be
lifted, he now spends four years undermining David and building his
own reputation. Finally, Absalom conducts his coup. He travels to
Hebron and declares himself king. David flees Jerusalem, leaving ten
concubines behind at the palace. (Remember these unfortunate la-
dies.) David weeps again. (I've got an idea for a great Bible drinking
game. Have a shot every time David cries.)

David is a shell of his usual arrogant self, resigned and plagued
by doubts he never had before. As David travels through the countryside, a relative of Saul named Shimei chucks rocks at him and screams
curses: "You criminal. You villain!" David's men ask his permission
to kill Shimei, but David—weary and philosophical—tells them not

to. David says the man is cursing him because the Lord told him to curse David, and maybe some good will come of it.

Back to those ten poor concubines. When Absalom captures Jerusalem, he immediately and publicly beds them—thus fulfilling an earlier prophecy that David would lose his wives to another man.

Absalom and David finally fight a battle, and David's men are easily victorious. As Absalom rides away on his mule, he runs into the low branch of an oak tree. His hair gets caught in the tree, the mule keeps going, and Absalom is left hanging preposterously from the oak by his hair, like one of the Three Stooges. David had ordered his generals to "deal gently" with Absalom, so when one of David's soldiers sees Absalom hanging, he doesn't kill him, but merely reports it to General Joab. Joab, who doesn't know from "gently," immediately races to the tree and thrusts three spears into Absalom's heart.

A messenger brings David the news of his death, which prompts his famous cry of mourning: "My son Absalom, O my son, my son Absalom! If only I had died instead of you, O Absalom, my son, my son." Again, we feel the force of repetition in the Bible, though it's slightly different here. Usually in the Bible, the name is repeated. Here it is "my son" that gets doubled up. The plaint suggests that David is mourning the loss of a son, any son—not that David had a special love for Absalom, who, after all, was a scoundrel. (William Faulkner, unlike the Bible, doubles up Absalom's name for the title of his book. I don't know why, because that's another book I've never read.)

As David keeps weeping and keening, Joab rebukes him. Joab complains that David cares more for the son who hated him than for all the soldiers who love and fight for him. Joab says, "You have made it clear today that commanders and officers are nothing to you. I am sure that if Absalom were alive and the rest of us dead, you would have preferred it." Joab tells David to pull himself together and start appreciating his loyal soldiers. Joab is an awful man in many ways—violent, impatient, suspicious—but he's one of the Bible's great pragmatists. He is more interested in results than in methods, more interested in rough honesty than foolish sentiment. In this way, he is arguably the first true Israeli.

When David recaptures Jerusalem, he locks his ten unfortunate, now slightly used, concubines in the palace, keeping them under house arrest till they die. The sexual taboos were rough, back in the day.

CHAPTER 21

Giants. Lots and lots and lots of giants. David is challenged by the Philistine giant Ishbibenob, but the king is too old for slingshots. He ducks combat and has someone else fight in his place. Then we learn that maybe David didn't even kill the Philistine giant Goliath. According to verse 19, someone named Elhanan killed Goliath. What are we supposed to make of this unexplained contradiction? Could there have been two giants named Goliath? And now here's a third enemy giant. He's my favorite one yet, because he has six fingers on each hand and six toes on each foot.

CHAPTER 24

The book of 2 Samuel finishes with a baffling story. It's a flashback to early in David's reign. The Lord orders David to take a census. David does so, but when he finishes, he feels guilty for having done the count. The Bible doesn't explain, doesn't even hint at, why David would feel bad for taking a census. Then it gets even harder to follow. The prophet Gad informs David that the Lord is furious about the census—but this makes no sense, since He ordered it. Gad tells David he can mollify God's anger by choosing one of three punishments—the divine retribution version of *Let's Make a Deal*. Behind curtain number one: three years of famine for Israel. Behind curtain number two: three months harried by enemies. Behind curtain number three: three days of pestilence.

Perhaps figuring that three days is a pretty short time, David picks the pestilence. But he forgot the kind of God he is dealing with. This is no seventy-two-hour flu. The Lord's angel kills 70,000 Israelites in three days. David, seeing the carnage, begs the angel to lay off the Israelites and punish him instead. "I alone am guilty, I alone have done wrong; but these poor sheep, what have they done?" (I think "sheep" is meant as a compliment to his people, referring to their gentle, innocent spirit, not their stupidity.) David finally ends the plague by building an altar in the barn of a local farmer.

This is a confusing incident all the way around: the Lord exacts terrible revenge for no apparent sin. The only way the story would make sense is if the Lord didn't order the census. In that case, the census might be David's attempt to aggrandize himself at the Lord's expense. Then David would feel guilty, the Lord would be rightly angry, and the punishment would be deserved. But if the Lord ordered the count, then David is being punished for obedience. And the Lord and His prophets have told us repeatedly that obedience to God is the highest good.

TEN

𝔗𝔥𝔢 𝔅𝔬𝔬𝔨 𝔬𝔣 1 𝔎𝔦𝔫𝔤𝔰

Kings of Pain

In which David dies and is succeeded by Solomon, the world's wisest man; He builds the Temple, marries 700 wives, welcomes the queen of Sheba, and almost cuts a baby in half; Israel splits into two kingdoms after Solomon's death, a mostly wicked Israel in the north and a mostly faithful Judah in the south; there are lots of really terrible kings; the prophet Elijah battles evil King Ahab and Queen Jezebel.

CHAPTER I

Like my grandma, old King David is always cold, no matter how many sweaters he's wearing. Unlike my grandma, King David has procurers who find the hottest young virgin in the land and order her to cuddle up with him. But when they bring lovely Abishag—nice face, shame about the name—to his bed, David doesn't even make a pass at her. David—who used to unsheath his sword for anything in a skirt, who picked up not one but two of his wives at funerals, who had so many concubines that he could cast off ten of them and not miss a beat—can't even wink an eye at the foxy, naked virgin in his bed.

These verses tell us everything we need to know about the state of David's kingship: the royal scepter is limp.

But he's not quite dead. David's wives and kids are lobbying him furiously to settle the succession in their favor. The eldest surviving son, Adonijah, raises a militia, recruits General Joab as his commander, and holds a grand animal sacrifice to affirm his status as heir. Alarmed by Adonijah's scheming, the prophet Nathan advises Bathsheba to push her son onto the throne. So Bathsheba "reminds" David that he had promised that Solomon would succeed him. Perhaps David actually did make this promise, but it was never mentioned earlier, and it seems more likely that Bathsheba is duping a forgetful old man. Nathan, colluding with Bathsheba, also reminds David of his supposed vow. David falls for their scam and has Solomon anointed king. This is, of course, another retelling of the story of Jacob and Esau. As in Genesis, a scheming mother gets her vulnerable, possibly senile, old husband to favor a younger son over an older one. Like Jacob, the younger son, Solomon, is a pawn, passively going along with mom's scheme. Solomon, fated to become the wisest man on earth, reveals no wisdom at all during this drama. He manages to become king without saying a single word.

Once Solomon is anointed, Adonijah realizes the jig is up and seeks sanctuary by grabbing the horns of the altar. Adonijah asks for Solomon to spare him, and Solomon does.

CHAPTER 2

David's deathbed is a heartfelt scene that suddenly turns Mafia. It starts with David counseling Solomon to follow the laws of Moses. Out of nowhere, David interrupts his own profound advice and starts telling Solomon which scores he should settle. Solomon should make sure to kill Joab—who has been Israel's best soldier—because Joab committed pointless murders in peacetime that disrupted David's diplomatic efforts. More disturbingly, David also orders Solomon to kill Shimei, the relative of Saul's who cursed David during Absalom's coup.

If you remember that strange encounter, David was actually quite resigned to the curses, and seemingly untroubled by them. Later, David had even vowed not to take revenge on Shimei, saying: "I will not put you to death with the sword." So, it's incredibly slimy—dare I say Clintonian?—for David to circumvent this promise by ordering Solomon to execute Shimei. It reminds us just how cruel and self-centered David can be.

Then David dies. Like Moses, Joseph, and Abraham, David is a hero who seems even larger in the real, messy Bible than in its popular image. He's the most complete person we've met: flawed but wonderful, his great sins outweighed by his huge heart, his care for his people, and his passion for God. I'm prouder than ever to be a David, and I'm going to miss him.

The drama of his family never ends. David's not cold in the grave when his ousted son, Adonijah, visits Bathsheba. After he assures her that he has not come to kill her, he begs a favor: could she ask her son Solomon to let Adonijah marry Abishag (who's still gorgeous and still, apparently, a virgin). Bathsheba agrees to speak to Solomon on Adonijah's behalf. King Solomon, after assuring his mother that he will grant her any favor, explodes at Bathsheba's request: "Why request Abishag the Shunammite for Adonijah? Request the kingship for him!" Let's try to explain Solomon's rage. First, he's furious at Adonijah's sexual one-upmanship—angling to bed the woman his father couldn't bed and Solomon hasn't bedded. More important, Solomon surely fears that Abishag's connection to David will rub off on Adonijah. If Adonijah is permitted to take Abishag, who was more or less David's final wife, then he will gain status: sexual conquest could preview actual conquest.

So, Solomon orders Adonijah's execution. Isn't this an overreaction? Even if Adonijah was trying to score at Solomon's expense, doesn't this betray the safe-conduct promise he gave Adonijah in 1 Kings 1? Perhaps, but the most important lesson of 1 Kings: kill first, regret later.

Joab, hearing of Adonijah's death, realizes that Solomon is trying to settle all his scores at once, just like Michael Corleone at the end of *The*

Godfather, after *his* father's death. Joab flees to the altar for sanctuary. Solomon sends his hit man Benaiah, who also took out Adonijah, to assassinate Joab. Joab refuses to leave the altar and dares Benaiah to kill him on that sacred spot. Solomon tells Benaiah to go ahead and do it—an early indicator of Solomon's own casual attitude toward the Lord. Solomon's third victim is Shimei, who at first is merely held under house arrest. But the minute Shimei violates this arrest by pursuing some escaped slaves, Solomon gleefully takes his revenge. Enter Benaiah, carrying a sword.

Exit Shimei.

CHAPTER 3

Solomon marries Pharaoh's daughter. What about God's laws against intermarriage? What about His fear that miscegenation would turn His people into idolaters? What about His loathing of alliances with heretics? Apparently Solomon doesn't think that any of this applies to him: he chooses the realpolitik marital alliance over Mosaic law.

God seems relatively unbothered because Solomon (at least for the moment) is otherwise a faithful steward. God appears to Solomon in a dream and asks what he wants. Demonstrating his canniness, Solomon says that he's just a "young lad" and he needs "an understanding mind" so that he can rule justly over his people. This impresses God to no end: He was expecting Solomon to ask for wealth or long life. "I grant you a wise and discerning mind; there has never been anyone like you before, nor will anyone like you arise again." But wait, it gets better: "And I also grant you what you did not ask for—both riches and glory all your life—the like of which no king has ever had."

Solomon's first opportunity to show off his brains comes later in 1 Kings 3. The king is petitioned by two women fighting over a newborn. Both have just given birth. One baby has died. They both claim the surviving son. There's no DNA testing available. What is Solomon to do? Now equipped with 100 percent divinely certified gray matter, Solomon devises the fabulous sword trick. He proposes to cut the baby in half. He immediately discovers the real mother, the woman willing to give up motherhood in order that the baby might live. It's a great stunt and reflects genuine wisdom. No wonder the Israelites soon "stood in awe of the king."

Here is the part of this that they forgot to mention in Sunday school. The two women are *prostitutes*. Perhaps the story is told about streetwalkers because it proves that Solomon cares about justice for even the lowliest of his people. Or perhaps there are just a lot of hookers in the Bible.

CHAPTERS 5–7

A hilariously magnificent passage pays tribute to Solomon's wisdom. It's essentially a list of everyone he is smarter than. His wisdom is greater than the combined wisdom of all Egyptians and all Kedemites. He's wiser than "Ethan the Ezrahite" (the Marilyn Vos Savant of his day) and "Heman, Chalkol, and Darda, the sons of Mahol" (who were presumably the Foer brothers of the ancient Near East). He writes 3,000 proverbs and 1,000 songs. He's a botanist, an ichthyologist, and an entomologist; a poet, a musician, and a judge; a joker, a smoker, and a midnight toker.

Solomon's kingdom is vastly bigger than David's, stretching all the way from Iraq to Egypt. Fulfilling a prophecy given to David, Solomon erects the first Temple. To build it, he imports cedar trees from Lebanon, signing a deal with King Hiram of Tyre. As payment for the materials, Solomon gives twenty Galilean towns to the king. This is the first recorded example of Israel trading land to its neighbors, and it doesn't go any better than the modern swaps. Hiram complains that the towns are dumps.

These chapters include the particulars about the construction and interior decoration of the Temple—interesting more for *Architectural Digest* subscribers than the casual reader. By far the most remarkable detail is this: the Temple is only sixty cubits by twenty cubits— ninety feet by thirty feet—much smaller than your average McMansion, and an anthill compared with the size of Jerusalem's Temple Mount. It seems especially paltry when we learn that Solomon has built a palace for himself that is more than twice as big.

CHAPTER 8

Like every building dedication in the 3,000 years since, the opening ceremony of the Temple has a big crowd, too many dignitaries, long speeches, and bad weather. (The cloud caused by the Lord's presence prevents the priests from performing the service.)

Solomon delivers a phenomenal speech—a long plea to God that is one of the most persuasive prayers in the Bible. A skilled debater, Solomon begins by acknowledging that God doesn't have to dwell here in the Temple or even notice the Israelites at all. He's God—He can do what He wants. Solomon acknowledges that even the universe can't hold Him, so it's silly to expect Him to bother with this little house in a suburb of Jerusalem. Still, Solomon begs, could You please be merciful enough to pay attention to the prayers from the Temple, to "heed and forgive" the worshipping Israelites? When an injustice has been committed, could You please listen and judge the evildoer? If the Israelites abandon You but then repent, could You please answer their prayers? If there's a drought, or a famine, or even "mildew," and the Israelites beseech You for help, could You please take action? He goes on in this vein for quite a while, building up to this final prayer, which is the most compelling of all:

> *When they sin against You—for there is no man who does not sin— . . . and they repent and make supplication to you . . . oh give heed in Your heavenly abode to their prayer and supplication.*

What grabs me in that verse is the parenthetical "for there is no man who does not sin." The greatness of Solomon's speech (and of Solomon generally) is his forthright acknowledgment of human frailty. God has often been impossibly demanding, issuing perfectionist laws and smiting humans for even minor transgressions. Solomon, by contrast, marries the ideal and the real. He's making a much more sophisticated religion. His prayer doesn't claim that the fallible Israelites are better than they are or pretend that they can follow God's laws steadily. The other lawgivers (notably Moses) begin with an assumption of perfect behavior and warn of the consequences of failure. Solomon begins with an assumption of failure and seeks mercy.

CHAPTER 10

Welcome to Israel, queen of Sheba. She hears of Solomon's wisdom and travels all the way from—well, where is Sheba, anyway? Ethiopia?—to test him with hard questions. Sadly, the Bible does not record what Sheba's questions were, only that Solomon answered all of them easily. I'm very curious about what she asked. Were they savant-type questions like: *What's the cube root of 98,543,306?* Or SAT questions like: *On the basis of the data supplied, what is the average speed of the oxcart between Jerusalem and Bethel?* Or Philosophy 101 questions like: *If God is all-knowing, all-powerful, and all-good, why does evil exist?* Or Jeopardy-style questions like: *Category is Patriarchs—he was the king duped by Abraham.* Or trick questions like: *Which is heavier, a pound of feathers or a pound of gold?*

The queen is so impressed by Solomon's wisdom that she is "left breathless." Is this a euphemism, too? Are we supposed to think she checked out more than his IQ? They lavish gifts on each other; then she heads home.

Solomon is wise, but he's not frugal. He blings out his throne: ivory covered in gold. His cups were gold; his knives and forks were gold (and thus probably got all bent out of shape by the dishwashers). "Silver did not count for anything in Solomon's days."

How can he afford it? Perhaps because he is the first successful international arms merchant. His dealers import chariots from Egypt at 600 shekels each, then resell them to the Hittites and pocket the profits.

CHAPTER 11

It's not just Sheba and Pharaoh's daughter who catch Solomon's eye. He "loved many foreign women." Like Samson, he doesn't really dig Jewish girls, preferring the transgressive thrill of the pagan. This preference gets Solomon into trouble, as it did Samson. Right after mentioning Solomon's love for foreign women, 1 Kings 11 restates God's warning to the Israelites not to consort with them, "lest they turn your heart away to follow their gods." But Solomon won't listen. With 700 idolatrous wives and 300 infidel concubines, Solomon finds himself corrupted in his old age. He starts worshipping the abominable Ashtoreth, Milcom, and Molech.

Solomon's idolatry raises a fundamental question about the difference between wisdom and faith. If Solomon were truly wise, presumably he would not build shrines to rival gods, because he would know—thanks to his great brain—that the Lord would punish him. Such idolatry is a terribly unwise move. The Bible clearly distinguishes Solomon's incomparable intellect from his unreliable faith. His mind is brilliant, but his soul is weak. Solomon's intelligence, like Samson's strength, is a godly gift that doesn't produce godliness. In fact, it may do just the opposite and encourage Solomon to stray: why does he need God when he's got an IQ of 194? The story of Solomon can be seen as the opening salvo in the war that still rages between reason and belief. Which does God ultimately favor? As I argued back in Genesis, God clearly feels fondly toward clever people. Particularly in the early books, He consistently favors smart people over moral ones. But now it's not so clear. God loved David more than He loves Solomon, presumably because David was always faithful to Him. Yet that's not the whole story, because though God loved David better, Solomon's rewards are greater: He's richer; his land is peaceful; he builds the Temple. And now consider the third variable: morality, which is separate from faith. Although David was more faithful than Solomon, he was also less good. David commited unspeakably immoral acts (see Uriah the Hittite), whereas the idolatrous Solomon lives a pretty righteous life. Except for taking a few scalps at the beginning of his reign, Solomon lives well and rules marvelously. Add it all up, and who wins? The Bible seems to side with David, whose unswerving faith counts more than Solomon's goodness and wisdom.

The Lord rages against Solomon's idolatry and vows to take the kingdom away from his descendants. Jeroboam rebels against Solomon. The Lord ordains that Israel be split, with Solomon's heirs ruling only Judah, and Jeroboam controlling the rest of the country. This division—the end of the unified kingdom of Israel—is the enormously high price the Chosen People must pay for Solomon's idolatry.

CHAPTERS 12–14

There's no sorrier figure than the incompetent son of a powerful man. King Rehoboam has inherited none of his father Solomon's gifts. Instead, Rehoboam is an Odai Hussein/Kim Jong-il type of son—megalomaniacal, jealous, incompetent, and surrounded by moronic yes-men. As soon as Rehoboam is crowned, his Israelite subjects petition him to reduce the forced labor Solomon imposed on them. Rehoboam's older advisers urge him to lighten the burden, assuring him that this will guarantee the Israelites' loyalty.

But the king's dumb homeboys—literally, "the young men who had grown up with him"—tell him, in the crudest possible way, that he should overwork the people instead. They advise him to tell the Israelites: "My little finger is thicker than my father's loins. Now whereas my father laid on you a heavy yoke, I will add to your yoke. My father disciplined you with whips, but I will discipline you with scorpions."

Look at that first sentence again. "My little finger is thicker than my father's loins." I wonder if the word "loins" is a translator's euphemism. Think of a male body part that is similar in shape to a finger and that an uncouth young man might brag about. Translators, am I right? The last sentence is also memorable: "I will discipline you with scorpions." It's a creepy reminder that horror-movie-style sadism has been around as long as there have been young men.

Rehoboam orders the Israelites to work harder (shades of Egypt here). That turns out to be a disastrous public policy. All the Israelites, except the tribes of Judah and Benjamin, rebel against Rehoboam, stoning his minister of forced labor to death and then inciting a civil war between Israel and Judah that will persist for centuries.

After the revolt against Rehoboam, the other ten northern tribes choose the rebel Jeroboam as their king. He's no prize, either. Jeroboam worries that his Israelites will keep making pilgrimages to the Temple, which is in Jerusalem, the capital of Rehoboam's Judah. These pilgrimages, he fears, will make his subjects side with the rival king against him. It's a choice between securing his power or honoring the Lord. Guess which he chooses. Jeroboam casts two golden calves and installs these idols in new temples that he builds at Bethel and Dan. More golden calves? The Israelites have learned absolutely nothing!

Yet God doesn't react to the two new golden calves with the genocidal rage he displayed when Aaron made one calf at Mount Sinai. The Lord is oddly quiet—and this raises a puzzling question about Him. In Genesis and Exodus, God retaliated as rapidly and ferociously as an assistant principal in a junior high school cafeteria. Utter a stray oath—He'd smite you. Light the wrong incense—He'd smite you. Grumble about Moses—the earth would swallow you up. He overlooked no misdemeanors; He gave no second chances. But here we have the king of Israel—the divinely anointed ruler of God's own Chosen People—rejecting the Lord in favor of golden calves, thus breaking the Bible's most important law, and He doesn't even toss a lightning bolt. Something has radically changed in the relationship between God and His people.

Why has the Lord withdrawn from the action? I can think of several reasons. First, like any good parent, He may have realized it's time to cut the apron strings. When they were in the wilderness, the Israelites really needed Him, so He was a daily, hectoring presence in their lives. Now they're rich and secure in Israel, and He's giving them space to make their own mistakes. Second, maybe He's disgusted with them. The Israelites have blown countless chances to obey His laws, and He's sick of dealing with them. Rather than smiting or haranguing them, He has decided enough is enough. He's done with them. They can worship calves, marry idolators, break the Sabbath, whatever—it's not His problem anymore.

Third—and this is the explanation I believe—we ascribe grandeur to the far past. The present, by contrast, seems mundane. The Bible was written down long after the events of Genesis, Exodus, etc.

supposedly occurred, but right around the time of the events in Kings. As we know from various religious and mythical traditions, events in the distant past—events passed down by oral tradition—become exaggerated and aggrandized. It's very easy to attribute ancient dramas to divine intervention. There was an earthquake or a plague? It must have been God's revenge for a rebellion. The Israelites fled Egypt? Well then, God held back the Red Sea. The passage of time allowed the authors of the Bible to see the hand of God everywhere. But as biblical events get closer to the time of writing, there are more obvious human explanations. That was surely as true for the authors of the Bible as it is for us, and that's probably why they imagined that God interfered so much in the Israelites' daily lives in Exodus, but was only a shadowy presence during their own time.

Bad King Rehoboam flouts the Lord by hiring "male temple prostitutes" who commit many abominations. Who are these prostitutes, and what do they do? Is this a *Midnight Cowboy* kind of situation? Is the problem their maleness or their prostitution? (On the upside, at least there's finally a prostitute in the Bible who's not a woman.)

Feckless Rehoboam loses a war to the Egyptians, who seize all the treasures from the Temple and palace—those twenty-four-carat ornaments so lovingly collected by Solomon. Rehoboam replaces what he can, but with bronze. Not gold but bronze—that tells us everything we need to know about the difference between Solomon and his son.

CHAPTERS 15–16

Let's pause for a brief word of explanation. The two books of Kings are a complicated double narrative following the rival kingdoms of Israel and Judah. The southern kingdom of Judah includes Jerusalem. Israel, to the north, is home to ten tribes and the majority of the people. In general, the books portray the kings of Judah as more appealing and faithful than the vicious, idolatrous kings of Israel. There's an obvious historical reason for this, according to most biblical scholars. The books were compiled by editors from Judah after the northern kingdom had been devastated by the Assyrian conquest. The books justify the destruction of the northern kingdom by depicting it as corrupt and godless, while admiring the pro-God policies of Judah's kings and emphasizing the centrality of Jerusalem to the religion.

Here's an example. Judah's good King Asa expels the temple prostitutes, topples idols, and even ousts his own mother, who worships abominations. In the northern kingdom, by contrast, one thuggish king follows another. Baasha slaughters Jeroboam's whole clan. Zimri, in turn, assassinates the evil Baasha. Seven days later, Omri overthrows Zimri. Omri is a dreadful king, too. Pretty soon he dies, and his son Ahab succeeds him. Ahab's the worst of the lot. He erects an altar to Baal and marries Jezebel. (It's always a bad move to marry a woman named Jezebel.) Ahab "did evil in the sight of the Lord more than all who were before him." When you consider the louts who preceded him, that's an impressively large amount of evil.

CHAPTER 17

During the Passover seder, Jews pour an extra glass of wine for the prophet Elijah and leave the door open so he can drop in. But grab a shot of Manischewitz and crack open the front door, because Elijah has come early this year! He arrives at the beginning of 1 Kings 17, sent by God to bedevil King Ahab, who, quite frankly, deserves bedeviling. Elijah shows up, warns Ahab that God will send a drought, and immediately disappears into the wilderness. He takes refuge in a wadi, one of the riverbed canyons common in Israel. In an unexplained but mesmerizing passage, God orders the ravens of the wadi to feed Elijah. The ravens deliver bread and meat twice a day, a kind of happy reversal of *The Birds*.

Elijah is a proto-Jesus figure, performing miracles that Jesus will repeat in the New Testament. You've heard what Jesus did with loaves and fishes? Check out Elijah's trick with flour and olive oil. After Elijah leaves the wadi, which has dried up in the drought, he begs some bread and water from an old woman. She apologizes that she has no food left to give him. Her olive oil jug is almost empty, and she's down to her last few crumbs of meal. No problem for Elijah, who conjures up a never-ending oil flagon and an all-you-can-eat flour jar. And he's not finished. The woman's ailing son dies, and she blames Elijah. Elijah lies down three times on the corpse and prays for God to revive the boy. God brings him back to life. Take that, Lazarus!

CHAPTER 18

This is a great chapter. It has the Bible's most thrilling "me against the world" climax. When the chapter starts, the drought has not ended, and Baal-worshipping Queen Jezebel is murdering the Lord's prophets. Elijah visits Ahab and Jezebel to rebuke them. As soon as Elijah walks into the room, he and the king start slinging insults as if they're playing the dozens. Ahab greets the prophet, "Is that you, you troubler of Israel?" Elijah responds, "It is not I who have brought trouble to Israel, but you." Elijah explains the reason for his visit. He wants a showdown with Jezebel's priests, her 450 prophets of Baal and 400 prophets of Asherah. So Jezebel's prophets and the people of Israel gather at Mount Carmel. Elijah issues his challenge—my God versus yours, for all the marbles. "How long will you keep hopping between two opinions? If the Lord is God, follow him; and if Baal, follow him." Elijah proposes an incineration contest. He'll get one bull and the 850 prophets of Baal and Asherah will get another. Each side will call on its god or gods, and whichever side can make the animal go up in flames worships the true Lord.

The rival priests go first. They shout to Baal all morning long, to no effect. Elijah interrupts their fruitless prayers with a ripsnorting insult-comic routine, a hilarious, sardonic attack on Baal and his silence. When noon comes, "Elijah mock[s] them, saying, 'Shout louder! After all he is a god! But he may be in conversation, he may be detained, or he may be on a journey, or perhaps he is asleep and will wake up.'" Reading this, you can imagine exactly what kind of man Elijah was—brilliant, blunt, and sarcastic. (Oh, and even better: "on a journey" is an ancient euphemism for "in the bathroom." Baal is on the pot!)

The priests of Baal become increasingly frantic, cutting themselves with swords and raving to their god. But, of course, Baal doesn't answer. Then Elijah takes center stage. A superb showman, he has the Israelites gather close around him, heightening the drama. Then he builds an altar with twelve stones—one for each tribe—and soaks the altar and the bull three times with water, so there will be no possibility of spontaneous combustion. (For all you animal rights activists, I should note that the bull is already dead.) The Lord ignites the bull, the stones, and even the water. The Israelites fall on their faces and pray to Him. At Elijah's urging, they seize the 850 false prophets and slaughter them. Then, in a glorious denouement, a small cloud on the horizon grows bigger and bigger and bigger, and a heavy rain falls, ending the terrible drought.

This is a marvelous story—inspiring and funny, cruel to the pagan priests yet merciful to the Israelites. And it's told with extraordinary dramatic skill and eloquence, from Elijah's sarcastic asides to the vivid description of the rain cloud appearing: "A cloud as small as a man's hand is rising in the west."

CHAPTER 19

After Elijah executes her false prophets, Jezebel vows revenge. Elijah takes refuge in a cave till the Lord summons him to meet on a mountain. Elijah walks forty days to get there (again forty). A huge wind gusts on the mountain, then a giant earthquake shakes it, then a fire rages, but Elijah knows that none of them is God. After the fire dies down, Elijah hears a soft murmuring. That whisper, Elijah recognizes, is the Lord. This is a powerful moment. Often in the Bible, God appears in an awesome way, marking his presence with an earthquake, a fire, a plague, or a pillar of smoke. This gentle murmur reminds us that He is also a God of small things, a Lord who cares as much about the little as the great, who is—implicitly, I suppose—the God of love and beauty and not just fear and might.

God commands Elijah to anoint Jehu as the new king of Israel and Elisha as his own successor as prophet. Elijah finds Elisha—a boy plowing a field way out in the sticks. Elisha immediately slaughters his team of oxen and holds a feast for his neighbors. This feast illustrates the carnivorous law of the Bible. Whenever the book mentions a domestic animal, you can be pretty sure that the beast is going to have a knife in its neck and its leg on a spit within a couple of verses. Vegetarians they weren't, those Israelites.

CHAPTER 21

Many Americans are outraged about a recent Supreme Court decision granting government expansive rights to seize private property. But the Bible has the world's first such case, and gets it more right than our justices did. When the story begins, King Ahab covets the vineyard of his neighbor Naboth, wanting to turn it into a vegetable garden. Naboth, speaking for property owners everywhere, tells him to buzz off: "The Lord forbid that I should give up to you what I have inherited from my fathers." Ahab, who lacks the single-minded obsession of his namesake in *Moby-Dick*, gives up and goes home to sulk. But his wife Jezebel tells him to stop moping, because she will take care of it. The queen writes a letter to the town elders, instructing them to frame Naboth for blasphemy. (Pause to consider the irony of Jezebel, who worships Baal, accusing anyone of blasphemy. Also chilling is Jezebel's canny manipulation of the Mosaic legal code. She makes sure to get *two* men to testify to Naboth's blasphemy, ensuring that the charge will stick.) The elders frame and convict Naboth, and then have him stoned to death. Ahab immediately seizes the vineyard. The Lord is appalled. He dispatches Elijah to threaten the king: "In the very place where the dogs lapped up Naboth's blood, the dogs will lap up your blood too." Ahab puts on sackcloth and ashes. The Lord accepts his humility and delays revenge. But make no mistake: the punishment will happen.

CHAPTER 22

In fact, here it is. Ahab makes an expedient alliance with King "Jumping" Jehoshaphat of Judah to take back a town captured by the Arameans. All the prophets but one advise them to launch their attack. The last prophet, Micaiah, warns that the other prophesies are flawed and that Ahab will die in the battle. Ahab ignores the caution, instead sending Micaiah to prison with orders that he not be released "until I come home safe." To which Micaiah wittily and cruelly responds, "If you ever come home safe, the Lord has not spoken through me."

Of course, Ahab dies in the battle. As the Lord predicted, "the dogs lapped up his blood." Even worse, "the whores bathed" in it. Though this is an extraordinarily gruesome image, it doesn't actually make sense. Why would a whore—or anyone—bathe in blood?

ELEVEN

The Book of 2 Kings

The End of Israel

In which the prophet Elijah is taken up to heaven and succeeded by Elisha; many terrible kings rule Israel, which is eventually conquered and depopulated by Assyria; various bad and good kings rule Judah; Josiah tries to save the kingdom by restoring God's law, but it's too late; the Babylonians overrun Judah and exile most of the population, ending Jewish rule of the Promised Land.

CHAPTER I

This book picks up where 1 Kings left off, with a terrible monarch. This time it's Ahab's son, clumsy King Ahaziah, Israel's Gerald Ford. Ahaziah falls through a window, and as he lies injured, he asks Baal if he will recover. Wrong god. Elijah cheerfully informs Ahaziah's flunkies that because the king prayed to the false deity, he'll die. Hoping for a stay of execution, Ahaziah dispatches fifty men to arrest Elijah. The prophet has them incinerated with divine fire. Another fifty men are sent, and there's another fifty-man barbecue. Elijah accompanies the third squadron back to Ahaziah. The prophet again tells the king that he's doomed for worshipping Baal. Ahaziah dies.

CHAPTER 2

This chapter starts innocently, then finishes with one of the most gruesome passages in the Bible. The Lord is preparing to take Elijah up to "heaven," but his disciple Elisha refuses to leave his side. Elijah strikes the river Jordan with his mantle, the water parts, and they cross on dry land. (Oh, that old trick!) As they're walking along, a "chariot of fire" swoops down and carts Elijah up to heaven in "a whirlwind."

Let's consider Elijah's unusual departure. Where did this "chariot of fire" come from? It's a spectacular and memorable image, but it's like nothing in the Bible so far. When biblical folk die, they just—die. Even when prophets and patriarchs call it quits, they simply expire and are buried. Corporeal ascent is a new trick. Why would Elijah qualify for special thanatological transportation when even Moses didn't? (I assume, incidentally, that this is the source of William Blake's chariot of fire, and the movie, and "Swing Low, Sweet Chariot" as well.)

Second, what's this "heaven" Elijah is ascending to? Until now, the only afterlife mentioned is "Sheol," which is (1) down in the ground, and (2) where bad people end up. I suppose Elijah's heaven could simply be heaven in the secular sense, as in "the heavens." But that's not what it sounds like. It sounds like a special destination, a holy place. Do we Jews actually have a developed notion of heaven, up in the sky, where God's favorites go when they die? If so, it is news to me—and not good news. I've always enjoyed Judaism's focus on the here and now. If a Jewish heaven exists, who gets to go there? Just Hall of Famers like Elijah? Or all good people? And what's up there? Angels? Harps? Alternative theory: Elijah is not really dead, but in permanent retirement in the sky, and this is how he's able to visit us on Passover every year.

In the excitement, Elijah drops his mantle, and Elisha picks it up. He strikes the river with it. The waters part for Elisha, too. So this is where the phrase "picking up the mantle of the prophet" comes from.

Now we come to the crazy, horrifying finale. As Elisha is walking to

Bethel, a group of boys—"small boys"—starts mocking him: "Go away, baldhead! Go away, baldhead!" I've written before about the Lord's profound affection for bald men. Here He demonstrates that His fondness for them has veered into lunacy. Elisha turns around and curses the taunting kids in the name of the Lord. After his curse, "two she-bears came out of the woods and mangled forty-two of the boys."

So, the Lord sends bears to commit a mass mangling, all because of a joke about baldness.

After much head-scratching—bald-head-scratching, since I'm a bit of a Ping-Pong ball myself—I realized there's one possibly sympathetic interpretation of Elisha's behavior. He's new at being a prophet. He hasn't learned his own powers yet. Until he picked up Elijah's mantle, he was a regular guy. His curses had no more effect than ours do. But now he has superpowers, and his every action has consequences. His passing curse, presumably tossed off the way you might give the finger to a tailgater, suddenly has potency it never had before. He learns the hard way—or rather, the forty-two boys learn the hard way—that you shouldn't go around setting rampaging bears on every tyke who insults your haircut. In this charitable interpretation of the story, we must assume that Elisha is as horrified by the episode as we are, and that it helps him learn that he must use his powers only sparingly, and for good.

CHAPTER 3

The bad king of Israel allies with good King Jehoshaphat of Judah to attack the Moabites. The Jewish armies end up in the desert without any water. The Israelite king begs Elisha to save them. Elisha says he would let the Israelites die without a second thought, but because he admires Jehoshaphat, he'll help. (Again, Judah = good and Israel = bad.) Elisha then reveals himself to be a funky prophet: he can conjure the power of the Lord only when music is playing. A musician is summoned, and Elisha delivers a lifesaving flood of water.

The besieged Moabite king, on the verge of defeat, sacrifices his firstborn son as a burnt offering in plain sight of the Israelites. This turns the tide of the battle, and the Israelites flee. The theology here befuddles me. If the Moabite made his child a sacrifice to his own god, not the Lord, then it shouldn't have helped, since rival gods are presumably impotent. If the Moabite king made the sacrifice to the Lord, that shouldn't have helped either, because the Lord has made it very clear that He loathes child sacrifice. The only theory that makes sense is that the child sacrifice did not work theologically, but did work strategically. It scares the heck out of the Israelites, who figure: *If he'll do that to his own son, can you imagine what he'd do to us?*

CHAPTER 5

This chapter marks the start of a long, complicated war pitting Israel, Judah, Aram, and Assyria against one another in various combinations. Brief geography lesson. Aram is the kingdom just north and east of Israel—around modern-day Damascus. Assyria is a larger empire north and east of Aram. The Aramean commander Naaman is a leper, and at the beginning of 2 Kings 11 he hears of the healing powers of Elisha. So, Naaman writes a letter to the Israelite king asking for a consultation with Elisha. The king assumes this is a trap, designed to provoke a war. (Imagine Kim Jong-il making an appointment at the Mayo Clinic.) But Elisha, who has apparently taken the prophets' equivalent of the Hippocratic oath, has no problem prescribing treatment for the enemy: He says that seven baths in the Jordan River will clear up the skin problem. Naaman follows the advice and is healed. This persuades him that the Lord is God. He promises never to worship any other god, but begs Elisha for one free pass. He says that when the Aramean king forces him to go to the temple of Rimmon, the Aramean god, he will bow down in order to save his life and his job. Elisha says that's OK. This is the first recorded example of "passing." Naaman is the forerunner of the Marrano Jews, worshipping God in his heart but avowing another religion publicly. I always wondered about the biblical justification for this kind of deception, and here it is.

CHAPTERS 6–7

Elisha shows off to his disciples by making a metal ax float on water. This prompts a question: why can the prophets do so few tricks? They multiply food, they raise the dead, they purify foul or poisoned liquids, they manipulate water (walk on it, part it, have something float on it). That's it. And all of them seem to have roughly the same talents. Why aren't the prophets more like the Justice League or the X-Men, with a diversity of God-given abilities? It would be more exciting if one prophet could stop time, another fly like a bird, another turn men into stone, another shoot fire out of his eyes, etc.

CHAPTER 8

The Aramean king Ben-Hadad falls ill, and Elisha, again a doctor without borders, travels to Damascus to help him. While he's there, Elisha has a conference with Hazael, the Aramean heir apparent. Elisha weeps during the meeting, because, as he tells the Aramean, he knows that Hazael will be an even worse king than Ben-Hadad, inflicting horrific agonies on the Israelites: "dash[ing] in pieces their little ones, and rip[ing] up their pregnant women." This prophecy cheers up Hazael, who promptly returns to the palace, suffocates Ben-Hadad, and takes the throne.

CHAPTERS 9–10

The first of several fiendishly complicated, soap-operatic chapters detailing the shenanigans of various Israelite and Judahite kings. One high point: the return of Jezebel. I've missed that hussy! A would-be king of Israel, Jehu, rebels against the current king, Joram, Jezebel's son. They meet in the vineyard of Naboth, the land stolen by Ahab and Jezebel in 1 Kings. When Joram sees Jehu, he asks timidly, "Is it peace, Jehu?" Jehu shouts back, "What peace can there be, so long as the many whoredoms and sorceries of your mother Jezebel continue?"

That's a "your mother" insult no loyal son would countenance, but cowardly Joram flees. Jehu shoots an arrow into his back, then chucks his corpse onto Naboth's property. For good measure, Jehu also murders visiting King Ahaziah of Judah, making this a two-regicide day! (This is not the same Ahaziah as the equally unfortunate monarch who fell down in 2 Kings 1.) Jehu then marches to Jezebel's palace. Jezebel, hearing of his approach, slathers on makeup. (She's the first biblical character to wear makeup, and it is implicitly linked to her evilness. To this day, some American Christians associate makeup with wickedness and harlotry because of Jezebel.) Jehu stands beneath Jezebel's window and yells, "Who is on my side? Who?" Jezebel's eunuchs hear him and toss her out the window, where her corpse is trampled by horses, then eaten by dogs. This is why you don't name your daughter Jezebel.

In a sublime act of cunning—one our wit-loving God must have appreciated—Jehu announces that he's going to worship Baal instead of the Lord. Jehu invites all Baal's followers to a grand temple consecration. Once they're assembled in the hall, Jehu orders his eighty guards, who have been waiting outside, to murder them. Creepy! Finally, Jehu's men topple the temple and turn it into a latrine.

CHAPTER 12

How's this for confusion? A little boy named Joash seems to have become King Jehoash of Judah, but he is also sometimes called King Joash. Meanwhile, the Israelites anoint a new king called Jehoahaz. When Jehoahaz dies, his son, also named Jehoash, becomes king. So, there are "Joash-Jehoash," "Jehoahaz," and another "Jehoash." And the high priest is named Jehoiada. (On the other hand, there are four David Plotzes in my family, so I'm no one to talk.)

Still, let's not let a few confusing names distract us from the real significance of this chapter, which marks the official invention of fund-raising. The Temple is in disrepair, so Jehoash-Joash orders the priests to earmark certain sacred fees for fixing it. (The first building fund.) As you'd expect in a world without auditors or capital improvement budget committees, none of the repairs actually gets done. The priests spend the money elsewhere. (Versace sheets? Vacation homes?) So Jehoash tries an experiment: He places a box with a hole in the lid next to the altar, and the temple guards deposit all donations in it. When enough cash accumulates, the high priest counts the money and hires a contractor to do repairs. Invented in one short chapter are the building fund, the in-house auditor, and the collection box—all institutions that are still with us today.

CHAPTERS 14–16

Second Kings is the same story over and over again. A king does "what was evil in the sight of the Lord." Then he loses a war and is assassinated. Another king, who's slightly less bad, replaces him and shatters idols erected by his predecessor. Then there's another war, and another bad king, and so on.

Let's take just 2 Kings 15 as an example. One king catches leprosy and dies. Another is assassinated and succeeded by his assassin. A month later, this new king is assassinated and succeeded by *his* assassin. He dies, and his heir is promptly assassinated and succeeded by *his* assassin. Then this king is also assassinated and succeeded by *his* assassin.

As the Israelites busy themselves with regicide, the Assyrians exploit the chaos. It's very World War I. Anticipating an Assyrian invasion, the Israelites ally themselves with their old enemies the Arameans, who are also being harried by the Assyrians. The kingdom of Judah, in turn, signs a peace treaty with the Assyrians, swearing fealty to them. So Judah and Israel, the Lord's two kingdoms, have become mortal enemies. Of course they've brought their misfortune on themselves by worshipping idols, abandoning the Lord, and selecting wicked kings. The alliance of Judah and Assyria—the southernmost and northernmost kingdoms—squeezes Aram and Israel in the middle. The Assyrians quickly conquer Aram and sack Damascus.

Having conquered Aram and forced Judah into vassalage, the Assyrians prepare for the destruction of Israel.

CHAPTERS 17–19

Reading these last few chapters of 2 Kings is like reading a history of Germany in the 1930s. A terrible ending waits just around the corner, and you hope that it's somehow going to be averted, that God will somehow redeem the situation. But He doesn't. Chapter 17 brings the first blow: the Assyrians conquer Israel and deport all the Israelites to Assyria. This marks the end of the ten northern tribes of Israel. The Israelites deported to Assyria vanish from history. They are the "lost tribes." Now only the people of Judah and its capital, Jerusalem, survive. They will endure to become the Jews of today.

After the Assyrian conquest of the north, life briefly improves in Judah. King Hezekiah eradicates pagan shrines and demolishes the bronze serpent that saved the Israelites from the plague of snakes in Numbers. (Too many Judahites were worshipping the serpent as an idol rather than recognizing it as a tool of the Lord.) The Assyrians turn on their old allies in Judah. They march against Jerusalem. Hezekiah temporarily buys peace by paying a huge bribe. The Assyrians besiege the city again, and this time the Lord afflicts 185,000 enemy soldiers with a mysterious plague. The Assyrians withdraw, and aren't heard from again. But Judah is not safe. A worse fate awaits it.

CHAPTER 20

On his deathbed, King Hezekiah weepingly begs the Lord to grant him a reprieve. The Lord listens and sends the prophet Isaiah to heal him. Hezekiah has a terrible rash, so Isaiah prescribes a fig paste, and the king heals right away. Is there any medical foundation for this figgery? Does the fig contain some powerful medicine, some kind of figgy steroid? I doubt it, though the Fig Newton is a divinely good cookie.

Hezekiah shows off his city and palace to a delegation from Babylon. This turns out to be a huge mistake, like introducing your hot girlfriend to George Clooney—your chance of keeping her immediately drops to zero. The Babylonians see Jerusalem, covet it, and start making plans to take it.

CHAPTERS 22–23

Judah makes one last, desperate attempt to save itself. The new king, Josiah, and his priests suddenly discover the "scroll of the Teaching" in the Temple. I cheated a little and checked the commentary on this, and there's general agreement that this scroll is the book of Deuteronomy. (Some scholars believe Josiah had Deuteronomy written and then claimed to discover it; more literal-minded readers believe he actually rediscovered it.) Josiah reads Deuteronomy, and it hits him like a ton of bricks. He realizes his people are doomed unless they mend their ways. They are breaking every law on the scroll. No wonder the Lord is so furious at them. A woman prophet, Huldah, says the Lord has doomed Judah—the land will become "a desolation and a curse." Josiah rends his clothes in sorrow.

Still, Josiah tries to change God's mind. He reads the whole scroll out loud to the Judahites, then topples all the idols (again), knocks down the temples of the male prostitutes, destroys the pagan monuments built by Solomon, unearths pagan cemeteries, and even restores Passover. Josiah is like no king before or after—so faithful that he's almost a second coming of Moses—but it's too little, too late. "The Lord did not turn away from His awesome wrath."

This seems very unfair of God. Josiah does everything possible to restore his people to God's good graces. He follows all of God's orders. By the time of Josiah's death, the Judahites are as holy as they have ever been. Even so, God doesn't forgive! It seems oddly merciless. If He won't save the faithful, what's the point of believing?

CHAPTERS 24–25

The end. Nebuchadnezzar of Babylon invades and makes quick work of Judah. His army takes the king prisoner, deports all able-bodied men to Babylon, sacks the Temple, and executes the priests. Jerusalem is turned into a ghost town, with only its poorest inhabitants left to till the fields. The hope and opportunity presented in the first five books of the Bible have been squandered. Ten tribes have been wiped off the Earth by the Assyrians, and the few remaining Jews have been packed off to exile in Babylon. Yet this turns out to be Judaism's finest hour. On the brink of annihilation, Jews sustain their faith. The survivors believed so deeply that they wrote down holy books—the very books we read today—preserving the memory of God's love through the exile to come.

The book of 2 Kings ends with a heartbreaking vignette. After the conquest of Judah, the new king of Babylon—the delightfully named Evil-Merodach—releases the deposed king Jehoiakim from prison and keeps him as a courtier in Babylon. King Evil lets Judah's former monarch eat at his table and gives him an allowance. The last king of Judah is a pet, a domesticated animal, serving a pagan master. This is the fate of God's Chosen People.

TWELVE

𝔇igging the 𝔅ible

In which I search for the Bible in Israel.

As I've been reading the Bible, I have been feeling an overwhelming urge to *see* it. I don't mean I want to go spelunking in caves in search of the lost ark of the covenant or that I expect to discover the remains of Noah's boat, but I want to stand where the Temple stood, and walk where David walked. I don't exactly know what I would get out of being in the land of the Bible. Would I suddenly believe it all when I see where it happened? Could I get closer to the truth of the Bible by visiting the Promised Land? I'm not sure, but I want to go, so I hop a flight to Israel.

The morning I arrive, I take a walk through Jerusalem and stumble on the Monastery of the Cross, a 1,500-year-old Eastern Orthodox chapel in a scrubby valley about a mile from the Old City. In a doorway of the monastery, I come across an extraordinary sign. It tells the following story. After Lot committed incest with his two daughters in Genesis, the sign says, he asked Abraham how he could absolve himself of the sin. Abraham owned three staffs, gifts from the angels who visited him to announce the coming of Isaac. (Those angels were, in fact, the Trinity.) Abraham handed the three staffs to Lot, and told him to plant them in this valley and irrigate them with water from the Jordan River. (The Jordan is thirty miles across searing desert from this valley, you protest? Just be quiet and enjoy the story!) Lot did as he was told. Though the devil himself tried to stop him, Lot eventually coaxed the staffs to blossom. They wound themselves around each other and became a single tree of three woods: pine, cedar, and cypress. Some 1,800 years later, that tree was chopped down and fashioned into the cross on which Jesus was crucified.

Needless to say, I don't believe a word of the sign, and I can't imagine how anyone could. (It's not a story mentioned anywhere in the Bible.) But I soon realize that wishful thinking is the foundation of Bible tourism. From the very beginning, travelers have been coming to Israel to see the Holy Land, and they discover what they want to find.

I'm hardly the first person to come to Jerusalem with a Bible jones. In the early fourth century after Christ, Saint Helena, mother of Emperor Constantine, came here for some biblical investigation. She is said to have discovered the site of the crucifixion of Jesus, the remains of the true cross, and possibly the tomb of Adam; and she built a church that still stands today. Not a bad month's work. And what were the Crusades if not a very long, ill-planned Bible tour, complete with surly innkeepers, overpriced food, and an unrealistic itinerary? With the dawn of scientific biblical scholarship in the nineteenth century, explorers returned to the Holy Land to *prove* the Good Book by finding archaeological evidence. Some of their discoveries were spurious; some were real. Explorers found several Mount Sinais and several Mount Ararats. On the other hand, explorers on the Dead Sea located Masada, the site of the famous Jewish mass suicide, which had been lost to history for 1,400 years. And some findings were unfalsifiable. There's a "valley of Elah" in Israel, but is it the place where the future King David defeated a giant named Goliath? Who knows? But you can visit it today, and collect five smooth stones from the streambed, just as David might have.

I make a date with Ian Stern, an American-born Israeli in his early fifties who operates Dig for a Day, probably the biggest archaeology outreach program in the world. Every year, Stern's dig is visited by 30,000 to 50,000 tourists—most of them American Jews. They do spadework for Stern's academic research, get a hands-on crash course in archaeology, and explore their own history in the dirt.

We drive an hour south from Jerusalem to the Maresha–Beit Guvrin national park, where Stern runs a huge archaeological dig. As we approach the park, even my rookie eyes can spot where an ancient town once stood. There's a hill that doesn't have the smooth roundish top that Mother Nature would specify. Instead, it's squared off, like a military haircut, as a result of centuries of human building. That is Tel Maresha, the oldest site in the area, where a Judean town stood 2,800 years ago. Ian gives me a quick history of the site. Almost 3,000 years ago, Solomon's son King Rehoboam of Judah fortified Maresha and neighboring towns as a bulwark against the Philistines. A century later, in the eighth century BC, the Assyrians conquered the region during the invasion that wiped out the ten northern "lost" tribes of Israel. And a century after that, the Babylonians conquered Maresha; probably, that conquest was doomsday for the town's Jewish population. Maresha rebounded and reached its heyday a couple of hundred years before the birth of Christ. By then dominated by Idumeans ("Edomites" in the Bible)—although perhaps with a Jewish minority—the town opposed the Jewish Maccabean rebellion against Israel's Hellenistic rulers. The Maccabeans won, and took their revenge. Around 112 BC, King John Hyrcanus, the nephew of Judah Maccabee, ordered the non-Jews of Maresha to convert, leave, or be killed. (Here the Old Testament intersects with the New. Among those who chose to convert were the grandparents of Herod, the king who, in the gospels, ordered the slaughter of the innocents. Herod himself was probably born at Maresha.)

What makes Maresha extraordinary is what's under our feet. Starting around 800 BC, Mareshans began digging into the soft limestone bedrock to quarry rock for their homes. This digging left bell-shaped underground caverns. According to Ian, who has been excavating here for twenty years, we are standing on a honeycomb: There are 170 cave systems in the area, comprising 3,000 to 5,000 underground rooms. These caverns, protected from the desert heat, proved to be perfect workshops and storage spaces—an underground city. Ian has found enormous olive presses, cisterns for water storage, and columbaria for raising turtledoves. He shows me the jaw-dropping Bell Caves, which have ceilings sixty feet high. (True cinephiles may know that Sylvester Stallone rappelled down into them during *Rambo III*.) When early European explorers came to Maresha, they believed the Bell Caves verified the stories about giants told in Numbers and Deuteronomy. (Now we know that the caves were dug by ordinary men, and not till hundreds of years *after* those biblical events supposedly would have taken place.)

At the time of Hyrcanus's conquest, around 112 BC, residents of Maresha dumped their possessions into their basement caves— leaving ten, twenty, or thirty feet of detritus that has not been touched since. The Dig for a Day visitors, like me, are cleaning out this ancient garbage dump. Ian and I clamber down a ladder into cave system 169. Carrying flashlights, pickaxes, buckets, and hand shovels, we make our way to a far corner and start digging. Within a minute I see a sharp-edged rock that looks like pottery. I fish the piece out of the dirt and push on it, as instructed, to see if it crumbles. If it did, it would just be limestone. But my piece firmly resists, so I brush the dirt off till I can see smooth pottery, one side black, the other brick red.

I hand it to Stern. He glances at it, and says, "Cooking pot. See the black part? That's where it carbonized. Probably 2,200 years old, time of the Maccabees," the Jewish heroes of the Hanukkah story. He tosses my shard into a plastic collection bucket. "That's why this place is so great. It has instant gratification. There's a biblical connection. There's a Hanukkah connection. You can come here and dig up pottery from the time of Judah Maccabee. He fought a battle near here. Now I am not saying he ate out of that pot, but you see and hold this pottery, and he is not a fairy-tale figure anymore. He is *real*."

After fifteen minutes, I have filled three buckets with dirt and found several pieces of bone and half a dozen more pottery shards. (Pottery,

Ian observes, is the plastic of the ancient world. It's everywhere and it's impossible to destroy.) We tote our buckets up the ladder to the surface, where we shake our diggings through a screen, discovering a few more shards, including a red piece of imported pottery, some charcoal, and a fragment of plaster. I'm embarrassed at how thrilled I am about our banal finds. *I'm the first person to touch this potsherd in 100 generations!* The Diggers for a Day routinely unearth genuine treasures. They've uncovered an ancient marriage contract (not Jewish), coins, gold earrings, seals of kings, a circumcised phallus, and literally thousands of complete pottery vessels. ("The groups get incredibly excited when they find a whole pottery piece. I don't tell them that we have boxes piled as high as the ceiling filled with complete pieces," says Ian.) It's an exciting experience, yet a confusing one. As Ian says, it does make history seem more real to me, because this pottery really was here during the time of Judah Maccabee. On the other hand, it doesn't actually make God or the Bible more real to me—this pottery would have been here if God was helping His Chosen People, or if He was just a figment of their imagination.

I experience this confusion even more severely when I spend a day with David Ilan, who directs the Nelson Gleuck School of Biblical Archaeology at Hebrew Union College in Jerusalem. I ask him to show me a conflict between biblical archaeology and politics in modern Israel. To do that, Ilan takes me down to the City of David, an archaeological park just south of Jerusalem's Old City. As soon as we enter the park, he walks us over to a metal grate and points down a dozen feet to a shadowy stone wall, the remains of what definitely is, or possibly might be, or is highly unlikely to be the palace of King David.

Don't shout this in the pews on Sunday, but when it comes to the fun parts of the Bible—from the Garden of Eden to Mount Sinai—the "facts on the ground" are scarce. Archaeologists have discovered no significant evidence for Noah's flood, for Sodom and Gomorrah, or for Abraham, Isaac, or Jacob. They don't believe that Jews were enslaved in Egypt, wandered in the desert, or even conquered the Promised Land. Much evidence has survived about later books—the cut-rate monarchs and latecomer generals we've just read about in First and Second Kings, for instance—but the most celebrated biblical heroes remain stuck in the world of myth.

The dividing line between myth and history is King David. Essentially nothing and no one until the time of King David can be confirmed, but much that comes after him can be. David himself is a gray zone. Little evidence exists that Israel's greatest king, the uniter of Israel, ever lived. Archaeologists have found several inscriptions that seem to refer to David, but they all date from a century after his death. Moreover, Ilan says, many scholars are skeptical about the idea that there ever was a united kingdom of Israel. The archaeological evidence suggests that the north (Israel) and the south (Judah) were separate kingdoms. Only after the northern kingdom had been destroyed did the scribes of Judah invent a history of a unified nation led by the great David. So to prove the existence of David would be a magnificent feat, and a blow to skeptics. It would push the true Bible all the way back to the book of Samuel, and show that even if Abraham, Moses, and Joseph are myth, at least one of the Bible's most vivid heroes— perhaps its most vivid hero—is real. To confirm the identity of David, a man who talked to God, killed Goliath, and united Israel, would be like winning the biblical lottery.

This is why it was astonishing and controversial when the Israeli archaeologist Eilat Mazar announced in 2005 that she had discovered what could be the palace of King David, here in the City of David. According to Mazar, the walls Ilan is showing me and the pottery shards unearthed near them indicate that a monumental building was erected here around the tenth century BC, the time of David.

But many archaeologists doubt that this is David's palace. Ilan stares through the grate, looking skeptical. "I see walls," says Ilan. "But the evidence is ambiguous. I look and I see shards and something that seems like a building that may be from the ninth or tenth century, but that is as much as I can tell you. [Mazar] found what she was looking for. You have a biblical text and an archaeologist who *wants* to find David's palace, and, bang, there it is." Ilan cites evidence that the palace dates from a century after David's death, and emphasizes that

Mazar did not find written inscriptions or more intact pottery vessels that would connect the building to the king.

"Probably twenty percent of archeologists would say, yes, it is the palace of David. And ten percent would say, no, it definitely isn't. And seventy percent of us would say we don't know."

Whether or not the palace is the palace of David, the City of David is a wonderland of biblical archaeology. There's an ancient house perched on the hillside beneath the (possible) palace. Ilan points to the right of the house, where there is an ancient outhouse. Some archaeologists excavated the sump beneath it, and learned which parasites and lice were feasting on Jerusalemites 2,500 years ago. Ilan walks me through a recent discovery, the enormous fortification protecting the town spring from invaders. Its towers were built around 1600 BC—a full 600 years *before* David would have conquered the city.

Putative Bible, possible Bible, and actual Bible—they're all here. We peer down a stone shaft above the spring. Some early archaeologists, says Ilan, speculated that this hole was the site of one of the most daring battles in the Bible. According to 2 Samuel 5, David conquered Jerusalem by infiltrating a commando team into the city via a water shaft. Was this where David's Delta Force penetrated the city? Almost certainly not, says Ilan, but it's a fun story.

Then he shows me a tunnel with a more solid biblical provenance. In 2 Kings 20, King Hezekiah of Judah digs a water tunnel, perhaps to help Jerusalem withstand the Assyrian siege of 701 BC. *Voilà*! Here's a tunnel that bores almost 2,000 feet through solid rock, channeling water from the spring to a protected pool on the far side of the town.

Ilan and I take a back way out of the archaeological park. It leads us into the heart of Silwan, the Arab town that surrounds the City of David. Silwan was captured by Israel in 1967, and much of the world does not recognize Israelis' right to build or live here. The excavations in the City of David are actually funded by a right-wing, pro-settlement group that aims to take back the area for Jews and has already helped move Jewish settlers into Silwan. Not surprisingly, the pro-settlement Israelis are thrilled by the biblical findings here, believing they confirm an ancient Jewish claim to the land. The Palestinian neighbors, by contrast, see the Bible digs as purely political, an excuse to drive them from their homes.

Nowhere is the conflict between the reality and the hope of the Bible clearer than at Jerusalem's Bible Lands Museum, which collects artifacts from across the biblical world, from Iran in the east to Greece in the west. The museum is a hodgepodge—sculpture, prayer figurines, mummies, idols, cuneiform texts, coins—with each room related loosely to a particular biblical verse. A room of ancient seals, for example, is crowned with a quotation from the story of Tamar, about how Judah gave her his seal as payment for sex. The collection is gorgeous, but there is an obvious problem: it contains almost nothing about Israelites. The Sumerians, Hittites, Egyptians, Romans, Greeks, Canaanites, and Philistines are well represented, but the people who wrote the Bible are essentially absent. The only obviously Jewish relics are postbiblical. These include coins from the period of the Roman occupation. (My favorite is one commemorating the Roman conquest of Judea and the destruction of the Second Temple. Inscribed "Judea Capta," it shows the emperor standing triumphant, while a Jewess weeps underneath a palm tree.)

There's a good reason for the absence of the Israelites. The Bible notwithstanding, there was never a long-lasting or distinct Israelite civilization. For all the grandeur of the Bible, for all that it tells us of a mighty nation that destroyed Pharaoh, killed 185,000 Assyrians in a night, and exterminated every non-Jew in the Promised Land, the physical evidence suggests that Israel-Judah was a tiny, short-lived nation. It existed for a few hundred deeply troubled years, buffeted by mightier surrounding civilizations. The Bible is telling a skewed version of history. Maybe it's something like your own autobiography. Your memoir would make you a central figure in the world, important, interesting, essential. Something similar seems to have happened with the Bible. The stories we've been reading exaggerate the role and the importance of Jews in the biblical world, because Jews wrote the book.

This realization leaves me feeling oddly alienated from the Bible, as if it's just a trick. I need some other way to look at it, and so I ask Ian

Stern to take me down to Qumran, where the Dead Sea scrolls were found. The scrolls are a collection of hundreds of texts and fragments of text discovered in caves near the Dead Sea during the late 1940s and 1950s. Most scholars believe they were compiled by a strange Jewish sect known as the Essenes who lived in Qumran from the second century BC until around AD 70. The scrolls include portions of every book of the Hebrew Bible except Esther and Nehemiah—the glory is a complete copy of the book of Isaiah—as well as apocrypha and the sect's own rule books.

The Dead Sea scrolls are by far the earliest surviving versions of biblical text, a full 1,000 years older than the next oldest Hebrew Bible. Because the scrolls were discovered at the very moment the state of Israel was born, they exert a profound pull on Israelis, helping confirm their sense of continuity with their new land. Even secular Israelis I know—people who would eat a bacon cheeseburger on Yom Kippur—revere the Dead Sea scrolls.

Ian and I drive ninety minutes from Jerusalem to Qumran. It's hard to overstate how hostile the place is. It's a godforsaken slab of rock on the northwestern shore of the world's evilest body of water, a sulfurous sea so cruel that it gave birth to the legends of Sodom and Gomorrah. (The pillars of salt on the southern coast were thought to be Lot's wife.) The Essenes fled Jerusalem to build their own, untouchable community here. Away from corrupt civilization, they would sanctify themselves and wait for the apocalypse to come, at which point they would rebuild a better, purified Temple in Jerusalem. The apocalypse did come, but only for them. Around the time Rome sacked the Second Temple to suppress the great revolt of Jews, its legions also obliterated the Essenes. They were wiped off the face of the Earth. But they saved their precious library, secreting parchments in cliff caves around their settlement, where the arid climate protected them for 2,000 years. The remains of Qumran have been excavated, showing a small, dense settlement, with ritual baths and a communal dining room, and, most poignantly, a scriptorium where the scrolls may have been composed.

What's immediately obvious from Qumran is that the Essenes—heroic because they saved the book, stirring because they remind us of the dawn of our civilization—were some very weird cats. The tourist terminology for them is "sect," but the right word is "cult." They followed a "teacher of righteousness" to this hellish place to wait for the end of days. They surrendered all their possessions, took vows of celibacy, and engaged in religious practices that suspiciously resemble obsessive-compulsive disorders. They took ritual baths all the time—Qumran has more bathrooms per square foot than a McMansion in Phoenix. They were freaky about urine and excrement. They did not relieve themselves on the Sabbath—at all. And they wouldn't relieve themselves inside the city walls: they schlepped up the hill behind a big pile of rocks to do their business. This, Ian tells me, may have been a dreadful mistake. The Essenes buried their excrement in the hill above the town. When the rains came, filling the Essenes' ritual pools, the parasites in the feces were washed down the slope into the bathwater. According to recent research, Ian says, the Essenes had a much shorter life expectancy than their neighbors, probably because their habitual washing and crazy toilet habits made them sick.

The Dead Sea scrolls themselves are now housed at the Shrine of the Book in Jerusalem, next door to the Bible Lands Museum. Since I've come to Israel to get as close as I can to the Bible, and the Dead Sea Scrolls are the first Bible, I make a visit to the shrine. Housed at the Israel Museum in Jerusalem, the shrine is visually arresting, a stark black slab standing next to a low white dome. I enter the round chamber beneath the dome, where I am surrounded by the cases holding the scrolls. At the center of the chamber stands an elevated platform, on which is a circular case displaying the entire scroll of Isaiah (actually, a reproduction, since the scroll is too fragile to be displayed whole). As you'll read in the next chapter, I'm not wild about the book of Isaiah—the apocalyptic visions that endeared it to the Essenes are exactly what leave me cold—but it's a profound experience to see the text unrolled like this. The scroll is an altar. Visitors shuffle around it, murmuring in hushed voices, those who can read Hebrew bending close to decipher the text.

As I circle this oldest Bible book in the world, I am struck again by the very unlikely survival of the Jews. The difference between us and the Canaanites, Moabites, Edomites, and all the other tribes who bedeviled us in the Bible is that we wrote the book, and they didn't. Jews survived not because we went forth and multiplied—we didn't— but because we kept going to the library. Again and again, Jews as a people have barely survived extermination at the hands of the Assyrians, the Babylonians, and the Romans. We were scattered by diaspora, savaged by the Inquisition and the Holocaust. If you are religious-minded, you may believe that Jews survived because God chose us. But even if you're not, you must acknowledge that the holy books are the root of our survival. Jews endured because our book endured. We remained a people because we preserved a culture, and we preserved a culture because we kept a book.

On my only Friday in Israel, I stroll in the late afternoon through Jerusalem's Old City to the Western Wall. Jews worship at the Western Wall because it is the accessible place closest to where the Temple's Holy of Holies would have stood, before the Romans destroyed it in AD 70. It's not a biblical site, or even a very old site, as sites go. Jews have prayed here for only 800 years.

I put on a yarmulke and wiggle my way through the crowds of Sabbath worshippers to the wall itself. It's an amazing spectacle, a cross section of world Jewry—the men, anyway, since women worship separately—from the vast bearded Hasidic Jews in their black frock coats and fur hats to the orthodox Litvaks in their dark suits and sharp fedoras, to Israeli soldiers with guns and yarmulkes, to Americans celebrating bar mitzvahs in Jerusalem, to ancients rolled up to the wall in their wheelchairs, to tourists in polo shirts like me. I arrive at dusk, as the afternoon sky turns cobalt and then black over the Temple Mount. I find a spot at the wall, put my hand on it, and offer what little prayer I know. I say the Shema. I sing a few verses of "O God Our Help in Ages Past," my favorite Christian hymn, which seems kosher since it is based on Hebrew Bible verses. I feel holy, calm, and warm.

I also feel like a cheat. In my heart, I know there is no reason for me to treat this as a special place. I don't believe God ever lived in the Temple here, no matter what it says in my Bible. I don't believe the

God of the Jews is any closer to the Wall than he is to my attic. This is a sacred place only because other people genuinely, truly believe that God chose our people as His, and picked this spot for His home on earth, and because we wrote a book about it. Because *they* believe, they come here and pray. And because they come here, I come here and am moved. But I am freeloading on the faith of others. I have come to Israel to see the Bible, and I have seen it gloriously—as history, anthropology, and tradition, but not as belief. I leave Israel thrilled—amazed to have had the chance to dig where Judah Maccabee stood, amazed to have seen the first books of the Bible, amazed to have walked through the ruin of the palace where David might have lived—but I leave no more certain that God was here when it happened.

THIRTEEN

The Book of Isaiah

The Jesus Preview

In which the prophet Isaiah predicts disaster for Israel, and redemption on the day of judgment.

CHAPTER I

The Bible is (mostly) finished with the history of the Israelite people. We're moving on. The second half of the Hebrew Bible consists of the "Prophets" and "Writings," books of prophecy, poetry, and wisdom, with occasional stories and short historical books thrown in for leavening.

Isaiah is the first of more than a dozen prophetic books. All of them share a few essential traits. Let's preview them, to save time later. The author-prophet, channeling a very cantankerous God, exhorts the people and the king of Judah to obey the Lord or else face terrible consequences. (These consequences may include some or all of the following: exile, destruction, devastation, cannibalization, enslavement.) The prophets are a pretty gloomy group—not that you can blame them. They generally lived in bad times, the period between the eighth and sixth centuries BC when Israel was annihilated by Assyria, and Judah was conquered by Nebuchadnezzar and exiled to Babylon.

On to Isaiah, the first, most important, and most famous of the prophets. I mean no disrespect to Isaiah, who seems a mighty good poet and one heck of a prophet, but reading his book sometimes feels like being trapped in an elevator with Al Sharpton. Isaiah won't stop shouting, issuing an endless string of insults and threats. It's a bravura performance, very scary and sometimes quite beautiful, but not a lot of fun.

The book begins with some gloriously bitter bullying from God, who spews at His people: "I reared children and brought them up, and they have rebelled against me. An ox knows its owner . . . Israel does not know. Ah, sinful nation! People laden with iniquity! Brood of evil doers! Depraved children! . . ."—you get the idea. God is particularly annoyed at the Israelites' *superficial* obedience. They continue to make sacrifices to him and burn incense: "Though you pray at length, I will not listen; your hands are stained with crime."

Indifferent to the public obedience, God demands that His people change how they treat others. To regain His love, they must "cease to do evil, learn to do good, devote [themselves] to justice, and the wronged, uphold the rights of the orphan, defend the cause of the widow." Isaiah represents a growing sophistication in biblical theology. As far as I can remember, this is the first time that God has explicitly valued good deeds over professions of faith. Until now, the Israelites got into trouble only for disobeying God's law—idolatry, scoffing at the Sabbath, etc. But now, they're dealing with a "good works" God, who requires righteous behavior toward fellow men, rather than disingenuous prayer. The debate over whether God wants faith or deeds still rages today, but this may be the first time the Bible refers to it.

(Incidentally, you'll notice that God narrates much of the first chapter. Some of the prophetic books are in the voice of the prophet, some in the voice of the Lord, some in the voice of the Lord channeled through the prophet, and some in the voice of a third-person narrator.)

CHAPTER 2

Like Genesis, Isaiah suffers from the *Gone with the Wind* problem. It's so widely quoted that it now sounds like one long cliché. For example, at the beginning of Chapter 2, Isaiah looks forward to the establishment of the Lord's kingdom. "They shall beat their swords into ploughshares, and their spears into pruning hooks; nation shall not take up sword against nation, they shall never again know war."

(What's a ploughshare, you ask? I certainly did. It's the metal part of a plow that actually cuts the soil.)

CHAPTER 5

Isaiah wasn't big on the Jerusalem bar scene, I guess. He indicts those "who are heroes in drinking wine and valiant at mixing drink." *Valiant?*

CHAPTERS 7–11

Isaiah counsels King Ahaz, "The Lord Himself will give you a sign of his own accord. Look, the young woman is with child and about to give birth to a son. Let her name him Immanuel." After Immanuel's arrival, Isaiah says, glorious days will follow. Hmm. What to make of this? Maybe it's a messianic prediction, maybe not. It's very ambiguous. The unnamed woman may be King Ahaz's own wife. Or she may be a metaphor, since the rest of the passage is all metaphor, with the Assyrians represented as bees and the Lord as a razor (don't ask).

What's undeniable is that Isaiah is shot through with prophetic language about a Messiah. For example, he predicts a savior who will comfort the meek. He prophesies happy days to come when "a child has been born for us, a son given to us . . . and he is named Wonderful Counselor, Mighty God, Everlasting Father, Prince of Peace. His authority shall grow continually, and there shall be endless people for the throne of David and his kingdom. He will establish and uphold it with justice and with righteousness from this time onward and forever more." Christianity adopted and updated Isaiah's imagery. This passage about the "Prince of Peace" is one of several from Isaiah included in Handel's *Messiah*.

And here's another famous proto-Christian verse, though it doesn't go the way you remember:

> *The wolf shall live with the lamb, the leopard shall lie down with the kid, the calf and the lion and the fatling together, and a little child shall lead them.*

What's missing here? Who is not lying down with whom? That's right: the lion does *not* lie down with the lamb! The leopard lies down with the kid, and the lion lies with the calf, but no lion and lamb.

The confusion about the lion and the lamb is a fascinating example of the Bible's extraordinary cultural influence. If you asked 100 people— even 100 literary scholars—ninety-nine of them would say that the lion lying down with the lamb is a line from the Bible. The very educated ones would even know it was from Isaiah. Yet it's a misquotation, or, perhaps something even better. At some point during the 400 years since the King James Bible was published, a clever soul did a Bible mash-up, tweaking a favorite verse to make it sound a little snazzier, adding alliteration to juice up the phrase. *Hmm. Wouldn't "lion and lamb" sound better than "leopard and kid"?* And all I can say to that inventor is: Thanks for the great rewrite.

CHAPTER 12

After eleven chapters of hectoring and screaming, Isaiah pauses for a chapter of quiet contemplation. It's brief, but very refreshing, like a ten-minute massage: The chapter is just six verses—perhaps the shortest in the Bible. Isaiah says (and I'm using the New Revised Standard translation here, as I will for much of Isaiah):

> *Surely God is my salvation;*
> *I will trust, and will not be afraid,*

For the Lord God is my strength and my might;
He has become my salvation.
With joy you will draw water from the wells of salvation. And you
will say in that day: Give thanks to the Lord.

The language of the chapter—salvation, joy, trust, thanks—is the language of modern worship, and that is probably why I like it. On the other hand, it's totally at odds with the rest of Isaiah. Isaiah is difficult to read not merely because it's a plotless prophetic poem, but also because the God of Isaiah is so cruel. He's God as Jack Nicholson. He has only two settings: angry and furious. Except for this all-too-brief chapter, He is never a God of love or mercy.

CHAPTERS 13–14

The first of a series of "pronouncements" by Isaiah. This one is the Babylon pronouncement, to be followed in later chapters by, to name a few, the Moab pronouncement, the Damascus pronouncement, the Egypt pronouncement, the Tyre pronouncement, and the Beasts of the Negeb pronouncement. These pronouncements vary a bit, but they're generally Isaiah prophesying exactly how an enemy of Israel will be punished by God. They correspond eerily to Israel's current foreign-policy complications: don't the Israelis dream of being rid of the problems of Babylon (Iraq), Damascus, Egypt, and Tyre (Lebanon)?

Anyway, back to the Babylon pronouncement. The Lord is really going to give those Babylonians a walloping. "Every human heart will melt. . . . [T]he sun will be dark at its rising, and the moon will not shed its light. . . . I will make mortals more rare than fine gold. . . . Their infants will be dashed to pieces before their eyes and their wives ravished." And so on. Babylon will be overrun by wild animals: "There ostriches will live, and there goat demons will dance"—how's that for a spooky image?

As you begin to see from this mouth-frothing above, the pronouncements resemble nothing so much as the obsessive, vindictive, logorrheic rants of sports talk radio. In place of the Babylon pronouncement, there's the "coach pronouncement": *Coach Jones is a frigging idiot. I can't believe he kept Smith in the game that long. He's going to get fired—he's definitely got to get fired if they don't beat the Redskins. A frigging goat demon could do a better job coaching than him.* Instead of the Damascus pronouncement, the "quarterback pronouncement": *Are you kidding me? I throw better than that joker. Heck, an ostrich throws better than him. They've got to trade him, right now, even if they just get a third-string safety. He's never going to be an NFL QB.*" Think of Isaiah as the world's angriest fan.

CHAPTER 22

Yet another disaster looms for the Israelites, and the Lord expects them to mourn and wear sackcloth. Instead they rejoice with a bacchanalian feast: "Eat and drink, for tomorrow we die." Interestingly, this phrase has come down to us as a good thing, a way to seize life in the face of adversity. (See countless war movies, *Casablanca*, any pop cultural representation of Vikings, etc.) The Lord is not charmed by the frenzied pleasure-seeking. He's infuriated, and vows not to forgive the feasters.

CHAPTERS 24–27

Chapter 24 gives us an end-of-days prophecy that is awesome in its menace. Because we have broken our covenant with God, He will break it with us. Nearly everyone will be wiped out: "Slave and master, handmaid and mistress, buyer and seller." But all is not lost. After "the gladness of earth is banished," the Lord will return, punish the wicked kings, and deliver justice to the poor and needy. "The song of the ruthless [will be] stilled." This is the big one, Judgment Day, when God "will swallow up death forever." Until Isaiah, the philosophy of the Bible has been that life is for the living; it has been relatively unconcerned with an afterlife. In Isaiah, by contrast, the Lord resurrects the dead, and eternal salvation is offered. This is one key reason why Isaiah feels so much more like the New Testament than other books of the Bible do, and why it's so popular with Christians.

Even as the Israelites rejoice in God's Judgment Day and wonder at His awesome achievements, they pause to give the poor Moabites one more kick. After lots of high-flown rhetoric, the final verses of Isaiah 25 gloat that the Moabites "shall be trodden down . . . as straw is trodden down in a dung pit." That's Isaiah in a nutshell: *All praise to our mighty God! OK, now let's go rub our enemies' faces in dung!* (Just another way, I suppose, that Isaiah is like football.)

CHAPTERS 28–29

Isaiah scorns the schemers and plotters who "scoff" at God:

> *Ha! Those who would hide their plans deep from the Lord, who do their work in dark places and say, "who sees us, who takes note of us?" How perverse of you!*

I love this passage. The opening "Ha!" is a favorite rhetorical gimmick of Isaiah's, and it's fabulous, a perfect combination of indignation and mockery. The closing "How perverse of you!" also has a wonderful condescending smirk. And the central point—that God is watching all the time, even seeing those who think they're hiding—is powerful. In Genesis and Exodus, God was everywhere, sniffing every animal sacrifice, smiting every violator of the Sabbath. But in recent books, God has been only an intermittent presence, dropping by occasionally to unleash a plague or two. Isaiah wants to make it clear that God is still watching. (As another great wordsmith wrote about a different religious figure: "He knows if you've been bad or good, so be good for goodness' sake.")

Here's an experiment, analogous to the fortune cookie game played in Chinese restaurants: Try adding "You idiots!" to the end of any verse in Isaiah. I guarantee that it will make the verse sound even more Isaiahish. I am doing it now. My finger landed on Isaiah 32:11:

> *Tremble, you women who are at ease,*
> *shudder, you complacent ones;*

strip and make yourselves bare,
and put sackcloth on your loins, you idiots!

CHAPTER 41

God mocks rival deities and challenges them to a fight. "Set forth your case, says the Lord; Bring your proofs. . . . Tell us what is to come hereafter, that we may know that you are gods; do good, or do harm, that we may be afraid and terrified." They can't take up his challenge, of course. The Lord dismisses them with a gloating sneer: "You, indeed, are nothing, and your work is nothing at all."

I know it's juvenile of me, but I love these catty biblical comments. They show God acting just as we would if we were God. The Good Book feels most real, and most persuasive, when it's funny, mean, and scornful. It reminds us that the Bible is not an idealization, but a book written by (and about) real people, who can be both scornful and kind, faithful and cruel, sarcastic and sweet—as their God can be, too. We've been sold an idealized Bible that's blander and kinder than the real thing. Instead, let's revel in its messiness, humor, and cruelty.

CHAPTERS 44–45

These chapters riff on how to make an idol. The carpenter cuts down a tree. He uses wood from the tree to bake his bread and warm himself, etc. It's not clear where Isaiah is going with this metaphor of carpentry, but then he pulls off a brilliant twist, a triple axel of a move: "The rest of [the wood] he makes into a god, his idol, bows down to it and worships it." What kind of moron, Isaiah is asking, would fall on his knees before a block of wood, would think that the kindling that cooks his food is a god?

Sometimes the Bible and modern geopolitics brush against each other. And sometimes they crash head-on as they do in Isaiah 45. The Lord sends a huge shout-out to King Cyrus of Persia. God promises to lead him to victory, "cutting through the bars of iron" to help him.

Why does God want to help this pagan king? Because Cyrus will conquer Babylon, free the Jews, end the Babylonian exile, and allow the
Israelites to return home to Zion. There are enough layers of irony and
analogy here to make biblical baklava. Cyrus remains a great hero to
modern Iranians as the father of Persia. Cyrus is also a hero to Jews,
because he liberated them, redeemed Jerusalem, and was famously
tolerant of Judaism. So, you have Iran, a nation led today by an anti-
Semite who calls for the destruction of Israel, sharing a hero with Jews,
who revere said hero for restoring Israel. And what did Cyrus conquer?
Babylon: modern-day Iraq. As I'm writing, Americans are fretting
about Tehran's rising influence in Baghdad and Iraq's possible transformation into a vassal state of Iran. Twenty-five hundred years later and
it's the same fights, the same land, the same people.

CHAPTER 48

The line so nice God uses it twice: " 'There is no peace,' says the
Lord, 'for the wicked.' " This is the closing verse of Isaiah 48, and of
Isaiah 57.

You'll notice I'm racing through Isaiah, skipping long passages of
exhortation, threat, and apocalyptic prophecy. These are the junk
DNA of the Bible. It's not that they're bad, but they are repetitive,
they serve no clear purpose after the fourth iteration, and they take up
a lot of space.

CHAPTERS 49–53

Until Isaiah, the Bible has addressed itself only to a small tribe of Israelites, embattled, struggling for survival. It never bothered to speak to
the rest of the world: non-Israelites were usually enemies and always
irrelevant to God's covenant. But Isaiah makes God a universal God.
In Isaiah 49, for example, God chooses a "servant" whose job is to
speak to the whole world. "I will give you as a light to the nations,
that my salvation may reach to the end of the earth." Moses and David

did not care an iota about universal salvation or the end of the Earth: they sought the survival of the Israelites in Canaan. Isaiah has repurposed God's mission for everyone. Not to belabor a point made by a million people before me, but it's certainly no surprise that Isaiah is popular with Christians, since the book teaches a proto-Christian, universalist theology, one very different from the insular, exclusionary message of the Bible's earlier books.

We have come to the most overt proto-Christian prophecy yet: The servant chosen by God is "despised and rejected by others." He is:

> *wounded for our transgressions, crushed for our iniquities . . . and by his bruises we are healed. . . . The Lord has laid on him the iniquity of us all. He was oppressed and he was afflicted, yet he did not open his mouth; like a lamb that is led to the slaughter. . . . Yet it was the will of the Lord to crush him with pain. When you make his life an offering for sin . . . through him the will of the Lord shall prosper.*

The earlier language in Isaiah that seemed to anticipate Christ was nothing compared with this. The notion of God sending a servant and making him suffer for our sins, so that we may be redeemed—the essential Christian idea about the redemptive suffering of Jesus—starts here in Isaiah.

CHAPTER 56

God promises eternal glory to "the eunuchs who keep my Sabbaths." Eunuchs? Where do the eunuchs come from?

CHAPTER 59

Isaiah asks a question that has plagued almost every child. If God is omnipotent, why doesn't He heed our prayers? If you've read Isaiah 1–58, you know how God is going to answer that one. *I don't pay attention because your sins are too great, your tongues too wicked, your hands too bloody. Shape up, and maybe I'll listen.* God's scathing denunciation is followed by this breast-beating passage, one of the most hauntingly beautiful in the Bible, in which the author acknowledges our failures:

> *We stumble at noon as in the twilight,*
> *Among the vigorous as though we were dead.*
> *We all growl like bears;*
> *Like doves we moan mournfully.*
> *We wait for justice, but there is none;*
> *For salvation, but it is far from us.*
> *For our transgressions before you are many,*
> *And our sins testify against us.*

"We stumble at noon as in the twilight." That's a powerful image!

CHAPTERS 60–62

Another description of Judgment Day. It will be good news for everyone, and particularly for the Israelites, who will finally reap the benefits of being God's Chosen People. For Israelites, these end times will be like being a senior during Senior Week, or a senator at a Washington cocktail party. All the other peoples of the world will pay tribute to the Israelites, tend their flocks, and treat them as God's own ministers on Earth. Speaking as a Jew, I must say: All right! Can we set a firm date? How's next Thursday?

CHAPTER 65

In the glorious, post-redemption Jerusalem, someone who dies at age 100 will be "considered a youth, and one who falls short of a hundred will be considered accursed." Sort of like Denmark.

CHAPTER 66

This final chapter nicely encapsulates the rest of the book. It includes marvelous verses about God's greatness and the super-fabulous post–Judgment Day future. But, of course, it also revels in carnage. After an ecstatic description of the coming of God's kingdom, the lucky survivors will go outside—to look upon "the dead bodies of the people who have rebelled against [God]." That's Isaiah: God, glory, and guts.

FOURTEEN

The Book of Jeremiah

The Prophet and the Lustful She-Camel

In which the prophet Jeremiah repeatedly predicts the destruction of Judah, and is shunned by his people; Babylon sacks Jerusalem and exiles most of the population; a few surviving Jews emigrate to Egypt.

Like Isaiah, Jeremiah is not a kittens, rainbows, and unicorns kind of guy. These two let-it-bleed prophets share a style (emphatic, metaphoric poetry) and a sensibility (gloom). But they're not identical twins—they're more like first cousins. Isaiah is bipolar, prone to wild mood swings, joyful when pleased, and a holy terror when angry. You might not always like Isaiah, but he'd often be entertaining company, especially if you could get him ragging on the Babylonians.

Jeremiah, on the other hand, is not the prophet you want to share a beach house with. He's entirely morbid. (They don't call them jeremiads for nothing.)

CHAPTERS 1–3

A century or so after Isaiah, around 600 BC, God summons Jeremiah to serve Him. Jeremiah aims to hector, nag, badger, noodge, and otherwise harass the increasingly unfaithful people of Judah to return to God before it's too late. Jeremiah is living during the darkest of times—the final few years before Babylon conquers Jerusalem and exiles the Jews—and he ultimately fails.

Jeremiah's endless rage may be explained by the hopelessness of his cause. He's warning the Judeans that the end is nigh, and they're still drinking date wine and worshipping idols. It infuriates him that the Judean people don't share his sense of urgency. As a result, Jeremiah suffers from the flaws that plague all whistle-blowers. Almost without exception, whistle-blowers are self-righteous and resentful. When they turn out to be right—and boy, does Jeremiah turn out to be right—everyone regrets not having listened to them. But there's a reason no one listens. Who wants to pay attention to a cantankerous rageaholic shouting doom in the bazaar?

In Jeremiah's first speech, he unloads on the wild, heedless idolatry of the Israelites, describing them as: "a lustful she-camel, restlessly running about." Now I personally have never seen a lustful she-camel or he-camel, but that is one vivid metaphor.

It's not just lusty camels that preoccupy Jeremiah. He has sex on the brain. A few verses before the she-camel, for example, he spews out that Israel "recline[s] as a whore." Chapter 3 begins with him frothing about Israel's "whoring and debauchery. He inveighs against the Israelites, "You had the brazenness of a street woman," and in Chapter 5 declares them "lusty stallions." (Are they camels? Are they stallions?) A few chapters later, they're harlots again. Then a few chapters after that:

> *I behold your adulteries,*
> *Your lustful neighing*
> *Your unbridled depravity, your vile acts.*

His combination of scorn and sex is very Church Lady—at once prudish and obsessed.

CHAPTER 4

God is disappointed with us not just because we're unfaithful, but also because we're idiots. "My people are stupid. . . . They are foolish children. They are not intelligent." This may be Jeremiah's cruelest cut of all, since we know how much the Lord values intelligence. God always rewards brainy people, even when they're wicked. His disillusionment about IQ is somehow more disturbing than His dismay over idolatry. He expects infidelity. But stupidity?

CHAPTERS 8–9

Jeremiah laments the suffering of his countrymen. He's miserable on their behalf and asks: "Is there no balm in Gilead?" He promises he would "weep day and night" for his people, moans at how heartbroken he is at their agony. Yet Jeremiah's histrionic mourning for the Jews becomes suspect once you notice how much delight he takes in enumerating their sins and threatening them. He's thrilled to be the bearer of bad tidings to Judah. He's like the gossipy classmate who, with a long face and a big hug, tells you that she saw your boyfriend making out with your best friend. You can be very sure that her glee outweighs her sympathy.

CHAPTER 13

A curious episode in which God orders Jeremiah to buy a loincloth, wear it for a while, and then hide it in a rock by the Euphrates River. Jeremiah is instructed to return to the loincloth some days later, at which point he discovers it is ruined. This loincloth, God tells us, is Judah. Judah was supposed to cling to God, the way the cloth clings to the loins—no boxer shorts back in the day, I guess—but because it has been ruined by sin, it's now just a worthless rag.

Jeremiah says the Judahites can't save themselves from their terrible fate because they have become evil to their core. The book asks, "Can the Cushite change his skin or the leopard his spots?" This is another example of a famous biblical phrase that isn't quite what I remember it to be. "Cushite" is a biblical term for Ethiopians or Nubians, and it complicates the passage for modern readers. Referring to the Cushites' skin does not mean the verse is racist—it's descriptive of skin color rather than derogatory. But it does muddy the cliché. I'm not surprised we've kept only the leopard. Can you imagine saying in conversation "Can the Ethiopian change his skin color?" That would be awkward.

CHAPTERS 18–20

Jeremiah is genuinely hurt that no one likes him. As soon as he curses a priest for arresting him, he chants a self-pitying lament, ruing the day he was born. He moans that he has become a laughingstock. ("Everyone mocks me.") He complains that whenever he's around, he hears people whispering, "Let us denounce him!"

Come on, Jeremiah! You must be kidding! You show up at the capital city, tell people that they're going to be disemboweled corpses in couple of years and that there's nothing they can do to prevent it. And then you're surprised that they don't like you?

CHAPTERS 26–28

The Lord instructs Jeremiah to wear a yoke and visit the kings of Moab, Tyre, Edom, and Judah. Jeremiah tells them that they must submit to the Babylonians, or else be annihilated. Let's linger here for a minute, because this is the passage where I finally recognize why Jeremiah bothers me so much. He's a Quisling, a Tokyo Rose. Jeremiah feels no loyalty to his land or his people. He's prodding his own countrymen to surrender to their mortal enemy.

In hindsight, Jeremiah picks the winners. The Babylonians do sack and slaughter, and the Jews are marched off into exile. But that almost makes Jeremiah's naysaying worse. He is rewarded by Babylon while his people suffer: King Nebuchadnezzar orders that Jeremiah is to be treated like a VIP, further evidence that he was an enemy of his own people. Perhaps Jeremiah was just a prophet, guided by God, who predicted Judah's fall. But maybe Jeremiah's predictions functioned as propaganda, weakening Jewish morale and hastening the Babylonian victory.

The Bible discovers a principled lesson in Jeremiah's betrayal of country, which is that all our quotidian bonds—to family, nation, and tribe—are nothing compared with our connection with God. Jeremiah believes Judah deserves to fall for failing God. But this doesn't solace me. I'm not strong enough in my faith to set aside family and country for God. And I wouldn't want to be. Jeremiah is a righteous prophet, but I can't help feeling that he's also a terrible traitor.

Random question: why was Jeremiah a bullfrog?

CHAPTER 29

From Babylon to Brooklyn, Jews have always found a way to prosper. It's pretty remarkable: No matter where we've been, and no matter what dreadful conditions we've lived under, Jews have thrived as traders, shopkeepers, bankers, and doctors—without losing our distinct identity as Jews. Why is our religion so mobile? Let me offer three theories. First, necessity: when you're being exiled and pogrommed you learn to adapt fast. Second, culture: because Judaism is a religion founded on writing and argument, Jews have always had high literacy rates and well-developed analytical skills, which have served them in business. And, third—this is right here in Jeremiah 29—our flexibility: it's built into the religion. Read this extraordinary passage from Jeremiah's letter to Judeans exiled in Babylon.

> *Build houses and live in them; plant gardens and eat what they produce. Take wives and have sons and daughters. . . . Seek the welfare of the city where I have sent you into exile, and pray to the Lord on its behalf, for in its welfare you will find your welfare.*

Modern victimology theory teaches that you can't move forward until you avenge a past wrong. But Jeremiah is saying, essentially, get over it, and find a new way to live for God. The passage anticipates the next 2,500 years of Jewish history. Jews have always found ways to be at home away from home, to be at once Jewish and American—waiting for Zion, but planting a garden in Babylon today.

CHAPTER 32

Just before the Babylonian conquest, one of his countrymen asks Jeremiah if he should sign a contract to purchase land—a chancy proposition given that Nebuchadnezzar is about to ransack Judah. But the Lord tells Jeremiah that the land sale should proceed. Jeremiah is understandably befuddled. He lavishly and sycophantically praises God for His wisdom and greatness—a sucking-up that goes on forever—and then at the end of it, asks: *What the heck are you talking about? Why should the Jews do land deals when they're about to get obliterated?* The Lord, sounding a bit like James Brown, first replies, "Behold I am the Lord. . . . Is anything too wondrous for me?"

Then He goes on to tell the prophet that, yes, Jerusalem is about to be obliterated, but this will be only a brief interruption of the Jews' time in Israel. This land purchase should go through, because after God has revenged himself on Babylon, the Jews will return to Zion, and all their old contracts and land arrangements will apply.

If you're seeking scriptural support for Jews' divine right to the land of Israel, it doesn't get any stronger than this passage. Even more than God's original grant of land to Abraham or the conquest of the Promised Land after Exodus, this passage guarantees permanent, divinely authorized inhabitation in Zion. No interruption—whether Babylonian or, presumably, Arab, whether 70 years or 700 years—cancels Jewish ownership.

CHAPTER 36

At God's command, Jeremiah writes a scroll of all his prophecies, then has his sidekick Baruch recite it at the Temple. The king of Judah's advisers seize the scroll, and the king orders that it be read to him. As each page is finished, the king tears it out and tosses it into the fire. Nice try, king! Jeremiah simply rewrites the scroll. This is a profound notion: no matter what kings may do, the book will survive. God's word endures, stronger than fire.

CHAPTERS 40–43

A historical interlude. When the Babylonians conquer and sack Jerusalem, they leave a Jewish regent, Gedaliah, to run the place. He promises the few Judeans who haven't been exiled that they will keep farming and thrive.

Gedaliah turns out to be a fool, laughing off reports that Ishmael (another bad Ishmael) plans to assassinate him. Ishmael promptly murders him, plunging Judea into a brutal civil war. Ishmael slaughters Temple pilgrims and tosses their bodies into a cistern. Finally, the noble Johanan rallies the army and overthrows Ishmael. I love this story because I have a beloved uncle-in-law named Johanan, who would also rally an army against tyranny, given half a chance.

Johanan asks Jeremiah whether the surviving Jews should remain in Zion under Babylonian rule or flee. Jeremiah prays for ten days, at the end of which God tells him that the Jews must stay in the Promised Land. If they remain, He promises to "rebuild" them and make them a great people once again. If they run away, He threatens, they will be afflicted by famine, war, and pestilence.

But Johanan doesn't believe Jeremiah. "You are lying," he tells the prophet. Johanan suspects that Jeremiah is setting him up, that as soon as Johanan tries to remain in Judea, the Babylonians will slay him and his small band of followers. So, Johanan and his remnant move to Egypt, leaving the Holy Land empty of Israelites. God vows to exterminate the emigrants for their disobedience.

We have to ask ourselves: Why would Johanan dismiss Jeremiah as a liar and assume the prophet was actually laying a Babylonian trap? The answer, I again suspect, is the troublesome personality of Jeremiah. The superficial lesson of this episode is that Johanan doubted God's prophet, and that his doubt caused him to disobey God's will. But the more profound lesson is about Jeremiah's tragic character. He's a terribly ineffective prophet, not because he's wrong, but because he fails to sell his message. He doesn't know how to win friends and influence people. He has been so negative and so unpleasant with the Judeans that he has squandered all his social capital. He has no buddies, no allies, no supporters. Is it any surprise the Judeans view him with suspicion? So what if he's always right? He's rotten to deal with. Moreover, he has a long history of siding with the Babylonians, so it's understandable that Johanan suspects him of being a double agent. The book of Jeremiah is supposed to be about our failure. Really, it's about his.

FIFTEEN

The Book of Ezekiel

God's Whole-Grain Hippie Prophet

In which Ezekiel has groovy, psychedelic dreams, then lies on his side for a year to symbolize the coming conquest of Jerusalem; Ezekiel tells stories about God's rage at His people; Ezekiel's wife dies; God leads Ezekiel to a valley of dry bones; and the dead are brought back to life.

CHAPTERS 1–3

Ezekiel—who has clearly been sprinkling something special on his matzo and brisket—has a vision of winged cherubim with four faces: one human, one lion, one ox, and one eagle. They're riding on gigantic beryl wheels, and inside each wheel is a "tall and awesome" rim that moves independently from the wheel. (Why do I linger on this detail, you ask? Because these self-propelled rims are a milestone in automobile and hip-hop history: They are the world's first spinners.)

The Lord instructs Ezekiel to go preach to the "impudent and stubborn" Israelites. God gives him a scroll containing His words and tells the prophet to eat it. "I ate it, and it tasted sweet as honey to me." Has there ever been a finer tribute to the glory of the holy book? The word of God tastes sweet as honey.

CHAPTERS 4–5

Ezekiel is God's grooviest, trippiest prophet. For Isaiah and Jeremiah, prophecy was speech—haranguing, arguing, badgering, indicting. For Ezekiel, prophecy is performance art. God has him build a model of Jerusalem out of brick and make a metal plate that represents the Babylonian siege works. Ezekiel then lies on his left side with the brick-and-metal plate resting on him. He stays in this position for 390 days, representing the 390 years of Israel's punishment. Then he lies on his right side for forty days, representing the forty years of Judah's punishment.

During this period of self-mortification, Ezekiel consumes the first macrobiotic diet, eating only bread made from wheat, barley, millet, and spelt, and drinking only water. I tried the prophet's meal plan, buying a box of "Ezekiel 4:9" cereal, a nourishing breakfast treat based on Ezekiel's whole-grain regimen. The cereal looks like gravel and tastes only slightly better. Imagine Grape-Nuts, but even less fun. My daughter, Noa, ate a few bites and grudgingly pronounced it "OK." When I asked her how she'd like to eat it every day for a year, she exclaimed, "Uck, no!" (The maker of Ezekiel 4:9, a scripture-minded company called Food for Life, produces a variety of Ezekiel-inspired products, such as pasta and English muffins, as well as a Genesis 1:29 bread. Personally, I prefer my Bible food with a little more sugar— whatever happened to the land of milk and honey?)

When he finishes his 430-day tableau of Jerusalem, Ezekiel shaves off his hair and beard—God, again, loves the baldy—and divides the clippings in three parts. He incinerates one third inside Jerusalem, strikes the second third with a sword outside the city walls, and scatters the last third to the wind. What does this represent? Anyone? Anyone? Yes: one-third of Judeans will die in the city, one-third will be killed in battle, and one-third will be scattered throughout the world.

I don't know about you, but I'm very moved by Ezekiel's performance prophecy. In journalism, we are always reminded, "Show, don't tell." Ezekiel understands this, recognizing that his actions speak louder than other prophets' words. What's more, Ezekiel has profound humility. Jeremiah and Isaiah are smug with angry certainty. Ezekiel isn't like that. He puts his body where his mouth is, truly making himself suffer for his people.

CHAPTERS 8–9

Ezekiel has a vision of abominations in the Temple (idols, loathsome animals, sun worship, etc.). In the vision, an angel walks through Jerusalem and marks the heads of all "who moan and groan" at the Temple abominations. Then the Lord orders his executioners to strike down every man, woman, and child who does not bear the mark. This slaughter, of course, reminds us of the final plague in Egypt, when the Israelites marked the doors of their houses with blood, so the angel of death would pass over them and kill only Egyptian children.

More important, it's another example of how the prophetic books are theologically more sophisticated than the earlier ones. In Egypt, survival was based on nothing more than genes. Being an Israelite protected you from the angel of death. But now God demands more. The fact that you were born a Jew is not enough. You must love God so much that you sorrow at the contamination of His Temple. In short, these two mass killings demonstrate a profound shift between the Judaism of Exodus and the Judaism of Ezekiel: the transition of Judaism from an immutable ethnic identity to a freely chosen religion, from blood to belief.

CHAPTER 14

Ezekiel is truly the prophet of redemption, a more merciful and forgiving messenger than his predecessors. At the beginning of the chapter, several Israelite elders request a meeting with him. The prophet is dubious, because these elders are notorious idolaters. But, in a Nixon-goes-to-China moment, God tells Ezekiel he of course must minister to these heretics. Ezekiel reminds them that they can still be saved if they reject idols and abominations. Ezekiel is always willing to offer a second chance, always holding out the possibility of grace. This puts him much more in line with modern religious practice than unbending Isaiah and Jeremiah were.

CHAPTER 15

This just slows us down on the way to my new favorite biblical chapter, Ezekiel 16.

CHAPTER 16

First of all, read this chapter yourself. Come on, just go read it. Right now. It's so good that you won't begrudge the five minutes.

You're back! How did you like it? Wasn't it as good as I said it was? You think it's a little bawdy? A little rude? Maybe, but doesn't it sound true?

Ezekiel 16 is the story of the world's most dreadful marriage, as narrated by the wronged husband. The husband is God. The wife is Jerusalem. They meet cute in the desert when she's just a baby. He mentors her. She grows up into a raving beauty. What hair! What a figure!

Soon the mentor becomes a lover. (Isn't it always that way?) "I passed by you again and looked on you; you were at the age for love." The Lord marries her: "You became Mine." It's all wine and roses for a few years. He buys her "fine linen . . . and rich fabric," hand-tooled shoes, and incredible jewelry. She even gets a nose ring: "I put . . . a ring on your nose.") Men all around the world hear about the Lord's bride and what a hottie she is.

But—there is always a "but" in these stories—everything soon sours. "You trusted in your beauty, and played the whore because of your fame, and lavished your whorings on any passerby." She makes male idols and plays with them. She's a nymphomaniac—"insatiable."

She prostitutes herself to the Egyptians and Assyrians, but that isn't enough. "You multiplied your whoring" with the Babylonians.

At this point the divorce lawyers should have been called, and restraining orders should have been issued, but instead the fight continues. Imagine the worst marital fight you've ever heard, and multiply by a thousand. It's a conjugal Armageddon. (It's as though every husband in the universe suddenly said, "You're just like your mother," and every wife said, "That's no way to load a dishwasher.")

"How sick is your heart, says the Lord God, you did all these things, the deeds of a brazen whore." Then He realizes she's even worse than a whore, because at least a whore gets paid. She does it for free.

God invites all her lovers to visit her. They strip her naked and set a mob on her to cut her to pieces. At last, God's rage is exhausted. At the end of Ezekiel 16, He promises to remarry her—but only if she shuts up: "I will establish my covenant with you, and you shall know that I am the Lord, in order that you may remember and be confounded, and never open your mouth again because of your shame, when I forgive you all that you have done."

This chapter is like the bad parts of *Portrait of a Lady*, *Madame Bovary*, and *Married with Children* rolled up into a ball of rage. It's the first story to correctly understand that the psychological relationship between God and His people is not parent and child, but spouses. For most of the Bible, God is a furious father, disappointed in his faithless children. But in this chapter He is a jealous husband, a role that is much more terrifying and persuasive. "Jilted husband" makes more sense as a role for God than "angry dad." Parents are disappointed and frustrated with their kids, but rarely so furious with them that they kill them, banish them, or humiliate them. Husbands and wives do this to each other all the time, and God has been doing it to His people throughout most of the Bible. Sexual jealousy is the greatest crazy maker we have. What is God's fury at our idolatry if not sexual jealousy? We have found other deities to satisfy our deepest needs. He's so enraged at our betrayal that He wants to kill us.

Ezekiel 16 is unsettling in its violent misogyny and sexist in its depiction of marriage. But it's psychologically penetrating like few other chapters in the Bible. I can't get it out of my head.

CHAPTER 23

Several male friends—with nudges and winks—recommended this chapter to me as the sexual high point of the Bible. They hinted that it was a chapter to which they had paid, um, special attention as teenage boys, if you catch my drift. I confess that I'm a little disappointed. Ezekiel 23 is just a sluttier version of 16. It's Chapter 16, but with twins. The gist is this. There are two sisters, Oholah and Oholibah. Oholah is Samaria, and Oholibah is Jerusalem. Both of them get married to the Lord. They proceed to put the "ho" back in Oholah and Oholibah. It turns out that they were prostitutes in Egypt before they married God, and they haven't mended their ways. After the wedding, they turn tricks with Assyrians. I suspect boys like this chapter because the language is cruder than that of Ezekiel 16: men "fondled [Oholah's] virgin bosom and poured out their lust upon her"; men "whose members were like those of donkeys, and whose emission was like that of stallions." But the message is the same: the Israelites betrayed God with other gods and bad allies. As in Ezekiel 16, they are cut to pieces for their "wanton whoring."

I can see why Ezekiel 23 catches the eye of fifteen-year-old boys—especially since many translations render "bosom" as "nipples"—but it doesn't move me as much as Chapter 16. Ezekiel 16 is a more sophisticated, passionate, and dramatic version of the same story: it is God's failed marriage, as told in the *New Yorker*. Ezekiel 23 is God's failed marriage, as told in *Hustler*.

CHAPTER 24

Unlike Jeremiah, who was celibate by God's order (or, more likely, because no woman could stand him), Ezekiel is a family man. That is why this chapter is so sad. Ezekiel's wife dies during the siege of

Jerusalem. God forbids him to mourn or weep. All Ezekiel may do, God says, is "sigh, but not aloud." God immediately dispatches the widower to preach to the Jerusalemites, and Ezekiel obediently does it. If you're searching for a pleasant interpretation of the story, tell yourself that Ezekiel is a workaholic and he found solace in returning immediately to prophecy. In any case, this episode is a reminder of what a mensch Ezekiel is. Unlike the icy, vengeful Jeremiah and Isaiah, Ezekiel is fully human, and thus a much more tragic figure. This is why I've cut Isaiah and Jeremiah from my list of acceptable Bible names for kids, and added Ezekiel.

CHAPTER 25

Once again, the Lord vows revenge against the Edomites, Moabites, Philistines, and Ammonites. This wouldn't be especially interesting, except that Ezekiel 25 plays a minor but spectacular role in the history of American pop culture. It's a key source for *Pulp Fiction*. In an unforgettable scene, Jules Winnfield, the hit man played by Samuel L. Jackson, says:

> *There's this passage I got memorized. Ezekiel 25:17.* "The path of the righteous man is beset on all sides by the iniquities of the selfish and the tyranny of evil men. Blessed is he who, in the name of charity and good will, shepherds the weak through the valley of the darkness. For he is truly his brother's keeper and the finder of lost children. And I will strike down upon thee with great vengeance and furious anger those who attempt to poison and destroy my brothers. And you will know my name is the Lord when I lay my vengeance upon you." *I been sayin' that shit for years. And if you heard it, that meant your ass. I never gave much thought to what it meant. I just thought it was some cold-blooded shit to say to a motherfucker before I popped a cap in his ass. But I saw some shit this mornin' made me think twice. See, now I'm thinkin', maybe it means you're the evil man, and I'm the righteous*

man. And Mr. 9mm here, he's the shepherd protecting my righ-
teous ass in the valley of darkness. Or, it could mean you're the
righteous man and I'm the shepherd and it's the world that's evil
and selfish. I'd like that. But that shit ain't the truth. The truth
is you're the weak. And I'm the tyranny of evil men. But I'm
tryin', Ringo. I'm tryin' real hard to be the shepherd.

Not to be pedantic here, but I feel obliged to point out that most of
the quotation is spurious. Only parts of two sentences ("lay my vengeance") actually come from Ezekiel.

CHAPTERS 26–27

This episode, the Babylonian sack of Tyre, is unusual for public policy
reasons: It is one of the few Bible stories to celebrate capitalism.
According to these chapters, Tyre was the Shanghai or New York of its
day, a port city that was the economic engine of the world around it.
In mourning Tyre's destruction, Ezekiel offers an economist's-eye view
of the city, listing all its trading partners, detailing the various kinds
of products it exports and imports, applauding its magnificent harbor
and clever merchants. It's a very enthusiastic and emphatic litany,
written by someone who truly seems to admire the free market.

CHAPTER 28

Whoops! I spoke too soon. This chapter reverses all the Adam Smith-
ery of Chapter 27. Mercantile success, Ezekiel declares, made the king
of Tyre "haughty" and idolatrous. Tyre's grand commercial achievements produced only "lawlessness." That's why it deserved to fall.

CHAPTER 34

A long, wonderful analogy compares the kings of Israel to shepherds
and the Israelites to sheep. The shepherds have neglected their flock,
exposed them to wild animals, failed to feed them, and never culled

the bad animals from the herd. So God is firing the shepherds and doing the job Himself. "I will look for the lost, and I will bring back the strayed; I will bandage the injured, and I will sustain the weak." This is among the most loving depictions of God in the Bible. Isn't that what you want God to be, a kind, nurturing shepherd, protecting poor dumb us from harm?

CHAPTER 37

Ezekiel 37 features one of the Bible's most famous images, especially beloved by Christians. God leads Ezekiel to a valley filled with desiccated bones. (It's the source for "Dem Dry Bones.") God tells him to summon the bones back to life. At the prophet's words, the bones sew themselves back together, and flesh and skin cover them. Then Ezekiel orders breath into them, and the corpses come alive, a mass reincarnation that symbolizes the restoration of Israel. The valley of dry bones is also an emphatic tribute to the power of scripture: God's words are so powerful that they bring dead men back to life.

The remainder of Ezekiel is pretty dull. Even so, I'm going to miss this warmhearted, whole-grain, hippie prophet.

SIXTEEN

The Minor Prophets

All Those Books You've Never Heard Of, Plus Jonah and the Whale

In which a dozen prophets predict catastrophe for the Jews; Jonah is swallowed by a whale and preaches in Nineveh; Amos quotes Martin Luther King Jr. (or maybe vice versa); Satan makes his first appearance.

THE BOOK OF HOSEA

Again with the prostitutes. God's first instruction to Hosea is: *Go find yourself a whore and marry her.* Hosea picks up a streetwalker named Gomer—ancient Hebrew for "Candee," I guess—and they quickly have a son, whom Hosea names Jezreel. (Remember that Jezreel is where Ahab and Jezebel committed one of the Bible's most loathsome crimes, in 1 Kings.) Hosea names their other kids "Not Accepted" and "Not My People," to symbolize God's rejection of the Israelites. (Why couldn't he just name them "Brianna" and "Madison" like everyone else?)

The hooker wife, Gomer, represents the faithlessness of the Israelites, which is the main theme of Hosea. It may be theologically illuminating to have a metaphor for a spouse, but it must make life around the house unbearable. In Chapter 2, for example, Hosea unloads on Gomer for her harlotry, then threatens to leave her in the wilderness to die of thirst. The squabble between Hosea and his wife resembles Ezekiel 16, when God has a similar fight with His wife, Jerusalem. I find the version in Hosea much more unpleasant. The fight in Ezekiel was between God and a city. But in Hosea, the wife is the putatively real prostitute Gomer, and the husband is the real prophet Hosea. That lends it a note of genuine domestic horror that the story in Ezekiel lacks. Still, Hosea eventually persuades Gomer to stop sleeping around with other gods. So it's a happy ending, of a sort.

There's a curious proto-Christian moment midway through the book, the first of many in the minor prophets. Hosea instructs the Israelites to return to the Lord, telling them, "On the third day He will raise us up, and we shall be whole by His favor." Am I crazy to think this has overtones of the resurrection of Christ?

The closing lines of Hosea are the best in the whole book.

He who is wise will consider these words, He who is prudent will take note of them, For the paths of the Lord are smooth; The righteous can walk on them, while sinners stumble on them.

I like those verses for their measured tone. There is none of the maniacal rage of Jeremiah here, none of the trying-too-hard threats of Deuteronomy. Hosea sounds like a prosecutor calmly summing up his case. He is speaking from a position of quiet confidence: *If you're smart, you'll listen to me.* This straightforward appeal to rational self-interest—as opposed to love, fear, hate, anxiety—is rare in the Bible, and surprisingly refreshing.

THE BOOK OF JOEL

Joel is the prophet of green. His brief (four-chapter) book glows with images of nature—as destroyer and redeemer. It's astonishingly beautiful. In the first two chapters, Joel depicts an invasion of locusts that is followed by widespread natural calamity: the fig trees droop, "the seeds shrivel," and—in a spookily brilliant image—"even the flocks of sheep are dazed." The natural destruction signals human disaster: "joy withers away."

This eco-catastrophe is a prelude to the Day of Judgment, which Joel also depicts as an environmental disaster. The Lord arrives as a thick, dark cloud and sends fiery warhorses to incinerate the land. (You're worried about your carbon footprint? Blazing horse armies sent by God to set the world on fire—that's global warming!) Earthquakes and solar and lunar eclipses follow.

But our God is a recycling God, and His redemption is also depicted in environmental terms. His salvation of Israel is represented as a Greenpeace, complete with lush grasses, fruiting trees, and abundant rains. I suspect Joel is a favorite book of the budding religious environmentalist movement, Creation Care.

THE BOOK OF AMOS

Dentistry must not have been a divine priority. God lists all the suffering He has inflicted on His people. He says He blighted orchards, sent plagues, caused droughts, starved towns, destroyed cities, cleaned teeth—excuse me? Yes, the Lord, like the British government, considers white, cavity-free, periodontally sound chompers to be a punishment. "I . . . have given you cleanness of teeth in all your towns, and lack of food in all your settlements."

Actually, I suspect "clean teeth" is a version of "empty stomach." It signifies hunger rather than hygiene.

My goodness, Amos can write! He describes the Day of Judgment as a world in which terrors never end: "As if a man should run from a lion and be attacked by a bear; Or if he got indoors, should lean his hand on the wall, and be bitten by a snake!" Isn't that creepy? The success of horror movies depends on their ability to tamper with our sense of relief: just when the heroine believes she has finally found a haven, evil strikes. That is exactly what this verse captures: you've finally escaped the bear and found shelter in the safety of home, but then a snake bites you.

Even better, Amos delivers an invocation of justice so magnificent that Martin Luther King Jr. borrowed it for both the "I Have a Dream" and the "I Have Been to the Mountaintop" speeches: "Let justice well up like water, righteousness like an unfailing stream."

THE BOOK OF OBADIAH

One chapter. Yup. The whole book is one measly chapter. It's about Jacob and Esau. This nothing-burger rates inclusion in the Bible, yet the Hanukkah story doesn't.

THE BOOK OF JONAH

At last, a minor prophet who's not minor at all. It's been seven books and a trip to Israel since I've read a Bible story that I was familiar with. The last one was Solomon threatening to cut the baby in two, in 1 Kings. So, howdy, Jonah! Greetings, whale!

It's even better than I remember from Hebrew school. God orders Jonah to Nineveh (near what is now Mosul, Iraq) to warn that the Lord is going to brimstone the city for its sins. Like some folks recently, Jonah isn't thrilled about his assignment in Iraq. So he goes AWOL, jumping a ship bound across the Mediterranean for Tarshish. The aggrieved Lord sends a mighty storm, and the sailors pray for rescue. But as the ship tosses, what does the prophet do? He heads belowdecks to take a nap! Jonah's snoozing signals his deplorable tendency to flee from difficulty, to avoid trouble at all costs.

It doesn't work, of course. The captain wakes him up. The sailors cast lots to determine who caused their misfortune, and Jonah comes up snake eyes. At last, the prophet faces up to his duty. He offers to be chucked overboard to appease God. The sailors are reluctant— admirably reluctant—to toss him, and they try to row their way out of the storm. These sailors are the uncredited heroes of Jonah's tale, brave, moral, careful. Finally, after pleading not to be held responsible, they throw him into the sea, and the storm lifts.

The Lord "provided a large fish to swallow up Jonah." The word "provided" is marvelous, with its echo of "providence." That's because the fish is not the punishment: the fish is the salvation. Jonah spends a long weekend in the big fish, praying the whole time. He thanks God for rescuing him from the edge of death. God commands the fish to spit Jonah up on the shore. This story gives biblical literalists fits—you can't imagine the somersaults some perform trying to find a fish with the right specs—but I am not going to spend any time arguing with them about the truth or science of Jonah. I don't believe a word of it. It's impossible. But hey, that's why they call them miracles.

My childhood memory of Jonah stops with him gasping on the beach, but the story continues, and actually gets even better. The regurgitated prophet makes his way to Nineveh, stands in the middle of the city, and announces that God's going to smite it in forty days. The people of Nineveh heed his warning. The king wears sackcloth, squats in ashes, and orders the entire population to fast in order to gain God's mercy. Why do the Ninevites even pay attention to Jonah? It makes no sense. He's a foreigner—he may not even speak their language—he prays to an alien God, and he's a stranger. How could he mesmerize an entire city? His success seems especially unlikely given our recent experience with prophets: from Isaiah to Jeremiah to Obadiah, prophets are notable principally for being ignored. It's inexplicable that Jonah would be the exception to that rule.

In any case, the Ninevites' prayer works. God relents and pardons the city. This leads to the funniest part of the book. Jonah is furious when God forgives Nineveh because His mercy turns Jonah into a false prophet. Jonah has been screaming about the city's doom, and instead nothing happens. Jonah looks like a fraud. Jonah kvetches that that's why he fled the Lord in the first place, because he knew God would be compassionate and not actually punish the city. His pettiness— a combination of utter self-involvement and indifference to the saved

Ninevites—is awful and yet recognizably human. Jonah is a character right out of a Woody Allen movie.

Showing keen psychological perception, God decides to teach Jonah a lesson about selfishness. He sends Jonah to the desert, and provides him a ricinus plant for shade. Jonah loves the plant. God—sly deity!—then kills the ricinus. Jonah freaks out, and whines melodramatically that he's so sad about the plant that he wants to die. At this point, God delivers the knockout punch, in the final verses of the book: "You cared about the plant, which you did not work for and which you did not grow, which appeared overnight and perished overnight. And should not I care about Nineveh, that great city, in which there are more than one hundred and twenty persons who do not yet know their right hand from their left, and many beasts as well!"

Jonah really is the perfect Bible story. God is demanding yet merciful, wise yet tricky. The tale is suspenseful from beginning to end. The hero is deeply flawed, mostly learns his lesson, and behaves with both the grace and the selfishness that are in all of us. There is no unnecessary violence. And it's extremely funny.

THE BOOK OF MICAH

I don't envy Micah: Jonah's a hard act to follow. Rather than trying to match Jonah fish for fish, Micah reverts to the usual prophetic clichés, giving us the same old enigmatic metaphors about God's coming vengeance against Jerusalem. Along the way, Micah even plagiarizes the entire "swords into ploughshares" speech from Isaiah.

At one point, the Lord declares that he is filing "a suit against Israel." This is the third or fourth reference to lawsuits in the Bible, and at least the second, I think, that proposes litigation between God and His people. Is the idea of God and His followers in a *legal* dispute unique to Judeo-Christian tradition? Do other holy texts use the same courtroom metaphor? I wouldn't be surprised if it's particular to us, because of the fundamentally contractual nature of God's relationship with his Chosen People. He and they are constantly making covenants.

He promises land or redemption or love. They promise faith and obedience to law. One side or the other then breaks the contract and tries to argue its way out of the deal. I suspect that this ancient litigiousness helps explain why Jews continue to be overrepresented in legal and argumentative professions. The very foundation of our faith is contract law. After you've gone toe-to-toe with God in the courtroom, even Justice Scalia must seem like a pussycat.

THE BOOK OF NAHUM

Never heard of him. But I'm delighted to meet him. If the Bible were a bit better organized, Nahum would directly follow Jonah, because he is a gruesome response to the jolly optimism of the whale prophet.

Nahum begins with a spectacular litany of praise to the Lord. There have been lots of hymns to God in the Bible, but this is the most over-the-top in its hyperbolic, florid grandiosity. Nahum was the Muhammad Ali of his day. A taste of his shtick: "He travels in whirlwind and storm, and clouds are the dust on His feet. He rebukes the sea and dries it up. . . . The earth heaves before Him. . . . Who can stand before His wrath? Who can resist His fury? . . . No adversary opposes him twice."

This patter segues into a denunciation of the Lord's chief enemy, which is—Nineveh! Yes, the very city that Jonah helped save is now on God's do-not-call list. Nineveh has conquered Zion, and the Lord wants payback. (Nahum does not explain how the God-fearing Nineveh of Jonah's story has become the enemy.)

Nahum is both the Muhammad Ali of the Bible and the Ernest Hemingway, because he can also write in a spare, compelling style. From Chapter 2: "Desolation, devastation, and destruction! Spirits sink. Knees buckle. All loins tremble. All faces turn ashen." From Chapter 3: "Ah, city of crime, utterly treacherous, full of violence, where killing never stops!"

God promises to "lift up" Nineveh's skirts and humiliate her, also to devour her, also to scatter her people like sheep. The final verse of

the book encapsulates the stiletto genius of Nahum. Discussing Nineveh's destruction, he writes: "All who hear the news about you clap
their hands over you. For who has not suffered from your constant
malice?" What a shame this book isn't better known; it's so muscular
and brilliantly written.

THE BOOK OF HABAKKUK

Give Habakkuk credit for posing one of the most important theological questions of the Bible: If you're so good, God, why are you "silent
when the wicked swallow those more righteous than they?" This is
probably the biggest question there is about God, and one that still
puzzles many believers today. Even so, Habakkuk is a whiner and
gloomy Gus, griping about how long he has to cry to the Lord for relief. Eventually, he decides to stand in a watchtower until God answers
his complaint.

THE BOOK OF ZEPHANIAH

They call these twelve the "minor prophets," but that term doesn't do
justice to the dinkiness, the negligibility, the puniness of Zephaniah.
He's not minor-league; he's Cape Cod league. His three, mercifully
short, chapters are third-rate Isaiah, a completely familiar prophetic
poem: God's going to destroy mankind to punish worshippers of Baal.
He will trash the Israelites, the Moabites, the Ninevites, etc. Then He'll
redeem Zion. Nothing you haven't heard forty-seven times, and better,
before.

THE BOOK OF HAGGAI

A confusing but lively story, whose chief lesson is: rebuild the Temple,
guys!

THE BOOK OF ZECHARIAH

Enter Satan. In a dream, Zechariah sees the high priest of Israel facing off against Satan, who goes by the professional wrestling–style nickname "the Accuser." This makes sense because, according to the footnotes in my Bible and my Hebrew-speaking wife, "Satan" does not mean devil or Antichrist or anything like that. It is just a Hebrew word meaning "accuser" or "adversary." The Accuser is no horn-sprouting, pitchfork-wielding, brimstone-stinking, red-satin devil. He appears to be more like God's lawyer. He's "standing at His right hand"—God's right-hand man. The Accuser doesn't say a word in the chapter. In fact, he just stands by while one of God's angels cross-examines Joshua. Still, it's momentous to witness Satan's first appearance. Question: How did this abashed, impotent Accuser turn into His Satanic Majesty? (Christian readers may be wondering why I've overlooked the appearance of Satan in the book of Job. As Jews read the Bible, Job comes after the minor prophets, almost at the end of the book. So we'll get to it later.)

Zechariah, who's prone to seriously weird visions (a giant flying scroll and a woman in a lead-sheathed tub representing wickedness), declares that a man called "the Branch" shall rebuild the Temple and rule Zion. David Koresh's Branch Davidians—who believed the Branch is Christ—took their name from here.

That's not the only proto-Christian prophecy in Zechariah. Another is that the new king of Israel shall ride into Jerusalem on a donkey. The more I read of the prophets, the more it becomes clear that the Christian tradition borrows heavily from them. (I know, I know—this is a blindingly obvious observation.) Why does Christianity tell stories about Christ riding a donkey, or coming from Bethlehem, or suffering for our sins—all notions forecast in the prophetic books? Perhaps because all those stories about Christ are true. Or perhaps because the early Christian writers wanted to place Christ emphatically in the Jewish prophetic tradition. They could do this by matching up his biography to predictions in the Hebrew Bible, legitimizing Christ as a Jewish messianic figure.

THE BOOK OF MALACHI

The final prophet! Hallelujah!

God is sick of our heresy and backsliding, our feeble sacrifices and worthless professions of faith. "You have wearied the Lord with your talk," Malachi chides. When the Lord's redemption comes, the good will finally take their revenge: "You shall trample the wicked to a pulp."

SEVENTEEN

The Book of Psalms

150 Short Poems about God

In which the Lord is my shepherd.

PSALM I

Because this book consists of 150 poems in no particular order, there isn't a compelling reason to start at Psalm 1 and read through to Psalm 150. You might as well start at Psalm 47 and then read 112 and then 6 and then 65 and so on. But I'm trying to march directly through the Bible, so I'll dutifully begin with Psalm 1 and trudge forward. The first psalm advises that a righteous man studies the Lord's teaching "day and night." It's eleven-thirty PM, so that's me.

PSALM 3

The first of many psalms "of David"—psalms that King David supposedly wrote. Given David's not inconsiderable ego, it's hardly surprising that the main theme of David's psalms is: *Poor me, I have so*

many enemies, even though I'm such a righteous man. Thanks for killing those
enemies, God!

I love this wonderfully modern line at the end of Psalm 3, where
David praises the Lord: "For You slap all my enemies in the face."

PSALM 6

Another psalm of David. It opens: "O Lord, do not punish me in anger,
do not chastise me in fury. Have mercy on me, O Lord." This is an interesting appeal to the Lord. God often reacts too quickly in the Bible,
immediately flying into a rage at human sin and frailty. What's so appealing about this verse is that David is not denying his own
wrongdoing—he knows he's a sinner—but he wants God to count to
ten before smiting, perhaps hoping that the Lord's fury will subside. As
always, David is a superb psychologist, daring to understand, and
manipulate, the Lord.

Also, a literary point. Note that the first line—"do not punish me in
anger"—is followed by a line that means the same thing: "do not chastise me in fury." This similar but not identical repetition is a common
device in biblical poetry. (Psalm 3, for example, begins: "O Lord, my
foes are so many! Many are those who attack me.") If I remember
correctly from my oral literature class in college, such repetition is
common in song-poems everywhere. "Oral formulaic" poems contained
repetitions so that the bards who performed them could remember
them more easily. When the song-poems were eventually written down,
the repetitions came along.

PSALM 18

The longest and most spectacular psalm yet, it's actually an almost
word-for-word copy of 2 Samuel 22. It opens with David rattling off an
amazing series of nouns to praise the Lord: "my crag, my fortress, my
rescuer, my God, my rock in whom I seek refuge, my shield, my mighty
champion, my haven."

It then turns into a story of how God "bent the sky and came down" to rescue David. Egomaniac David, naturally, thinks he deserves nothing less, because he is a "blameless" man. "The Lord rewarded me according to my merit."

PSALM 22

This psalm surely has special meaning for Christians. David, complaining again, opens the psalm by crying: "My God, my God, why have You forsaken me?" Even I know these are Jesus's last words, according to one account in the Gospels.

It is not the only line in this psalm that relates to the death of Jesus. David imagines his killers "casting lots for my garments"—which is what the Roman soldiers did over Jesus's clothes.

PSALM 23

Probably the most famous poem ever written: "The Lord is my shepherd, I shall not want . . . green pastures . . . still waters . . . valley of the shadow of death . . . my cup overflows," etc. A key question for a lay reader is: why is this psalm world famous and 149 others are not? I have a theory. Psalm 23 is a pacific poem. One of the revelations I've had in reading the Bible is that its most famous passages are almost always its most loving ones. Although there are certainly famous Bible stories that are disturbing—Noah, Sodom, etc.—the celebrated bits are far milder than the book as a whole. ("Swords into ploughshares," for example, is the most famous verse in Isaiah, and also one of the few nonviolent ones.) Psalm 23 is another case of this whitewashing, presenting a God who is loving, forgiving, and openhearted—even though the God of most psalms, and of the Hebrew Bible generally, is quick to anger, furious, and unforgiving. This God of Psalm 23 is certainly better for marketing.

The King James version famously and majestically refers to "the valley of the shadow of death." My Jewish Publication Society translation instead offers "a valley of deepest darkness." I assume my translation is more accurate, but it's so—blah.

PSALM 25

"O my God, in you I trust." Let's stamp that on some coins.

PSALM 29

The usual formula so far is:

> *Dear Lord,*
> > *Please be my salvation and smite my enemies.*
> > > > > *Sincerely,*
> > > > > *David*

This quirky psalm breaks the mold. Instead, it's a poem about God's voice. Just His voice: "The voice of the Lord is powerful; the voice of the Lord is full of majesty. The voice of the Lord breaks the cedars. . . . The voice of the Lord flashes forth flames of fire. The voice of the Lord shakes the wilderness. . . . The voice of the Lord causes the oaks to whirl, and strips the forest bare." Stupendous! No wonder they always want Morgan Freeman to play God.

PSALM 34

Though you can't tell from the English translation, this is one of several psalms that are acrostics. In the original Hebrew, each stanza begins with a different letter, starting with "aleph" and going right through the alphabet. (What's next, sudoku psalms?) The word game doesn't do much for the poem itself, which is a workmanlike version of the usual prayer for redemption.

PSALM 37

The premise of Psalm 37 is: Don't worry about the wicked, because God is going to get back at them, big-time. Verse 11 reads: "The meek shall inherit the land." Did you know that Jesus had borrowed from this psalm for the Sermon on the Mount? I didn't. Isn't it a bit of a cheat to steal your best lines from someone else?

PSALM 38

Doctors, nurses, please gather around. This patient presents with an extraordinary and alarming set of symptoms. We need a diagnosis and a treatment plan. Patient David R., please tell us how you feel.

"My wounds foul and fester."

Really? Please continue.

"My loins are filled with burning."

Hmm. Yes. That sounds quite unpleasant.

"There is no soundness in my flesh."

What do you mean by that? Could you elaborate?

"There is no health in my bones."

What about your heart? Do you have any pain there?

"My heart throbs."

It sounds dire, colleagues. My initial diagnosis was a sexually transmitted disease. The burning loins are significant, and patient David R. has a long history of extramarital sexual activity. But I wonder if focusing on that sexual history distracts us from his other symptoms. After all, he seems to have severely infected wounds, suggesting that we may be looking at septic shock ("no soundness" and "no health"), along with damage to the heart ("throbs"). I advise a course of intravenous antibiotics, with constant monitoring in the ICU.

Update, 16:30 hours. Patient David R. has refused treatment, yet heartbeat and other vitals have suddenly returned to normal. He appears delusional, insisting that someone he calls "God" is healing him. "It is for you, O Lord, that I wait. It is you, O Lord my God, who will answer." Hospital attorneys advise patient David R. that hospital cannot be held liable for complications, disability, pain, suffering, and death that may result from his refusal of treatment. Patient David R. insists that he understands risks, signs waiver, demands return of crown and scepter, and checks himself out.

PSALM 51

A psalm attributed to David, as he did penance for Bathsheba. David begs for mercy and confesses his terrible sins. Sincere or not, David's powerful confession is a source of remorseful language we still use today. David begs to be "whiter than snow." He asks God to make a "pure heart" for him. Most interestingly, for those who believe in original sin, he says, "I was born guilty, a sinner when my mother conceived me."

PSALM 53

OK, these are getting kind of dull. Reading one psalm is a joy, reading two is a pleasure, reading three is a chore, and reading a dozen or more at once is like sitting next to a desperate insurance salesman on a transatlantic flight.

PSALM 58

The Bible describes violence and revenge better than any other book I've ever read. It's bloodier than Stephen King, icier than Cormac McCarthy. Here the psalmist asks God to take out his enemies: "[B]reak the teeth in their mouths . . . like grass let them be trodden down and wither. Let them be like the snail that dissolves into slime. . . . The righteous will rejoice when they see vengeance done; they will bathe their feet in the blood of the wicked."

PSALM 65

A psalm for farmers. What a beauty! It thanks God for irrigating the land, providing grains, "softening" the soil with gentle rain, providing grass for the flocks. "You crown the year with your bounty." Amen to that.

PSALM 69

The chief theme of Psalm 69 is loneliness, which is perhaps the underlying subject of all the psalms. Again and again, the psalms give us an embattled, solitary soul, clinging to love of God even as the rest of his world crumbles around him. In this poem, he has broken with his family. In others, he is beset by enemies or disease. Always, he has no one to talk to except God. I suspect that reading the psalms on assignment, as I am doing, does an injustice to them, because it deprives them of their unique power and value. In fact, people who love the psalms tell me, the poems are best read when you're feeling alone and seeking consolation from distress—comfort that only God can provide. Reading for obligation misses the point.

PSALM 84

One day in God's presence "is better than a thousand elsewhere."

What is it about 1,000 to 1? It's the magic ratio. Helen's was the face that launched 1,000 ships. A picture is worth 1,000 words.

PSALM 89

This is one of the most subversive chapters in the entire Bible. The usual narrative of the Old Testament is: we break our covenant with God, but He relents and lets us back into His favor. But here the psalmist reverses that story. The poem begins by praising God lavishly, admiring Him for His strength and wisdom, thanking Him for His goodness, and applauding Him for making a *permanent* covenant with David and David's descendants. All this sounds good, right?

Suddenly, the poet turns on Him. He points an accusing finger at God. "You have renounced the covenant." God has "exalted" Israel's enemies and shamed the house of David. We didn't break the deal, God—*You* did!

The psalmist reminds God of His younger and better days: "Where is Your steadfast love of old; which by Your faithfulness You swore to David?"

The last verse of the psalm reads: "Blessed be the Lord forever. Amen and Amen." Perhaps this is a sincere attempt to soothe the Lord. I don't know. You could also read it ironically, as a jab in the holy ribs.

PSALM 90

I know nice Jewish boys like me aren't supposed to have favorite hymns, but I attended an Episcopalian high school, and if there's anything I learned in four years of mandatory chapel, it's that those Christian composers sure could write a tune. All of which is to say: I'm thrilled to discover that my favorite hymn, "O God Our Help in Ages Past," was inspired by Psalm 90. The lyricist, Isaac Watts, actually improved on the Bible text. This is the King James verse: "For in your sight a thousand years are like yesterday that has past, like a watch of the night." Watts jazzed it up into *this*: "A thousand ages in thy sight are like an evening gone; short as the watch that ends the night before the rising sun." Now imagine it with a pipe organ.

PSALM 104

This is a glorious one, a tribute to God as provider and creator. "You make springs gush forth in torrents." You make the wind. You make the grass for cattle, trees where birds can build their nests, high mountains for the wild goats, and the crags "as a refuge for the rock badgers." (What's a rock badger?)

This psalm, in addition to being a thing of beauty and a joy forever, neatly encapsulates the conflict between creationists and evolutionists. For a creationist such as the psalmist, the orderliness of the world is evidence that God made it. How else would the rock badger survive, if God hadn't made the crag for it? Where would the stork make a home, if God hadn't kindly provided the juniper tree? But to a Darwinist, these are post hoc explanations: the crag wasn't created by

God to give the rock badger a home; the rock badger evolved to exploit the opportunity offered by the crag.

All sides, fortunately, can agree that Psalm 104 is a pretty darn spectacular tribute to nature, whether nature created by God or nature left here by chance.

Another line worth mentioning: God makes the "wine that cheers the hearts of men." Take that, my teetotaling friends.

PSALM III

"The fear of the Lord is the beginning of wisdom." That wouldn't be a popular sentiment today. We'd replace "fear" with "love." Still, it's very true to the Bible. So far, God has been much keener on scaring us than hugging us.

PSALM 114

This is my mother's favorite. We include it in our Passover seder every year, and she always likes to read it. When the Israelites left Egypt, the psalm says, "The sea saw them and fled, Jordan ran backward, mountains skipped like rams, hills like sheep." My mother is bewitched by the image of mountains skipping like rams. I am too.

PSALM 117

At two verses and only twenty-six words, the shortest chapter in the whole Bible. It's too dull to quote.

PSALM 118

Almost every line in this psalm is familiar. Christian pastors must have some Amway-type arrangement with Psalm 118 whereby they get a bonus each time they quote it. A couple of the greatest hits:

The stone that the builders rejected has become the chief corner-
stone.

This is the day that the Lord has made.

I don't think this psalm has as much sway over Jews, perhaps because of its heavy emphasis on rebirth, a more popular theme with
Christians than with us.

PSALM 119

So it's the end of the day—a day that the Lord has made—and I can't
wait to shut my Bible and head home for dinner, when all of a sudden I
encounter this psalm. It couldn't make a worse first impression. In
Hebrew, it's an acrostic: the first word in each line of each stanza starts
with the same letter. Also, it's the longest psalm in the book of Psalms
and the longest chapter in the Bible. As you can imagine, an endless
acrostic is not what I want to be reading at quitting time. But after a
few stanzas, I realize that this is one weird psalm. I gradually catch on
that it's a love poem, but not a regular moon-swoon-June verse. It's a
love poem, written to—guess who.
   No, not Him.
   Not him, either.
   Give up?
   It's a love poem to God's laws—a sweat-soaked, *9½ Weeks* ode to
His commandments, decrees, and rules. Imagine Supreme Court Justice David Souter falling head over heels, and you get some idea of this
psalm. Here is just a small sampling of the adoring verses:

I take delight in Your laws.

Your decrees are my delight, my intimate companions.

I cling to your decrees.

I prefer the teaching You proclaimed to thousands of gold and silver pieces.

O how I love your teaching!

And in verse 131: "I open my mouth wide, I pant, longing for your commandments." Now that's a psalmist you'd don't want to let too close to your Torah.

It is, of course, easy to mock this kinky legalism, but let me try to restrain myself. I want to try to appreciate Psalm 119 for what it's trying to do. Over the weekend I listened to a CD of Leviticus in the car. As I listened to Leviticus 19, perhaps my favorite chapter in the Bible, I got chills. The Levitical laws mandating justice, generosity to the poor, and decency to the blind and deaf are as inspiring as the Bill of Rights. I don't always keep all the commandments, but I remain astonished that my ancestors wrote down, 3,000 years ago, laws which still guide our behavior today. Those laws—whether dictated by God or merely inspired by faith—are monumental and beautiful. They are our greatest heritage. We *should* pant for them, longingly.

PSALM 127

A poem about the blessing of having sons. "Happy is the man who has a quiver full of them." Possibly true, but I know a family with five boys, and "happy" is not the first adjective that comes to mind.

PSALM 133

The last section of Psalms includes many short, imagistic poems. Their stanzas are bit like modern poetry—a metaphor or two, and not a lot of explanation. This psalm, for examples, anticipates the unification of Israel, saying that reconciliation will be "like the precious oil on the head, running down upon the beard, the beard of Aaron, running down over the collar of his robes." What a combination of strangeness and grandeur!

Can't you see the oil glistening, the beard shiny and matted with it, and the joyful smile on Aaron's face as he is anointed as God's priest? The prayer captures God's blessing, Aaron's gratitude, and—most of all—the physical sensation of that oil: slick, golden, glorious.

PSALM 137

A very important psalm for Jews. Even an ignoramus like me knows its opening line, "By the rivers of Babylon—there we sat down and there we wept when we remembered Zion." A mournful song of exile, the poem insists that we never abandon Israel: "If I forget you, O Jerusalem, let my right hand wither! Let my tongue cling to the roof of my mouth, if I do not remember you." The psalm, as you can imagine, is beloved by Zionists. In his book *Prisoners*, Jeffrey Goldberg writes wonderfully about how Psalm 137 made him decide to move to Israel. Actually, Goldberg had his revelation when he listened to the Melodians' reggae version of the psalm, "Rivers of Babylon," which is on the soundtrack of *The Harder They Come.*

But the Melodians omit the last verses of Psalm 137, and I suspect most modern readers do the same. That's because the last verses are monstrous. After the heartfelt versifying about Zion, the author addresses the poem's final lines to the Babylonian enemy: "Happy shall they be who take your little ones and dash them against the rock." This juxtaposition of personal sorrow and grotesque revenge—infanticide! with rocks!—perfectly captures the cognitive dissonance of the psalms. These poems appeal to the best in us, and the worst, often at the same time.

PSALM 150

The book ends with a romping, stomping hoedown of a psalm. It lists all the instruments that we should play while honoring God. "Praise Him with trumpet sound; praise Him with lute and harp! Praise Him with tambourine and dance; praise Him with strings and pipe! Praise Him with clanging cymbals; praise Him with loud clashing cymbals!"

EIGHTEEN

The Book of Proverbs

Chicken Soup for the Hebrew Soul

In which Solomon writes the first self-help book.

CHAPTERS 1–3

According to the opening verses, Solomon wrote Proverbs in order to teach "wisdom" to his people. It's the world's first self-help book, and it offers surprisingly sensible advice throughout: practice prudence, never panic, don't quarrel "without cause," don't plot against your neighbor, "do not envy the violent." Why doesn't some sly publisher put this between covers, throw a catchy title on it (*The Way of the King: The Timeless Wisdom of Solomon*), and rake in the bucks? It couldn't possibly be worse than *The 48 Laws of Power*.

Proverbs 1 includes a superb after-school-special moment. Solomon advises kids that if a gang of roughnecks should ask for help in mugging passersby, just say "No!" That's because such thugs will get their comeuppance. In the most after-school-special moment of all, Solomon says that the would-be muggers have "set an ambush—for their own lives! Such is the end of all who are greedy for gain." (Can't you hear the basso narrator, pausing pregnantly before saying, "for their own lives"?)

CHAPTERS 4–5

The code of behavior in Proverbs is monkish in its self-denial: wisdom comes from talking little and minding your own business. The word "discipline" appears in chapter after chapter. In a typical passage, Solomon advises: "Let your eyes look directly forward, and your gaze be straight before you. Keep straight the path of your feet, and all your ways will be sure. Do not swerve to the right or to the left."

It's odd to hear this call for self-restraint coming from our putative author Solomon. He was a king notorious for excess—too many wives, too much gold, too big a house, too much talking. And you could argue that those very excesses—his swerves off the straight and narrow, his flirtations with other gods and other women—were what gave him such an active mind and curious spirit. In other words, his own wisdom came from habits exactly the *opposite* of those he is teaching. He *didn't* look directly forward. He *didn't* avoid the adulteress. He denied himself nothing. And yet he grew in wisdom.

Another example of the Solomonic paradox is this passage about marriage: "Rejoice in the wife of your youth, a lovely deer, a graceful doe. May her breasts satisfy you at all times; may you be intoxicated always by her love." May you, indeed! But wouldn't Solomon's plea for uxorial satisfaction be more convincing from a man who didn't have 700 wives and 300 mistresses?

CHAPTER 6

I must quote the following passage in full, because (1) it's great advice; and (2) it captures something fundamental about Proberbs:

> *There are six things that the Lord hates, seven that are an abomination to him: haughty eyes, a lying tongue, and hands that shed innocent blood, a heart that devises wicked plans, feet that hurry*

*to run to evil, a lying witness who testifies falsely, and one who
sows discord in a family.*

Don't get too hung up on those numbers—is it six or seven hatreds,
Lord? Instead, let's talk about the first five abominations—haughty
eyes, lying tongue, bloody hands, wicked heart, evil feet. Solomon is
reminding us that the physical *is* the moral. Again and again, Proverbs
uses images of the body to describe moral behavior. ("Let your eyes
look directly forward"; "turn your foot away from evil"; etc.) Our age
celebrates the supremacy of the mind and holds that morality is
founded in thought and feeling. But I like the model in Proverbs,
which recognizes that it is the *body* that sins, *not* the vague, incorpo-
real mind.

CHAPTER 7

Solomon watches a sexy young thing seduce a dumb guy walking
down the street. Her husband's away, so she has tarted herself up and
decorated her house like a bordello, and she proposes to the stupid
buck: "Let us delight ourselves with love." He follows her home "like
an ox to the slaughter." His sin will "cost him his life." It's not clear if
the romp will literally get him killed, because the cuckolded husband
will murder him, or if he only dies a moral death, losing God's favor.

CHAPTERS 10–11

Solomon starts tossing off snappy one-liners, the proverbs that give
the book its name. "A wise child makes a glad father, but a foolish
child is a mother's grief." (I'm not really sure what that one means,
but it sounds good.) A few of my favorites in these chapters: "Love
covers all offenses." "Lying lips conceal hatred." "Like vinegar to the
teeth, and smoke to the eyes, so are the lazy to their employers."
That last one was probably the corporate slogan of the Judean version
of FedEx.

That proverb about vinegar in the teeth is an excellent reminder that the Bible, among its other achievements, is also a pretty good guidebook for ethical behavior in business. Throughout the book, but especially in Leviticus and here in Proverbs, there are instructions on how to do business honestly. For example, the first proverb in Chapter 11 is: "A false balance is an abomination to the Lord, but an accurate weight is his delight." Think how important true weights and measures are to any society. We have electronic scales and the National Institute of Standards and Technology. The Israelites didn't, so God makes honest scales His business.

Here's a doozy of a line: "Like a gold ring in a pig's snout is a beautiful woman without good sense."

CHAPTER 17

God is not a big fan of schadenfreude: "Those who are glad at calamity will not go unpunished."

Great proverb: "Better to meet a she-bear robbed of its cubs than to confront a fool immersed in folly."

CHAPTER 20

Proverbs is not keen on alcohol. Here it says, "Wine is a mocker, strong drink a brawler." And Proverbs 23 teetotals more emphatically, vividly describing the symptoms of both a hangover ("Who has redness of eyes?") and drunkenness ("Your mind utter[s] perverse things. You will be like one who lies down in the midst of the sea.") Proverbs 23 rails particularly at "those who keep trying mixed wines." As any bartender will tell you, only a fool mixes his drinks.

But Proverbs does believe there is one group of people who *should* drink. After recommending that kings and princes avoid wine because they need their wits about them, the book urges us to ply the poor and miserable with liquor because it will help them "put their troubles out of their mind." In other words, when a panhandler begs for a buck, you should hope that he uses it to buy rotgut.

CHAPTER 23

The Bible enthusiastically endorses corporal punishment: "Do not withhold discipline from your children; if you beat them with a rod, they will not die. If you beat them with the rod, you will save their lives from Sheol." That's pretty unequivocal.

CHAPTER 24

A lot of Proverbs sounds like something my Irish grandmother would say, if I had an Irish grandmother. "One who gives an honest answer gives a kiss on the lips."

CHAPTER 25

May I pause to pay tribute to the sheer common sense of Proverbs? It speaks up for modesty, humility, generosity, hard work, sympathy, and all the other virtues of moderation. Two gems in this chapter: "If you have found honey, eat only enough for you, or else, having too much, you will vomit it." "Visit your neighbor sparingly, lest he have his surfeit of you and loathe you."

CHAPTER 31

Proverbs is fascinating on the subject of marriage, alternating wild enthusiasm and *Married with Children* fury. Proverbs 21, for example, has this negative comment: "It is better to live in a corner of the housetop than in a house shared with a contentious wife. . . . It is better to live in a desert land than with a contentious and fretful wife." But Proverbs finishes with one of the most wonderful tributes to a wife ever written. The "capable wife"—"she is far more precious than jewels." The capable wife makes Oprah look like a bum: She gets up in the middle of the night to start her chores. She plants her own vineyard. She buys real estate. She operates a successful textile manufacturing business. She gives generously to the poor. And she's delightful company: "She looks to the future cheerfully. Her mouth is full of wisdom, her tongue with kindly teaching." She's not beautiful, but so what? "Beauty is illusory"! She loves God; she works hard; she does good. We should all want to marry her—or be her.

NINETEEN

𝕿𝖍𝖊 𝕭𝖔𝖔𝖐 𝖔𝖋 𝕵𝖔𝖇

God's Bad Bet

In which Satan wagers God that he can make Job curse the Lord; Satan kills Job's family, bankrupts him, and afflicts him with horrible skin diseases; Job complains incessantly and berates God for punishing him; Job's three friends tell him he deserves his suffering; Job insists he doesn't; God shows up and belittles Job's complaints, but then restores his fortune and family.

CHAPTER I

It is one of the embarrassments of my life that I've never read the book of Job. (Some other embarrassments, for those who are curious: repeatedly referring to Christian Scientists as "Scientologists" in an article for my college newspaper; a short-lived ponytail.) Job is a fundamental text of western civilization, the Bible book that even people who don't read the Bible have read. Yet I've managed to avoid it.

While not reading Job, I apparently developed a gross misconception about what was in it. Like everyone with a pulse, I knew the basic outlines: God bets Satan—a gentlegod's bet, no cash at stake—that

His most upright servant, Job, will remain faithful even in the face of catastrophe. God and Satan afflict Job, and he endures patiently.

But I seem to have wildly misunderstood the story in two ways. First, I assumed that the book was the story of Job's trials, an endless series of unfortunate events, punctuated by satanic (and divine) laughter. In fact, God and Satan wipe out Job by the middle of Chapter 2. The next forty chapters are just argument. Second, because I believe clichés, I thought that Job would be patient ("patient as Job"). In fact, it turns out he's the opposite of patient. He's frustrated, enraged, petulant, and agitated about his situation. He can't believe how badly he has been screwed, and he's desperate to fix it, right now.

Who is Job? And when did he live? The book does not give us many clues. Judging from the language and milieu, the book seems to take place before the time of the patriarchs, sometime between the Flood and Abraham. It's pretty clear that Job is not an Israelite, since the book doesn't mention the patriarchs, God's covenant, or Israel. Other evidence that it's pre-Abrahamic: the God of Job resembles the God of early Genesis, who intervened busily in earthly affairs, and concerned Himself with all humans, not merely His chosen Israelites.

Job lives in the land of Uz, which is not to be confused with the Land of Oz (though, as we shall see, Uz, like Oz, is vulnerable to sudden tornadoes that cause deadly building collapses). Job has "feared God and shunned evil," and his faithful goodness has made him the richest man in the east, the Warren Buffett of Uz, with 7,000 sheep and 3,000 camels. He also has seven sons and three daughters. (That numerical pattern of sevens and threes is odd—why are sheep like sons and camels like daughters?)

Meanwhile, over at God's house, some angels drop by for a social visit. Accompanying them is the Adversary, "Ha-Satan" in Hebrew, as we learned in Zechariah. Here is what this Satan is not: a fallen angel, wicked, omnipotent, demonic, living in hell, warring with God for dominion over the Earth, carrying a pitchfork, or dressed like an evil Santa. Here is what he is: argumentative, troublemaking. This is another example of the popular culture and Christianity oversimplifying and flattening a biblical character. Our modern Satan is a cartoonish incarnation of pure evil. The Bible's Satan is fascinating because he's ambiguous. He is actually the kind of guy any smart God would want around, because he questions authority. He asks the tricky, contentious questions that make God more thoughtful about His own work. Satan makes God uncomfortable, but only so God will do His job better.

The Lord asks Satan what he has been doing. Satan says he's been wandering around the world. The Lord asks if he ever got a chance to meet the star earthling Job. God starts bragging about how good Job is. Satan interrupts the love fest, jeering that Job loves the Lord only because God has given him so much wealth. If God takes away all this good fortune, Satan says, Job will curse Him. God accepts the wager. He tells Satan to do his worst but to not harm Job physically. The next seven verses are breathtaking. In short order, four messengers arrive at Job's house. The first announces that all Job's oxen and donkeys have been stolen; the next that a fire from heaven has incinerated his 7,000 sheep; the next that the Chaldeans have taken his 3,000 camels; and the last that a "mighty wind" has blown down his son's tent, killing all ten of his children. But Job does *not* curse God: He tears his clothes, cuts off his hair, and cries one of the most famous verses in the Bible: "Naked I came out of my mother's womb, and naked shall I return there; the Lord has given, and the Lord has taken away; blessed be the name of the Lord."

CHAPTER 2

Round one clearly goes to God. Job isn't cursing. But Satan isn't satisfied. He gibes God a second time. The only reason Job isn't complaining is that he still has health and life. "Lay a hand on his bones and his flesh, and he will surely blaspheme." God can't say no to a challenge. He says that Satan can do anything short of killing Job. Satan afflicts Job with wicked sores all over his body. Completely incapacitated, Job sits and scratches himself with a broken shard of pottery. His wife tells him he should curse God, but Job is philosophical: "Should we accept only good from God and not accept evil?"

We're only halfway through Job 2, and almost all the action of this book has taken place: the divine bet, the punishments of Job, and his per-severance. What's left to happen? Job's three friends Eliphaz, Bildad, and Zophar hear about his tragedies and show up at his house to console him.

CHAPTER 3

At this point, Job turns from prose to poetry. Both translations I am reading pause to observe, almost apologetically, that the poetic language of Job is very difficult and opaque. This must explain why the two trans-lations differ immensely from each other, and from other translations.

Job has not cursed God—in that sense, God is winning his wager with Satan—but Job certainly isn't taking his misery lying down. His first words to his three friends are, "Perish the day on which I was born." He asks why God let him live, only to make him suffer, and why God doesn't let him die now.

CHAPTERS 4–5

Job's three friends—who turn out to be more "frenemies" than friends—immediately lay into him. Eliphaz rebukes Job, setting out the argument that the friends will repeat for the next thirty-odd chap-ters. No innocent man was ever punished by God. If you're suffering, it is surely because you have done wrong. You, Job, are evil, as we are all evil: "For man is born to do mischief, just as sparks fly upward."

Eliphaz also suggests that Job should be grateful for God's punish-ment. The Lord is wounding him so as to heal him later. Eventually, God will give him wealth, protect him from violence, and, apparently, give him a lifetime supply of Viagra. ("When you visit your wife, you will never fail.")

CHAPTERS 6–8

Job is unimpressed by Eliphaz's Panglossian argument. He points out that his punishment is undeservedly great. He's suffering so much that he can't endure any longer. Job doesn't curse God, but he certainly waxes wroth against Him. "I will complain in the bitterness of my soul." His flesh is infested with maggots, happiness has abandoned him, and when he seeks comfort in sleep, God sends nightmares. In a wonderful passage, Job urges God to stop paying so much attention to man, since his attention is so unpleasant. Job sees God as Big Brother: "What is man, that You make much of him. . . . You inspect him every morning, examine him every minute. Will You not look away from me for awhile, let me be?" (This inverts, and mocks, a famous verse from Psalm 8: "What is man that Thou are mindful of him?")

The second friend, Bildad, now chimes in, also blaming Job, and telling him to shut up: "Your utterances are a mighty wind." Of course Job should suffer, Bildad says, because God would never "pervert justice." Job's sons probably died because they sinned. God doesn't punish the blameless.

CHAPTER 9

As I've mentioned, one repeated theme of the Bible is a lawsuit between man and God. Again and again, we are suing the Almighty or He is countersuing—usually for breach of covenant. Job 9 is the beginning of the most spectacular lawsuit of them all: *Job v. God.* The friends have urged Job to take his case to God. Canny lawyer that he is, Job recognizes that he faces impossible odds: "Man cannot win a suit against God," Job moans. God can move mountains; He can "command the sun not to shine." How can Job possibly argue with Him? How could Job possibly defeat Him? God would fix the outcome; He would cheat to win. Even though Job is innocent, Job says, "It will be I who am in the wrong." Even if Job washes himself, "You would dip me in muck." Again, Job doesn't exactly curse God, but he comes mighty close, accusing Him of injustice, of punishing the blameless and mocking the innocent.

CHAPTER 10

So far, Job has directed most of his comments to the friends, but now he whacks God directly. God knows he's innocent yet punishes him.

Job wonders why God would bother to make him—to fashion him "like clay"—just so that he can suffer. Job thinks it must be a game for God, an ego trip.

These complaints of Job's don't count as curses for the purposes of the bet between God and Satan. Why? Even though Job is angry at God, he still accepts God's authority. Job still appeals to God, still assumes that God can act to make it right. Truly cursing God would be abandoning Him. Job never gives up: he begs, berates, insists, and screams that God do better. But he always accepts that God is the decider.

CHAPTER 11

The bitter exchange between Job and his obnoxious friends continues. The three friends' relentless criticism of him seems particularly unfair when you remember that he's in mourning, having just lost all ten of his kids in a terrible accident (and lost his fortune, too). Miss Manners would take a hammer to the head of any funeral guest who behaved as rudely as Job's friends.

The basic pattern of the next twenty chapters is this: Jerk friend tells Job that he deserves his suffering because God always punishes the wicked; infuriated Job growls at the jerk friend, then asserts his innocence. Repeat.

CHAPTERS 12–14

Job vows to speak the whole truth to God—to say that God has wronged him. Job will speak out, he says, "come on me what may. I will . . . put my life in my hand. See, he will kill me; I have no hope; but I will defend my ways to his face. This will be my salvation." No one else in the Bible—except Moses in a few brave moments, Abraham in the memorable face-off at Sodom, and Gideon, briefly—has ever dared what Job dares here. Job refuses to flatter God, refuses to confess sins he didn't commit, refuses to compromise to win God's approval. He is placing truth above life, honesty above obedience. In doing this, Job is laying out what has become the modern idea of justice. There is a truth that's independent of power. The truth will set you free, even if it's painful for the king to hear it.

CHAPTERS 18–21

Bildad hits the usual theme: only the wicked and ungodly are punished. The friends' notion of justified punishment rings particularly hollow to me this week, when two good friends—two of the best people I know—were diagnosed with cancer. I don't know how anyone who has lived for any time on planet Earth could swallow the friends' argument. It's obvious that suffering and happiness are randomly distributed. Often the good suffer terribly and the wicked prosper mightily. No one but a fool would say otherwise. Any religion that hopes to succeed has to devise an explanation for that injustice. Usually, the explanation is: you'll get yours—and the wicked will get theirs—in the next world. The friends are claiming something manifestly false: that reward and punishment occur in our own lifetimes.

Job raises exactly this objection. "Why do the wicked live on, reach old age, and grow mighty in power? Their children are established in their presence. . . . Their houses are safe from fear. . . . Their bull breeds without fail. . . . They spend their days in prosperity."

Job concludes that it's all random. Some people die rich and happy, others poor and bitter, and there's no order or justice in it.

CHAPTERS 28–31

Job sets out to prove that he was a good man. When God was still with him—"when His lamp shone over my head"—Job led a worthy life. He enjoyed his riches, to be sure—his "feet were bathed in cream," and everyone heeded his orders—but he also did good, all the time. "I put on righteousness." He had a handout for every beggar, a job for every widow, new clothes for every orphan.

Job contrasts those glorious days with his fallen state. Now he is mocked by worthless young men. (He describes them memorably: "They do not withhold spittle from my face.")

At the end of Job's laundry list of good deeds, he rests his case. It's
a brilliant summing up: He has undeniably proved that he was a good
man. He's so persuasive, in fact, that he finally shuts up the three
friends. They fall silent, letting Job have the last word.

CHAPTERS 32–37

As soon as the three friends finally stop badgering Job, a whippersnap-
per named Elihu arrives to replace them. A know-it-all twerp, Elihu is
even more obnoxious than the other three—more aggressive, smug-
ger, and ruder to poor old Job. Elihu immediately takes issue with
Job's claim that God doesn't answer us. Elihu says the problem is that
Job isn't listening. God answers in dreams (where He "terrifies them
with his warnings"). God also answers in the form of physical illness,
sending pain and discomfort to those who are crossing Him. (I don't
know about you, but I find the argument that illness is divine punishment infuriating.) A little later, Elihu offers another explanation for
God's apparent indifference to the pleas of Job and others who are suffering. It's not that He's not listening; it's that their prayers are not
sincere. "God does not hear an empty cry." Elihu—who has the stam-
ina of Fidel Castro—rants on like this for six straight chapters. As
soon as he finally shuts his mouth . . .

CHAPTERS 38–39

. . . God Himself appears—in a whirlwind. He is not happy. The Lord
Most High does not appreciate Job's complaints. His opening line to
Job: "Who is this that darkens counsel by words without knowledge?
Gird up your loins like a man." Job wants to question God, but that's
not how it's going to be, the Almighty says. The Lord is going to be
the one asking the questions. His first query to Job is a tough one:
"Where were you when I laid the foundation of the earth? Tell me, if
you have understanding."

God continues in this swaggering vein for two chapters. It would
sound like bragging if He weren't, you know, God. He lists His cre-

ations and asks what Job has done that can compare: "Have you commanded the morning since your days began, and caused the dawn to
know its place?" "Have the gates of death been revealed to you? . . .
Have you comprehended the expanse of the earth? Declare, if you
know all this." Can Job move the stars? Is Job the father of the snow?
Does Job send rain to make the desert bloom? Does Job "know when
the mountain goats give birth"? Will the wild ass serve Job? Is it by
Job's wisdom that the hawk soars and the eagle commands the mountains? I don't think so.

God doesn't merely humble Job. He savors Job's humiliation, de-
molishing Job with sarcastic jabs: "Where is the place of darkness, that
you may take it to its territory and that you may discern the paths to
its home? Surely you know." That "surely you know" is so mean, so
petty. God takes too much pleasure in making Job feel like an ig-
noramous, like a mere speck.

Vicious, petty, cruel—definitely. But beautiful, too! God's self-
congratulatory speech is one of the most spectacular passages in the
Bible, a masterpiece of imagery and forceful language, one killer phrase
after another. Indulge me as I quote a favorite bit about the making of
the ocean:

> *Who shut in the sea with doors when it burst out from the womb?—*
> *when I made the clouds its garment, and thick darkness its*
>   *swaddling band,*
> *and prescribed bounds for it, and set bars and doors,*
> *and said, "Thus far shall you come, and no farther,*
>   *and here shall your proud waves be stopped"?*

"Thus far shall you come, and no farther"!

CHAPTERS 40–41

God bullies Job to answer His questions. "Anyone who argues with
God must respond." What do you have to say for yourself now, smart
aleck? You started the fight, Job, so let's hear it! Not so chatty, now,

are you, little fella? I'm very familiar with how Job must feel at this moment, since God sounds exactly like my wife when she knows she has defeated me in an argument. Much like me, Job stammers, stutters, and caves in. All his courage of Chapters 1–37 vanishes in the teeth of this divine hurricane. He is totally cowed. His grand oath in Chapter 13 to confront God goes out the window. He whispers that he has nothing to say. "I lay my hand on my mouth. . . . I will not answer."

That's not good enough for God, who wants to run up the score on Job. He redoubles His bragging. Can Job tame the Behemoth, the mighty creature with "limbs like bars of iron"? Can Job fish and catch the Leviathan, the giant sea monster with "flaming torches" in its mouth, which "laughs at" javelins and arrows? God seems to think He has won this round because He has reduced Job to a blubbering mess. In the keeping score department, God certainly has triumphed, because Job has given up. But God has won only in the way that the president "wins" when he argues with his assistants, or a principal "wins" when she suspends a student. The powerful can crush the impotent whenever they want. But an independent referee would give the victory to Job, because God's actual answer is unpersuasive. Job says that he is innocent, that he doesn't deserve God's punishment, and that God screwed up. God doesn't address any of these points. Instead He thunders: *I'm the mighty God of creation—how* dare *you question Me?* God's answer, as a lawyer might say, is "nonresponsive."

CHAPTER 42

But wait—even God apparently recognizes that He's in the wrong. Here in the final chapter, God rebukes the three friends and acknowledges that Job is "right." So all the bragging of Chapters 38 through 41 was just posturing, God flexing His big muscles before quietly admitting He screwed up. God restores Job's fortune. Job gets twice as many sheep and camels as before, and ten new children—seven sons, and three daughters, who are the most beautiful girls in Uz. (This is perhaps the only time in the Bible when we are told the names of daughters but not sons.)

I confess that I'm flummoxed by Job. Should we believe Chapters 38 through 41, when God tells us we're nothing, and that we have no right to question Him? Or should we believe Chapter 42, when God acknowledges that Job was right and settles the lawsuit? The God of Chapters 38–41 is petulant, arrogant, and wrong. The God of Chapter 42 is willing to correct His mistake. Also, the God of Chapter 42 admits that the three friends are fools. By rebuking them, He seems to be conceding that, in fact, the wicked *aren't* always punished and the good *aren't* always rewarded. But isn't such a concession impossible for God? If He disavows their arguments, isn't He saying that He's impotent—that He doesn't actually reward the righteous and upbraid the wicked?

Job is the paramount example of what I would call the Messy Bible, a story that's far more complicated, ambiguous, and confusing than its popular version. The principal task of priests and rabbis has been cleaning up the Bible, taking complicated stories and bringing order to them. But it is an artificial order, with a much neater morality that we find in the real book: Jacob good, Esau bad; Moses good, Pharaoh bad; God good, good, good. As we've seen, the actual text is much sloppier. Some of the heroes are intolerable; some of the villains are admirable, and God himself is often unreasonable. This Messy Bible is truer to our actual world—where the good do evil and the evil do good, where people suffer for no reason—than the idealized Bible is. The Messy Bible is the better Bible. That's why we should read the Good Book for ourselves, to confront the complexity that the idealized Bible avoids.

TWENTY

The Song of Songs

Hot and Holy

In which two lovers get hot and heavy, and Solomon drops by for a visit.

CHAPTER I

Like my grandmother's basement, which is crammed with jelly jars, eighty-three-year-old report cards, and failed perpetual motion machines, the Bible is a magnificent hodgepodge. It contains everything under the sun, from a creation story (or two), to law books, genealogical tables, prophecies, histories, ritual handbooks, self-help manuals, and now—erotica.

The Song of Songs—also called the "Song of Solomon"—is like nothing else in the Bible, a steamy poem narrated by two lovers. She is foxy, young, and dark. He is strong, sexy, and seductive. (He may even be Solomon, the purported author of the song.) Some biblical scholars, whose libidos we must question, insist that the song is merely an allegory, that the lusty verses are just enthusiastic prayers. No way. This is no religious metaphor. This is *Last Tango in Judah*.

The poem begins with her daydreaming. Imagine a young woman alone in her room, hugging her pillow: "Let him kiss me with the kisses of his mouth! For your love is better than wine." Now that's an opening line.

In one of my translations, our songstress describes herself as "dark and swarthy but beautiful." The New Revised Standard Version uses a saucier, modern coinage: "I am black and beautiful."

CHAPTER 2

She's very forward, our dusky beauty. She says her lover is an apple tree, "and his fruit is sweet to my mouth." (She follows this with the carnal imperative, "comfort me with apples," borrowed as a book title by both Ruth Reichl and Peter De Vries.)

In the middle of the erotic reverie, she catches herself, and sits up long enough to address a word to her young readers: "I adjure you, O daughters of Jerusalem . . . do not stir up or awaken love until it is ready!" She repeats this line twice in later chapters. What does it mean and why is it so important? She includes this caution to remind us that she can be wanton only because he is her true love. She guarded her heart and found the right man, and *that* has liberated her to indulge her sensual desires. She wants girls to be careful, not to give away their hearts, or their virginity, too easily. This lesson—that true love waits, to steal a phrase—makes the otherwise spicy poem suitable for church and synagogue.

A pretty exchange between the two of them—he's a gazelle; she's a dove—climaxes with a verse that has been co-opted by brides and grooms everywhere: "My beloved is mine and I am his."

CHAPTER 3

She can't sleep, so she gets out of bed and wanders the city, seeking him out. (See Patsy Cline, "Walking after Midnight.") She finds him, brings him back to her mom's house, and—well, you'll have to imagine the rest.

Meanwhile, Solomon's wedding procession comes to town. He's riding in a palanquin, and he has seriously pimped his ride for maximum scoring: "He made its posts of silver, its back of gold, its seat of purple; its interior was inlaid with love." Inlaid with love, oh my! On the back, Solomon attached a bumper sticker: *If this palanquin's a rockin', don't come a knockin'.*

CHAPTER 4

Now it's the guy's turn to praise his lover. Either he's not much of a wordsmith, or men chatted girls up differently back in the day. He says: "Your hair is like a flock of goats . . . your teeth are like a flock of shorn ewes." Your brow is like a "pomegranate split open." "Your neck is like the tower of David." You're so beautiful—your hair looks like goats! Your forehead is a pomegranate—a fruit that resembles, um, acne. And you have a neck made of brick. These lines wouldn't go over well at my house.

His most famous compliment is: "Your two breasts are like two fawns, twins of a gazelle." This isn't exactly insulting, but it is confusing. Fawns are bony, muscular, and jumpy—not at all how I would describe breasts. However, someone pointed out to me why the metaphor may work: "I've always thought that the comparison between breasts and twin fawns is more that they are soft-looking and symmetrical—and, in her case, similarly colored. If you see a fawn, don't you want to pet it? Especially two of them?"

When he calls her a "locked garden," that really turns her on. "Awake, O north wind, and come, O south wind! Blow upon my garden that its fragrance may be wafted abroad. Let my beloved come to his garden, and eat its choicest fruits."

CHAPTER 5

This is probably the hottest passage in the song. She recalls her beloved knocking on the door. Then he "thrust his hand into the opening, and my inmost being yearned for him. I arose to open to my beloved, and my hands dripped with myrrh, my fingers with liquid myrrh, upon the handles of the bolt."

She praises his good looks. Her compliments, unlike his, withstand the test of time. He's "radiant and ruddy." His hair is black like a raven's. His cheeks "are like beds of spices . . . his lips are lilies . . . his arms are rounded gold . . . his legs are alabaster columns." Is it any wonder the girl digs him?

CHAPTER 6

He is *her* true love. But is she *his* true love? In this chapter, he mentions sixty queens and eighty concubines, then says she's the finest of them all, the only woman he really cares about: "My dove, my perfect one, is the only one." Should we believe him? That depends on how you interpret the line about queens and concubines. If the author is just a regular guy, and he's saying that his love is more beautiful than any queen—the way you hear guys brag, "My girlfriend looks like Salma Hayek, only hotter"—then perhaps he does love her truly. But as I read it, the author—perhaps Solomon—is referring to these sixty queens and eighty concubines as *his own* queens and concubines. And that sets off the alarm bells. If he has already run through 140 women, he'll run through one more. (And if the author actually is Solomon, he'll run through 860 more women, since he ends up with 700 wives and 300 concubines.) All his sweet compliments mean nothing: they're just lines he's using to get her into his palanquin.

CHAPTER 7

In a wonderful passage, she proposes that they go for a walk in the fields and vineyards, to see if the blossoms have opened: "There I will give you my love."

CHAPTER 8

She wishes that her lover were her brother. Then they could be together in public and kiss in the street, and no one would notice. Doesn't this sound eerily like what must happen today, in Islamic nations such as Saudi Arabia that have turned ancient sexual taboos into the law of the land?

She says he can drink "the juice of my pomegranates."

And one final line plagiarized for weddings: "Set me as a seal upon your heart."

TWENTY-ONE

𝕿𝖍𝖊 𝕭𝖔𝖔𝖐 𝖔𝖋 𝕽𝖚𝖙𝖍

My Favorite Bible Story

In which two poor widows, Naomi and her daughter-in-law Ruth, move back to Bethlehem; while gleaning in the fields, Ruth meets Boaz, a relative of her dead husband; he falls in love with her; eventually they get married, and are great-grandparents to King David.

CHAPTER I

It's the time of Judges. There's a famine in Bethlehem, so Elimelech, his wife Naomi, and their two sons immigrate to Moab. Elimelech promptly dies. The sons marry Moabite girls—a brave move, since we know how the Lord feels about intermarriage with idolaters. Both sons die, though their deaths are not attributed to divine disapproval of the mixed marriages. This is our first sign that Ruth is not like other books of the Bible. God won't be the prime mover here. The characters in Ruth are faithful, but they make their own fate; the Lord won't make it for them. Ruth is a great book for agnostics, since it shows how good people should behave even when they don't expect God to intervene.

Naomi decides to return to Bethlehem, but before she leaves she gently tells her widowed Moabite daughters-in-law, Orpah and Ruth, to remain in Moab and remarry. Naomi isn't trying to ditch them for selfish reasons. On the contrary, Naomi knows that she herself is too old to marry again, and she doesn't want to burden the young women. They insist on going with her anyway. Naomi orders them not to follow her. Orpah finally leaves, but Ruth sticks to her like glue, delivering one of the most moving speeches in the Bible: "For wherever you go, I will go; wherever you lodge, I will lodge; your people shall be my people, and your God my God. Where you die, I will die, and there I will be buried." This speech is impressive in many ways, but perhaps most because of its insight into how people choose a religion. Ruth does not come to the Lord because He is the Lord. She comes because she loves Naomi. If Naomi worshipped Baal, Ruth probably would have become a Baalite. Sometimes theologians forget that religion is not a calculation: almost always, we come to God or Allah or the Buddha not because we have carefully analyzed the relevant laws, texts, and miracles but because someone we love leads us to him. Relationships, not theories, make religions grow.

Incidentally, this chapter is the source of the most famous quasi-biblical name of our time. Oprah Winfrey was officially named Orpah—it's on her birth certificate—but because of spelling confusion, the family called her Oprah instead.

CHAPTER 2

Naomi and Ruth return to Bethlehem during the barley harvest. They're flat broke. Ruth goes to glean in the fields, collecting the grain left behind by the harvesters. (Leviticus 19 orders farmers to leave gleanings for the poor. This is one of many passages in which Ruth shows us biblical laws in practice.) Ruth doesn't yet know it, but she happens to glean the field of Boaz, a relative of Naomi's dead husband, Elimelech. Boaz shows up in the field and hears that Naomi's daughter-in-law has been gleaning. He immediately invites her to drink his water and glean from all his fields. He calls her "daughter," a red herring that distracts us from the idea that they could ever marry. She asks why he's being so kind to a stranger, and he says he heard how good she was to his kinswoman Naomi. He invites her to eat and drink with him, then surreptitiously orders his workers to leave extra stalks so she can glean more.

CHAPTER 3

Naomi decides that Ruth needs to remarry, and that Boaz would be a catch. She has Ruth wash and dress up, then go to the barn where Boaz is spending the night, in preparation for a big day of threshing. Naomi instructs Ruth to uncover his feet, then to fall asleep at them. Ruth does this. He wakes up astonished, and asks who she is. She tells him to put his robe over her—a euphemism for "have sex with," perhaps?—because he is "a redeeming kinsman." This means he is a male relative of her dead husband and thus has an obligation to marry her. No spring chicken, Boaz is evidently thrilled to find a lovely young woman throwing herself at him. His first response is to thank her for not seeking a younger man. Then he hesitates. Because he's a deeply good and law-abiding man, he knows he can't say yes. Full of regret, he tells her that there is a "closer" male relative, who gets first dibs on her. He invites her to spend the night anyway. (As friends, I think. Boaz does not seem to want to get in her pants. In fact, he appears to be trying to protect her reputation.)

CHAPTER 4

The next day, Boaz waits by the town gate for the closer kinsman. When he arrives, Boaz offers him a deal: you buy Elimelech's land and marry Ruth, but any son you have with Ruth will inherit the estate. The relative, though tempted, says no. The relative then offers Ruth and the land to Boaz. Without hesitating a second, Boaz accepts. They seal the deal, with the other kinsman removing his sandal. (In discussing Deuteronomy, I made fun of the weird law by which a man refusing a levirate marriage has his sandal removed and is known as the "unsandaled one." And now, it has happened.) The townspeople cheer Boaz's announcement that he is marrying Ruth. He is the beloved old bachelor of Bethlehem, and everyone is overjoyed that he's finding happiness in his declining years. No one blinks at the idea of his marrying a Moabite: by her actions, Ruth has made herself as much a Jew as anyone. The women of Bethlehem congratulate Naomi, telling her that her daughter-in-law Ruth "is better to you than seven sons." True enough.

Ruth and Boaz have a son, whom they name Obed. He grows up to be the father of Jesse, who is in turn the father of King David. (Ruth, thus, is also an ancestor of Jesus, since he is descended from David.)

And that's it. That's the whole story. No smiting. No prophecies. No laws. No kings. No God. Just the story of one family and its two good women.

I had never read Ruth, so going into the story I didn't understand the fierce loyalty it inspired. But I do now. Like the Song of Songs, Ruth is very different from everything that precedes it. For starters, it's inspiring for observant Jewish readers because it shows biblical laws in action. We see how a nice family follows the Bible's (peculiar) rules about gleaning and levirate marriage and thrives as a result. The law is no longer an abstraction; it's alive, and it's good.

What's even more important and unusual about Ruth, and the reason why so many Christians and nonobservant Jews love it, is its domesticity. Ruth reminds me of nothing so much as a Jane Austen novel, compressing the whole world into the intimate details of family life. Grand national and religious politics are absent. Ruth revels in the small moments where love is forged. It holds out the prospect of redemption, but in the smallest, most personal way—for the young foreign widow, for the kind mother-in-law, for the lonely old bachelor. Ruth is the quietest of all Bible books, a short story that manages to combine extraordinary power and extraordinary serenity. Like an old country song, it leaves me feeling calm, joyful, inspired, and also a little bit melancholy—sad that the world can't always be so sweet.

TWENTY-TWO

The Books of Lamentations and Ecclesiastes

Bible Books for Rock Stars

In which Jerusalem's destruction is remembered again; a teacher wonders what the point of life is, since we all die anyway, then advises us to enjoy every day, since you can't take it with you.

THE BOOK OF LAMENTATIONS

As you might surmise from the name, Lamentations is not the cheeriest read. It begins "Alas," and goes downhill from there. Its five poetic chapters address the destruction of Jerusalem and the misery of the Jews. The first one, written in the voice of the Israelites, admits that God "is in the right" to punish Jerusalem, but it mourns because the enemy has conquered and humiliated the city. The lamenter tries to look on the bright side, begging the Lord to make Israel's enemies as miserable as the Israelites. Sometimes the Bible denounces schadenfreude, and sometimes that's the only item on the menu.

Lamentations is tossed way in the back of the Hebrew Bible, but it really belongs with the prophets, since it addresses the same depressing themes as they do: destruction, exile, God's disappointment with us.

THE BOOK OF ECCLESIASTES

Chapters 1–2

Ecclesiastes, like Deuteronomy, has a name that is at once familiar and nonsensical. Goodness knows I have heard "Ecclesiastes" a million times, but I couldn't for the life of me tell you what the word means. So, I Googled and learned that it's the Greek for "preacher," in turn a translation of the Hebrew *goheleth* or *koheleth*.

In the first sentence, Ecclesiastes announces that the book is "the words of Koheleth son of David, king in Jerusalem." This immediately sets wheels spinning, since the only son of David who became king is Solomon. Does that make Koheleth Solomon? One current theory is that Ecclesiastes was actually written hundreds of years after the time of Solomon, and was attributed to Koheleth in order to give it street cred. But other translations simply call him the Teacher or the Preacher.

In any case, Koheleth is a thoughtful, weary fellow, trying to come to grips with the fact that wealth, power, and wisdom don't seem to matter. In the end, we all make a meal for worms. The book mixes the contemplative, self-help style of Proverbs with a shrugging, though not cheerless, fatalism.

The second verse of the book is one of the most famous in the Bible, at least as the King James Version translates it: "Vanity of vanities, all is vanity." My translation renders it "Utter futility! All is futile!," which, I think, better captures the tone of the book. The King James Version suggests that Ecclesiastes is a hectoring book, but actually it's a hopeless one.

Koheleth's big question is: what does a man gain from all his work, prosperity, and success "under the sun"? The key phrase, which appears probably thirty times in the book, is "under the sun." Koheleth is interested in the here and now. "Under the sun" suggests brightness, joy, youth. He is seeking to sum up life at its best. How does it hold up?

Not well, apparently. Koheleth immediately concludes that generation after generation lives on Earth, but nothing ever changes: "There is nothing new under the sun." Koheleth studies wisdom, and realizes that it's pointless, because the wiser you are, the more heartache you suffer. He examines merriment—that's pointless as well. He builds houses, plants vineyards, buys slaves and cattle, amasses gold and silver. He gets nothing out of it except a little pleasure. It's futile, of "no real value under the sun!" At first he thinks the wise man is better than the fool, but then he realizes there is no difference, because "the same fate awaits them both." He decides that he loathes life because "all is futile, and pursuit of wind." Pretty bleak, eh?

Eventually, he decides to embrace a kind of nihilistic hedonism. If life is pointless, you might as well enjoy it. So eat, drink, be merry!

Chapter 3

Another of the most famous passages in the Bible—"there's a time for everything." (Ecclesiastes is, verse for verse, the most quoted book in the Bible.) There's "a time for being born, and a time for dying, a time for planting, and a time for uprooting the planted . . . a time for loving and a time for hating; a time for war and a time for peace." And a bunch more times, as well. If you're like me, you know this best as the Byrds' cover of a song by Pete Seeger. Modern readers view this passage as soothing: *Ah, look, the whole world fits together. There is a time for everything. Cool.* But Koheleth reaches a gloomier conclusion: If it's all put together by God, all planned out in this way, then what purpose is life? If the fix is in, we might as well just "eat and drink and get enjoyment." This is another case of the messy Bible being cleaned up.

Chapter 4

This chapter contains the Bible's finest tribute to family and love. Koheleth begins by deploring the "solitary individuals," who spend all their time working but have no one to share their wealth with. This flows into the following glorious passage:

> *Two are better than one, because they have a good reward for their toil. For if they fall, one will lift up the other; but woe to one who*

is alone and falls and does not have another to help. Again, if two
lie together, they keep warm; but how can one keep warm alone?

Chapters 5–6

Koheleth concludes that wealth and greed bring only dissatisfaction.
"A lover of money never has his fill of money." It's also pointless to love
money, because you can't take it with you. Ripping off Job—or being
ripped off by Job—he declares: "As he came out of his mother's womb,
so must he depart at last, naked as he came." (Job 1 says: "Naked I
came out of my mother's womb, and naked shall I return there.")

Chapter 9

I now understand why Ecclesiastes is the favorite book of the Bible
among people who don't strongly believe in God. It offers the only
genuine competition to the Bible's main theme of heaven, redemption, and judgment. If you *believe* in God, you can explain injustice
and wickedness on earth with Judgment Day, when the good get
their just deserts. But what if you don't believe? What if death is
just death? What if there is no afterlife, no second chance? How do
we live then? Ecclesiastes faces this head-on. Koheleth believes that
you die and that's it—"even a live dog is better than a dead lion . . .
the dead know nothing . . . their loves, their hates, their jealousies
have long since perished." Koheleth's answer is: seize the day.
"Whatever it is in your power to do, do with all your might."
"Enjoy happiness with a woman you love." This is all we get, so
make the most of it.

I am not criticizing one bit when I say that this is a godless philosophy. It is literally a way to live well without God. So, it raises an obvious question: what on Earth is it doing in the Bible? Why did the
rabbis and bishops keep Ecclesiastes all these thousands of years? I can
think of a couple of reasons. First, there may be a powerful agnostic
strain in the Judeo-Christian tradition—hey, that's certainly *my*
strain—and Ecclesiastes is a way to speak to this crowd, a way to acknowledge their doubts but keep them in the fold. (A few weeks ago,

an evangelical Christian friend told me that Ecclesiastes is his favorite book of the Bible. This makes me like him even more, but I wonder if his pastor should worry about him.) Second, maybe Ecclesiastes was kept in the Bible precisely because it's so provocative. It riles people up, it makes them think, and thinking may make them more active in their faith.

Chapter 12

The last chapter is a beauty. Returning to our key lesson—repeat after me, class, *Enjoy your days under the sun, because they are brief*—Koheleth delivers a poetic montage, a list of people, places, and things coming to their end. It has a relentless, gorgeous rhythm. It sounds exactly like a Bob Dylan song:

> *When the guards of the house become shaky,*
> *And the men of valor are bent,*
> *And the maids that grind, grown few, are idle,*
> *And the ladies that peer through the windows grow dim,*
> *And the doors to the street are shut—*
> *With the noise of the hand mill growing fainter,*
> *And the song of the bird growing feebler,*
> *And all the strains of music dying down;*
> *When one is afraid of heights*
> *And there is terror in the road . . .*
> *Before the silver cord snaps*
> *And the golden bowl crashes,*
> *The jar is shattered at the spring,*
> *And the jug is smashed at the cistern.*
> *And the dust returns to the ground,*
> *As it was.*

So live now! Live now, before it's too late!

That should be the end of Ecclesiastes, but it's not. There's a hilariously misplaced coda, seemingly tacked on by another author trying to make the book more palatable. It declares: "The sum of the matter, when all is said and done: Revere God and observe His commandments. . . . God will call every creature to account for everything unknown, be it good or bad."

Uh, dude, did you read the rest of the book? That's exactly what it *doesn't* say.

TWENTY-THREE

The Book of Esther

The First Miss Universe Pageant

In which the King of Persia divorces his wife, holds a beauty pageant, and marries the winner, a nice Jewish girl named Esther; her uncle saves the king's life; the new prime minister, Haman, hates Jews and orders their extermination; Esther and her uncle discover the plan and persuade the king that it's a bad idea; Haman is executed, his supporters are crushed, and the Jewish victory is celebrated with the holiday Purim.

CHAPTER I

Esther is one of the best stories in the Bible, but not because it teaches moral lessons, reveals human goodness, or glorifies the Lord. It's short on all three counts. Instead, it's a great story because it's got sex, subterfuge, violence, revenge, and four main characters straight out of Shakespeare.

We begin with a jerk. Not merely a jerk, but a vain, egomaniacal, fickle, childish cad. Ahasuerus is emperor of, well, everywhere. Based in Persia, he rules 127 provinces from India to Ethiopia. Notably for our purposes, he rules the Jews, who have been liberated from their Babylonian oppressors and now live throughout the Persian empire.

Soon after he inherits the throne, Ahasuerus decides to hold a six-month party in his capital, Shushan. The final week of Ahasuerus's party is a banquet, where, as during Mardi Gras and at the Sigma Chi house, "the rule for drinking was, 'no restrictions.'" On the seventh day of the feast, the soused king orders his queen, Vashti, to come and "display her beauty to the partygoers."

What does "display her beauty" mean, you ask? Good question. I don't know. Does he want her merely to be admired from afar? Or lasciviously ogled? Or does he actually expect her to strip for them? It's not clear, and we never learn the answer, because Vashti bravely refuses. Ahasuerus flips out. His ministers tell him that Vashti has not merely insulted her hubby but committed a crime against the empire, because now all women will think it's OK to disobey their husbands, and what a mess that will be. "There will be no end of scorn and provocation!"

Egged on by the prime minister, the king orders Vashti banished from his presence. He concludes, hilariously, that their divorce will improve marriages nationwide: From now on, "all wives will treat their husbands with respect." So ends our setup, one of the most entertaining chapters in the whole Good Book.

CHAPTER 2

Playing the role of royal pimps, Ahasuerus's ministers assemble all the beautiful young virgins in the empire, placing them under the care of the emperor's top eunuch. (This episode includes a fabulous line, one that reminds us just how little has changed in 2,500 years. The ministers instruct the eunuch to treat the girls right: "Let them be provided with their cosmetics.") When the virgins arrive at the harem, they don't go immediately to Ahasuerus's bed. Rather, they prepare for an entire year: "Six months with oil of myrrh and six months with perfumes and women's cosmetics."

It's the first Miss Universe pageant, complete with a tiara for the winner. (Plus one sleazy Persian monarch in the role of Donald Trump.)

And your new Miss Universe, 483 BC, is—Miss Shushan, Esther Cohen! Frankly, it doesn't surprise me that Esther turns out to be the most stunning girl in the empire. Not to reveal my biases, but have you seen how great-looking the Jewish women of that region are? Readers, I married one.

The emperor makes Esther his queen. A Jewish orphan, Esther had been adopted by her elderly cousin Mordecai. At Mordecai's urging, Esther "passes," not revealing herself as a Jew to her husband.

Loitering outside the palace gates one day, Mordecai overhears two eunuchs plotting to assassinate Ahasuerus. (And who can blame them? If someone made you a eunuch, wouldn't you want some payback?) He tells Esther, who reports it to her husband, who has the plotters impaled on stakes.

CHAPTER 3

The king appoints a new prime minister, Haman. (Boo! Hiss!) Everyone else in the court bows to Haman, but Mordecai refuses. The text doesn't say this, but I assume that Mordecai won't bow because Jews are supposed to bow only to God. Is that right? (Question: If that is the case, how does Mordecai get away with not bowing to the king?) The detestable Haman is "filled with rage" at Mordecai and plots to annihilate all the Jews in the empire. Haman casts lots to determine the date of the massacre. ("Lots" is *purim* in Hebrew; this is why the holiday inspired by Esther is called Purim.) Now Haman needs to get the king on his side. Haman tells Ahasuerus that the empire is filled with Jews who don't obey the king's laws but follow their own laws instead. The king mustn't tolerate such dissent.

What's curious is that Haman is half right. From Persia to Spain to the United States, we Jews have always set ourselves apart from the societies in which we live, following our own customs and laws (though also the laws of the host nation). That separation has allowed Jews to maintain their faith and culture through 2,500 years of diaspora. The question, of course, is what conclusion you should draw from the separation. In many places, wise rulers decided that Jewish separation posed no danger, because Jews contributed so much to the nation. But in other places, rulers exploited Jewish separateness as a threat and an opportunity. Jews could be scapegoated and attacked, and their difference was considered a menace to what should be a homogeneous society. (See Spain during the Inquisition, or Nazi Germany.) So the story of Esther is also a lesson in the virtue of diversity.

The king, an easily led fool, listens to Haman for about fifteen seconds and agrees that extermination of the Jews is a great idea. (Then, presumably, he immediately goes back to what really interests him—playing video golf or fondling the latest batch of virgins.)

Haman dispatches an order across the empire, under the king's signature, to "destroy, massacre, and exterminate all the Jews, young and old, children and women, on a single day." Those three verbs—"destroy, massacre, and exterminate"—are very powerful, emphasizing the existential menace of Haman. Remember that at this time there were no Jews anywhere else in the world. If you wiped out the Jews in the Persian empire, you wiped them out, period. It's not hyperbole to compare Hitler to Haman or Haman to Hitler.

Here's a fascinating verse. When the decree is announced in Shushan, the king and Haman sit down for a celebratory dinner, but "the city of Shushan [is] dumfounded." Presumably, this is because Shushan itself has a huge Jewish population. It must be the New York of Persia.

CHAPTERS 4–6

Jews grieve over their impending destruction, slated for the thirteenth day of the month of Adar. But they don't revolt. Why?

Mordecai asks Esther to intercede with the king. She quavers. She tells Mordecai that Ahasuerus has not seen her in a month, and she can't go to him on her own, because the penalty for seeing the king without having been summoned is death. Mordecai tells her she's going to die anyway if Haman isn't stopped—her position won't protect her—so she must petition Ahasuerus. She asks the Jews of Shushan to fast on her behalf, then agrees to take her life in her hands and visit the king unbidden. (Note the parallel between Vashti and Esther. Vashti risks her life by refusing to go to the king when summoned. Esther risks hers by going to the king when she has not been summoned.)

Esther shows up in the throne room. Ahasuerus, rather than chopping off her head, is thrilled to see her—she's a stone-cold Persian fox, after all—and says she can have whatever she wants, even half the kingdom. She asks only that the king invite Haman to a feast. At the dinner, she requests that Haman and the king return for another banquet the next day. Haman is delighted at the royal favor, until he runs into Mordecai, who again refuses to bow. Haman goes home in a sour mood and tells his wife that Mordecai is spoiling his good time. His wife and friends, who just want to cheer up gloomy old Haman, tell him to erect a stake seventy-five feet high and have Mordecai impaled on it the next day. "Then you can go gaily with the king to the feast." This puts a spring in Haman's step and a smile in his heart.

That same night, the king has a hard time falling asleep, so he asks his servants to read to him from "the annals": the history book–*Congressional Record–New York Times* where all important imperial events are recorded. His reader opens the book to the story of Mordecai averting the eunuchs' assassination plot. The king is dismayed to hear that Mordecai has never received a reward for his good deed. Haman happens to arrive at the palace at this moment to get a bright and early start on the impaling. The king summons Haman and asks him the best way a king can honor a man. In a wonderful case of mistaken identity, Haman assumes that Ahasuerus wants to honor *him* and says that the king should put that man in royal robes and crown, and parade him through town on a horse. The king then orders Haman to do this—for Mordecai. Haman gulps, but does it.

CHAPTERS 7–8

Esther holds her second feast for Haman and the king. Ahasuerus again asks what he can do for her. This time she pleads for her life and the lives of her fellow Jews, who are scheduled for extermination. The king—who is either amnesiac or criminally inattentive or a moron—doesn't seem to remember that he himself ordered the slaughter of the Jews, since he exclaims indignantly, "Who is he and where is he who dared to do this?" Esther replies—and you can imagine her pointing her bejeweled finger—"The adversary and the enemy . . . is this evil Haman." Haman cringes in terror. The king storms out of the room. Haman begs Esther to save him. In a marvelous moment—again, so cinematic!—Haman lies next to Esther on her couch and pleads for his life. At this moment, the king returns to the room and assumes that Haman is trying to rape Esther. "Does he mean . . . to ravish the queen in my own palace?"

It's curtains for Haman, as you can imagine. They impale him on the stake meant for Mordecai. The king gives all of Haman's property to Esther, who hands it over to Mordecai. The king names Mordecai as his new prime minister. With the king's OK, Mordecai sends out a new order telling the Jews that they can defend themselves if they are attacked. All of Shushan celebrates the reprieve.

If it ended there, the story of Esther would be a perfect set piece, with unambiguous moral clarity. But it doesn't. The first dark hints come in the last verse of Chapter 8, which says that many Persians now "professed to be Jews, for the fear of the Jews had fallen upon them."

CHAPTERS 9–10

On the day Haman scheduled for the Jewish extermination, the thirteenth of Adar, Jews muster throughout the empire and slaughter 75,000 people in a one-day spasm. The book is slippery: it never tells us whether the Hamanites actually attacked the Jews. As the last verse of Esther 8 hints, the enemies seem to have been thoroughly cowed by Mordecai's new power, suggesting that the Jews were taking vengeance against an already defeated foe. Given that the book doesn't report any Jewish casualties, it's pretty clear the fight was one-sided.

It gets worse. After the first day, Ahasuerus comes to Esther and tells her that 500 people have been killed in Shushan alone. He asks her what she wants now. The bloodthirsty queen says it's not enough. The Jews of Shushan must be given a second day to kill. Moreover, she wants all of Haman's ten sons impaled on stakes. The king says OK, and the massacre continues. The day after the murders, the Jews celebrate "with feasting and merrymaking," and Purim is declared a Jewish holiday for all time.

I'm from a family of lax Jews, and I'm sure our Purim celebrations weren't quite up to code. Even so, I am shocked at the difference between the Purim story I heard in synagogue and the Purim story in the Bible. At the synagogue, we certainly celebrated the death of Haman, but I don't recall hearing about the orgy of violence that followed. The 75,000 killed, Esther's insistence on a second day of slaughter, the vindictive impaling of Haman's sons—all that was underplayed or ignored in the kid-friendly Purim story I was raised on. Those horrifying acts make Purim a much more ambiguous, and troubling, holiday.

The Book of Daniel

Nice Pussycat!

In which Jewish Daniel is brought with three friends to the court of King Nebuchadnezzar of Babylon, then rises to power by interpreting the king's dreams; his friends are tossed into a furnace for refusing to bow down to a statue, but they survive; Nebuchadnezzar goes crazy, then regains his sanity by worshipping God; his faithless heir is warned by a ghostly hand; the Persians conquer Babylon and make Daniel minister; he is framed for a crime and tossed into the lions' den, which he survives; then he has many apocalyptic visions.

There are disappointingly few lions in Daniel, and they're bit players. Daniel is instead a version of Joseph's story: a holy man is held against his will in a hostile land, keeps his faith, loves God, and rises to power by interpreting dreams. Like Joseph, Daniel is about how people of faith are supposed to survive, and even prosper, in an alien land. It's about how Jews maintain their Jewish identity when society wants to erase it, and how they find strength in small groups. In short, Daniel is a manual for surviving a diaspora, and this must be why it has remained so popular for so long. It also helps that it's a thrilling story.

CHAPTER I

Having conquered Jerusalem and exiled the Jews, King Nebuchadnezzar of Babylon invites a few of the best young Jewish men to live at his
court and learn Babylonian ways. Presumably they'll serve as his ambassadors to the Jews, helping him co-opt and integrate them. This
tactic is straight out of Conquering 101: it's what all smart imperial
powers do. The English enrolled Indian rajas at their boarding schools;
the United States sent young Native Americans to learn the "white
man's way" at government academies. King Nebuchadnezzar's first
class of young Hebrews includes Daniel and three of Daniel's friends:
Hananiah, Mishael, and Azariah—soon renamed, in Babylonian, Shad-
rach, Meshach, and Abednego.

Daniel, who's one tough cookie, resolves not to assimilate and not
to betray God. He refuses to eat the *trayf* Babylonian food, and persuades their supervisor to let him and his three pals subsist on beans,
while all the other boys gorge on the king's bacon cheeseburgers and
lobster rolls. But God loves their kosher diet, and they prove healthier,
stronger, and wiser than the young courtiers. Daniel gains special favor for his ability to interpret dreams and visions.

CHAPTER 2

Nebuchadnezzar has a disturbing dream and orders his magicians to
explain it to him—or be torn limb from limb. The problem is that he
refuses to tell them what happened in the dream. So, they first have to
guess what his dream was, *then* interpret it. Impossible!

Well, not so hard if I were king, because I have the most literal
dreams in the world. My wife could do this guessing-interpreting
thing in a snap. Let's say I was anxious that our car was having problems; my morning conversation with Hanna would go like this.

David: *Hanna, guess what I dreamed last night?*
Hanna: *I bet you dreamed that the car was having problems and needed to*
    go to the shop.

David: *You're right! How did you know? What do you think it means?*

Hanna: *What it means, sweetie, is that you think the car is having problems and needs to go to the shop.*

The pagan magicians fail at the guessing game, naturally. So, Nebuchadnezzar flies into a rage and—like Pol Pot—orders all the wise men in the kingdom killed. But before that happens, Daniel visits the king and offers to interpret the dream. Aided by God, Daniel says that the king dreamed of a great statue of gold, silver, and bronze that was crushed by stone from a mountain. Then he says that the dream means the king's empire will be destroyed, and eventually another kingdom will rise to rule the earth. Nebuchadnezzar is so impressed that he appoints Daniel and Daniel's friends as top officials.

CHAPTER 3

Nebuchadnezzar, who appears to be painfully literal-minded, commissions a statue ninety feet high and orders his subjects to worship it. Anyone who doesn't bow down will be tossed into a fiery furnace. A few Babylonian anti-Semites inform the king that the Jews refuse to worship the statue. (Note the echoes of the book of Esther, in which Mordecai refuses to bow to Haman. Perhaps it is more accurate to say: note the echoes of Daniel in Esther. Daniel seems to have been written first.) Daniel's three friends are singled out for their refusal to bow down. Nebuchadnezzar orders them tossed into the furnace. They say that God will protect them. He orders the furnace turned up to extra-crispy—it's so hot that even the Babylonian guards are incinerated by the radiant heat. But when the three friends are tossed in, they relax in the blaze as though in a sauna. They emerge from the fire unscathed, and accompanied by a mysterious fourth man (Jesus, according to many Christians). Nebuchadnezzar is astonished, promotes them, and makes blasphemy against the Lord a capital crime.

CHAPTER 4

A weird chapter: All of a sudden, Nebuchadnezzar himself is the narrator. He has another dream, about a tree that's chopped down. Daniel is summoned. Anxious, he tells the king that he wishes the dream were about someone else. But it isn't. The dream means that Nebuchadnezzar himself will be chopped down by God. Sure enough, a year later the king is walking on the palace roof, congratulating himself on his power, when a voice from heaven rings out, "The kingdom has passed out of your hands."

At this point, Nebuchadnezzar goes cuckoo crazy, completely nutso. He becomes a homeless loon, eating grass like a cow, growing hair like feathers. It's very like *The Madness of King George*. After seven years, Nebuchadnezzar's sanity returns, as suddenly as it was taken away. Why does he get his marbles back? Because he embraces the Lord. Yes, his majesty Nebuchadnezzar of Babylon, the sacker of Jerusalem, the scourge of the Jews, the villain of the books of Kings, Isaiah, and Psalms, has suddenly become a worshipper of God! It's like Pharaoh coming to a seder.

CHAPTERS 5–6

Fast-forward several years. Nebuchadnezzar's son, King Belshazzar, holds a swanky banquet for 1,000 nobles, gets ripsnorting drunk, and tells his servants to bring out the gold and silver vessels looted from the Temple in Jerusalem. Bad idea. As the Babylonians toast their idols using God's cups, a ghostly hand appears in the room and scrawls a message on the wall of the palace (the original "writing on the wall"). It's a Stephen King moment, not least for the king, who is so scared that "his knees knocked together." None of Belshazzar's magicians or scribes can read the message. Finally the queen, who has more common sense than the rest of the court put together, tells the king to call Daniel. The king promises Daniel power and glory if he can read the inscription. Daniel first rebukes Belshazzar for rejecting God, reminding him how idolatry drove his father, Nebuchadnezzar, crazy. Then

Daniel translates the mysterious words, which are: "God has numbered the days of your kingdom and brought it to an end. . . . [Y]ou have been weighed in the balance and found wanting. . . . [Y]our kingdom has been divided and given to the Medes and the Persians." Strangely, the king isn't perturbed by Daniel's dire prophecy. He even makes good on his promise and names Daniel as one of his top ministers.

But Belshazzar is killed that very night, and Darius the Mede (of Persia) conquers the kingdom. Darius retains Daniel as his adviser. Daniel is at least the third such biblical hero to rise to prime minister in a foreign land. (Joseph and Mordecai are the others.) It's a curious role. I wonder if there is something in the nature of Judaism that makes this ministerial position so suitable. Perhaps Jews, when they're in the minority, must always balance power and modesty. Their learning (or, in this case, divine inspiration) prepares them for positions of authority, but their status as outsiders bars them from the top job. So they settle into power behind the throne. (See Henry Kissinger.) Or maybe I am making too much of a few examples.

In yet another Haman-like attempt to "entrap the Jew," envious Persian ministers scheme to oust Daniel from Darius's court. They have Darius issue a decree barring his subjects from addressing prayers to anyone except Darius himself. The penalty: a night in the lions' den. Daniel, though aware of the law, prays to God anyway. His rivals catch him and bring him to the king, who is dismayed that his favorite is in trouble. But the king can't undo his own law and has Daniel sentenced to the lions' den. (The king actually seals the mouth of the den himself, with a stone.) Darius can't sleep, and when morning comes, he races to the den and rolls back the stone—um, does this remind you of another Bible story?—and finds Daniel, fit as a fiddle. Daniel says that God sent an angel to shut the lions' mouths.

I always thought the story ended here, with Daniel's rescue and Darius's turn toward God. But, like many of the Bible stories I thought I knew but didn't, the lions' den has a gruesome coda. As soon as Daniel is rescued, Darius orders the arrest of the "men who slandered Daniel." (This, of course, is an unfair characterization of them. They did not slander Daniel. Daniel broke the law about prayer. It was a stupid law, but Darius signed it. They were just enforcing it.) The men—and their wives and children—are sentenced to the lions' den. "They had hardly reached the bottom of the den when the lions overpowered them and crushed all their bones." Good God. Add this to the biblical roster of excessive revenge and collective punishment.

CHAPTER 7–12

The rest of Daniel is a letdown after the preceding melodrama, though its prophecies are apparently important to Christianity. The second half of the book largely consists of trippy visions: winged lions and ten-horned beasties; a huge ram attacked by an enormous goat; a man with a body like beryl, a face like lightning, eyes like torches, etc. These visions are all about geopolitics and the end of days. Long story short: after a lot of geopolitical maneuvering, a great prince named Michael will show up, the dead will awaken, and the righteous will triumph. Do I even need to mention that there will be "appalling abomination[s]" all along the way?

TWENTY-FIVE

The Books of Ezra and Nehemiah

Coming Home

In which the Persian emperor encourages Jews to return to Jerusalem, where they rebuild the Temple; the scholar Ezra restores God's law and rails against intermarriage; the general Nehemiah rebuilds the city walls, over the objections of Arab neighbors.

The books of Ezra and Nehemiah recount much the same event—the repopulating of Jerusalem—from slightly different angles. The book of Ezra is told by a holy man. The book of Nehemiah is told by a politician. The first is more concerned with God and faith; the second with men and deeds. The books aren't hugely interesting—though at this late stage in my Bible reading, I must confess, Ezra would have to invent cold fusion and conjure up a magical army of Penélope Cruz look-alikes to get me really excited.

THE BOOK OF EZRA

Chapters 1–4

Having conquered Babylon, Emperor Cyrus of Persia invites all Jews to return home to Jerusalem and rebuild the Temple. More than 40,000

Jews return, and quickly rebuild the foundation of the Temple. They hold a buoyant, song-filled celebration. The oldest Jews, the ones who can still remember worshipping at the original Temple before Nebuchadnezzar sacked it, weep with joy when they see the new foundation. The younger Jews, meanwhile, shout with joy. This leads to a lovely verse: "The people could not distinguish the sound of the joyful shouts from the sound of the people's weeping." Isn't it wonderful the way memory, sorrow, joy, and the passage of time are all rolled up in that single sentence?

Chapters 5–6

There's a stop-work order on the Temple, because neighboring tribes object to the new building. (Even before zoning laws, there was NIMBY.) The new provincial governor, who doesn't want to be stuck with a half-finished building, overrules the neighbors. The empire mandates the death penalty for anyone who tries to stop the project. (A provocative idea: I'm surprised Phoenix or some other pro-growth city hasn't experimented with capital punishment for enviros and other bulldozer-blockers.) The Jews finish the Temple and celebrate the first Israeli Passover in a long time. This is the Temple that stood until the Romans sacked it 500 years later, the Temple where the miracle of Hanukkah occurred, the Temple where Jesus routed the money changers.

Chapter 7

The emperor dispatches the Torah scholar Ezra to Jerusalem, authorizing him to appoint judges and collect taxes. The emperor also declares that the Torah is the law of the land. It's the first official establishment of the Jewish faith outside a Jewish kingdom.

Chapters 9–10

As soon as Ezra arrives, he discovers that the earlier Jewish returnees— even the priests—have committed an abomination by marrying local Canaanite girls. The "holy seed" of the Jews has been contaminated. Aware of the Torah's teachings on mixed marriage, Ezra is beside himself. He tears his hair and beard out, apologizes to God for abandoning His commandments and polluting His land, and begs Him to have mercy.

What follows is an extraordinary (though appalling, for reasons we will discuss) act of collective responsibility. While Ezra is weeping and "throwing himself down before the house of God," all the Israelites gather to discuss their sin. They agree that they've wronged God with intermarriage but decide that there's still hope for Israel. In an astonishing consensus, they agree to banish the alien wives and the children of intermarriage. This will restore the Jews' blood purity and mollify God. In a rainstorm, all the Israelite men swear an oath to ditch their foreign wives. Then the book publishes a long, long list of men, followed by this verse, the final line in Ezra: "All these had married foreign women, and they sent them away with their children."

This is one of the very few times in the Bible that the Israelites accept responsibility for their sin and take strong, difficult measures to appease God. Yet it's also horrifying. I don't want to get self-righteous here. I took enough anthropology and history classes in college to know that group solidarity and blood purity are important to almost all cultures at almost all times. Only a few, rare societies, such as ours, welcome mixing and difference. So I know I'm imposing my patchwork-quilt idealism on my ancient ancestors when I say that it's sickening to imagine the wives and children expelled from Jerusalem for an accident of birth. (These days, the rabbis would enlist those gentile wives to bring the bagels for a post-Shabbat brunch.) This is yet another reminder of the Bible's radical morality. God does not put families first. He will let them be destroyed to preserve the faith.

THE BOOK OF NEHEMIAH

Chapters 1–2

Nehemiah, the Jewish cupbearer to the ruler of Persia, is heartbroken to learn that Jerusalem is a shambles. He's so sad that he can't even bear a cup without getting weepy. Rather than throwing him into a lions' den or impaling him on a stake—the usual response of Persian monarchs to dour underlings—Emperor Artaxerxes asks Nehemiah what's wrong. Nehemiah explains that he's bummed about Jerusalem. The king agrees to let Nehemiah return to rebuild the city and its walls. (The action of Nehemiah comes after the events of Ezra: The Temple has already been rebuilt in Jerusalem, but the city lies undefended.)

Nehemiah arrives in Jerusalem and rallies its Jews to join his wall project. But not all is milk and honey in the Holy Land. Nehemiah realizes that three non-Jewish local governors—Sanballat the Horonite, Tobiah the Ammonite, and Geshem the Arab—are seething about the plan to rebuild Jerusalem. They fear, quite reasonably, that a walled Jerusalem will be a mightier city, and a threat to its neighbors.

Let's pause for a moment to observe the entrance of the Bible's first and only "Arab." Arabia is referred to a few times in passing in various books, and anonymous "Arabians" are mentioned, but Geshem is the single named Arab. The whole scene is almost too depressing—or too funny—to believe. There is just one conversation between a Jew and an Arab in the entire Bible. When Geshem the Arab and his cronies hear that Nehemiah is rebuilding the wall, they "mocked and ridiculed" him. Nehemiah responds by saying: "The God of heaven is the one who will give us success, and we His servants are going to start building; *but you have no share or claim or historic right in Jerusalem.*" In what can be seen as a darkly humorous divine joke, the only Arab in the Bible turns out to be (1) an enemy of the Jews and (2) at odds with them over who should control Jerusalem. It's 2,500 years later: Has anything changed?

Chapters 3–6

Under Nehemiah's command, the Jerusalemites begin rebuilding the gates and walls of the city. Geshem, Sanballat, and Tobiah continue to mock and scheme. (To be fair to Geshem the Arab, the other two are much nastier. Sanballat, for example, mutters, "What are the miserable Jews doing?") The three enemies harass and terrorize the Jews so much that Nehemiah has to suspend the wall project. Eventually, Nehemiah sends his men back to the walls, but half of them have to provide security while the other half pile stones. Still, they manage to complete the wall in just fifty-two days. Nehemiah is the biblical role model for our ambitious big-city mayors, undertaking massive construction projects, fending off sniping critics, rallying the little guys without losing the elite—a Fiorello La Guardia of the Levant.

Chapter 8

Ezra kicks off the celebration of the wall's completion by reading the whole Torah to the assembly. The book inspires the Israelites, who realize while they listen that it's time for the holiday of Sukkoth, which they haven't kept for generations, although Sukkoth is mandated by the Torah. The whole country stops to observe the holiday—the same holiday that Jews celebrate today. It's fascinating, and rather humbling, to realize that once more *the book* guarantees Jewish survival. By reading the Torah, the Jerusalemites are able to make themselves Jewish again.

Chapter 13

The most interesting parallel between Nehemiah and Ezra is found in the last few verses of this final chapter. Like the book of Ezra, the book of Nehemiah ends with an uproar over intermarriage. Nehemiah notices that Jews are marrying Moabite and Ammonite women, and their kids can't even speak Hebrew. He gets the Jews to promise to stop intermarrying. Nehemiah cites the example of King Solomon, who despite being beloved by God and the smartest man in the world, was brought low by marrying foreign women. Nehemiah beats up, curses, and pulls out the hair of some of the intermarrying sinners. But let's notice how the episode does *not* end. In Ezra, all the foreign wives and children were exiled. In Nehemiah, there's no such purge. The Israelites promise not to sin in the future, but, unlike Ezra, Nehemiah doesn't break up the families. The infidel wives and half-breed kids get to stay. Perhaps that reflects the difference between the zealous priest and the pragmatic governor. The holy man Ezra can afford to be uncompromising in the service of God. But Nehemiah has to keep his citizens happy and maintain civil relations with his idolatrous neighbors. Nehemiah knows what every office-seeker since him has learned: a politician doesn't have the luxury of idealism.

TWENTY-SIX

The Books of 1 and 2 Chronicles

Return of the Kings

In which the events described in the books of Samuel and Kings are recounted again.

The Christian Bible locates the two books of Chronicles with the other historical books in the middle of the Old Testament. But Jews shove Chronicles into the trunk, at the very end of our Bible. The Jewish way makes more sense, I suspect. That's because Chronicles is largely a rehash of other books, mostly Samuel and Kings, but told more quickly and with less flair. It doesn't rate a place of honor.

THE BOOK OF 1 CHRONICLES

Chapters 1–2

The first five books of the Bible are condensed into two chapters of begats. The chief purpose of Chronicles is to glorify and legitimize the kings of Judah, so this elaborate genealogy is clearly intended to link Judah's monarchs by blood to the patriarchs. The family tree begins with Adam and follows the Chosen through Noah's son Shem to Abraham to Jacob to the twelve tribes and then down through Judah's line to King David.

Chapters 3–9
Because I could barely stay awake while I was reading this tedious section, I almost missed an extremely important moment of pop theology. 1 Chronicles 4 mentions a descendant of Judah named Jabez, who audaciously beseeches God: "Bless me, enlarge my territory, stand by me, and make me not suffer pain from misfortune!" God grants his prayer, and in so doing, the Lord lays the groundwork for *The Prayer of Jabez*, a gazillion-copy best seller in 2000.

Chapters 10–20
First Chronicles grooves into its real subject: the kings of Judah. The remainder of the book retells the story of King David, only minimally tweaked from the version in Samuel and 1 Kings. There are a few interesting new episodes. One is the Bible's version of a Congressional Medal of Honor citation: the heroic deeds of David's best soldiers are recounted. My favorite is the guy who killed both a lion and a giant.

Close your eyes, eleven-year-old girls: When David defeats a rival's 1,000-chariot army, he has all but 100 of the chariot horses hamstrung, a nasty chop to the leg that cripples but does not kill the animal.

Chapter 21
Remember how I puzzled about the end of 2 Samuel, when David angered God by taking a census. David was offered a choice of punishment: either famine, warfare, or plague. David chose plague. After thousands of deaths, he begged God to spare the innocent and punish only him, and God relented. In that discussion, I asked why God would get steamed about a census. That question is answered here, sort of. The chapter begins, "Satan arose against Israel and incited David to number Israel." So, God was angry about the census because it was actually Satan's idea!

Chapters 22–29
A bunch of very dreary chapters about the duties of each clan, which are decided by lot. (Shelemiah guards the east gate; Shebuel runs the

treasury, etc.) David favors a peculiar rotating bureaucracy. Each month, a new group of 24,000 clerks and parchment-pushers serves the king. There are obviously good political reasons to rotate jobs by tribe—he surely didn't want to irritate the Gadites by favoring the Reubenites too much—but can you imagine what a mess it was? Suppose you needed to pay the twenty-five-talent ticket you got last month for parking the ox on the wrong side of the street. When you show up at the office, you find that the entire Department of Unmotor Vehicles has turned over, and no one has any idea where the right scroll is.

THE BOOK OF 2 CHRONICLES

Chapters 1–4

Here's a disturbing episode. In 1 Kings, Solomon built the Temple using 153,600 conscripted laborers. Now Chronicles retells that story but adds a sinister detail. Solomon takes a census of all the foreigners in Israel, and those are the 153,600 people he sets to work building the Temple. How, exactly, is this different from the Egyptians enslaving the Jews to build their cities and temples? In each case, the king separates a minority foreign population and indentures it.

Chapter 5–9

The summary of Solomon's life and accomplishments in 2 Chronicles omits perhaps the key point made in the book of Kings: that Solomon ultimately betrays the Lord by marrying 700 foreign wives and building shrines to their gods all over Israel. Second Chronicles ignores those pagan wives entirely. That's a pretty important point to miss, don't you think? And that's not the only kingly misbehavior that the books of Chronicles overlook. First Chronicles, for example, recounts the life of David without mentioning the sleazy seduction of Bathsheba. I'm sure these omissions are intentional. The books of Chronicles clearly seem to have been written to glorify particular kings—notably David, Solomon, and various kings of Judah. The books burnish their reputations by leaving out their sins and infidelities.

Chapters 10–35

Unlike 1 and 2 Kings, which alternate between Judah and the northern kingdom, 2 Chronicles concerns itself only with Judah, the mightier and longer-lasting of the two countries. These chapters detail lots of kingly shenanigans, most of which we heard about in 2 Kings, and only a few of which are worth repeating. One is that King Jehoshaphat dispatches a cadre of priests and bureaucrats to teach the Torah to the Judaean people. As far as I can remember, this is the first (and only) systematic educational effort in the Bible.

Wicked King Amaziah of Judah captures 10,000 men of Seir and has them thrown off a cliff, so that they "burst open." Then King Uzziah, a great builder of war machines (a one-man Northrop Grumman), becomes so arrogant that he thinks he can perform incense ceremonies in the Temple. But only a priest may conduct these sacred rituals, so God afflicts Uzziah with leprosy.

A brief moment of sunshine. Hezekiah restores the Temple and celebrates Passover for the first time in memory. After the holiday, all of Judah goes out and smashes idols. Ah, good times!

And there is a genuine miracle. When Joash renovates the Temple, the project comes in *under* budget. (This is such a marvel that it has never been repeated since.) Joash spends the savings on gold cutlery.

Chapter 36

The final chapter of the Hebrew Bible. It retells history we have already heard several times—the Babylonian conquest, the destruction of the Temple, the exile. Then, in the final few verses, hope springs again. Persia conquers Babylon. King Cyrus restores the fortunes of the Jews. He says that God has ordered him to restore the Temple. Cyrus invites all of "His people" to return and help rebuild Jerusalem.

So we finish with a rebirth, a new creation story: God's few Chosen People, their covenant with the Lord restored, will return to the Promised Land to build His kingdom, again. At the start of Genesis, "In the beginning," God gave us life, land, and His love. And here He is at the end of His book, doing the very same thing.

Should You Read the Bible?

That's it! After thirty-nine books, 929 chapters, more than 600,000 words, and just over a year, I've finally finished reading the Bible—or at least the Hebrew Bible. The New Testament is not my Good Book; I'm going to leave it for another Bible amateur.

Should you read the Bible? You probably haven't read it. A century ago, most well-educated Americans knew the Bible deeply. Today, biblical illiteracy is nearly universal among nonreligious people. My mother and my brother, professors of literature and the best-read people I've ever met, have never done more than skim Genesis and Exodus. Even among the faithful, Bible reading is erratic. The obscure parts are virtually unknown. The Catholic church, for example, includes only a small fraction of the Old Testament in its official readings. Jews study the first five books of the Bible pretty well, but shortchange the rest of it. Orthodox Jews generally spend more time learning the Talmud and other commentary than the Bible itself. Of the major Jewish and Christian groups, only evangelical Protestants read the whole Bible thoroughly. That's why, when I finished my reading, I challenged some evangelical friends to a game of Bible trivia. It ended in a tie: I knew what kind of tree Absalom was caught in (oak); they remembered which king ruled Jerusalem when 185,000 Assyrians died in a plague (Hezekiah).

Maybe ignorance of the Bible doesn't matter, and maybe it doesn't make sense for most of us to read the whole thing. After all, there are so many difficult, repellent, confusing, and boring passages. Why not skip them and cherry-pick the best bits? After spending a year with the Good Book, I've become a full-on Bible thumper. Everyone should read it—all of it! In fact, the less you believe, the more you should read. Let me explain why, in part by telling how reading the whole Bible has changed me.

When I was reading Judges one day, I came to a complicated digression about a civil war between two groups of Israelites: the Gileadites and the Ephraimites. According to the story, the Gileadites hold the Jordan River, and whenever anyone comes to cross, the guards ask them to say the password, "shibboleth." The Ephraimites, for some unexplained reason, can't pronounce the "sh" in "shibboleth," and say "sibboleth" instead. When an Ephraimite fails this test, the Gileadites "seize him and slay him." I've read the word "shibboleth" a hundred times, written it a few, and probably even said it myself, but I had never understood it until then. It was a tiny but thrilling moment when my world came alive, when a word that had just been a word suddenly meant something to me.

And something like that happened to me five, ten, or fifty times a day when I was reading the Bible. It was as if I lifted a veil off my culture. You can't get through a chapter of the Bible, even in the most obscure book, without encountering a phrase, a name, a character, or an idea that has come down to us from 3,000 years ago. The Bible is the first source of so much: from the smallest plot twists (the dummy David's wife places in the bed to fool assassins) to the most fundamental ideas about morality (the Levitical prohibition of homosexuality that still shapes our politics, for example) to our grandest notions of law and justice.

Most of these cultural alerts occur on the back roads of the Bible. Just as an exercise, I thought for a few minutes about the cultural markers in Daniel, a late, short, and not hugely important book. What foot-prints has it left on our world? What bits of culture did I suddenly recognize after reading it? First, there are the "lions' den" and "the writing on the wall," two metaphors we can't live without. The "fiery furnace" that Daniel's friends are tossed into is the inspiration for the Fiery Furnaces, a band I listen to. The king rolls a stone in front of the lions' den, sealing in a holy man who won't stay sealed—foreshadowing the stone rolled in front of the tomb of Jesus. Daniel inspired the novel and the television show *The Book of Daniel*. It's a touchstone for one of my favorite good-bad movies, *A Knight's Tale*, in which the villain is always belittling our hero by declaring, "You have been weighed, you have been measured, and you have been found wanting"—exactly what the writing on the wall tells Belshazzar. And in the final days of the 2008 presidential campaign, Barack Obama used that same "found wanting" verse to describe John McCain's eco-nomic policies.

While reading the Bible, I often felt as though I was understanding my own world for the very first time. It was humbling. In reading, I learned that I didn't know the true nature of God's conflict with Job, which is the ur-text of all subsequent discussions of obedience and faith. I was ignorant of the story of Ruth. I was unaware of the radical theology of Ecclesiastes, the source of so many of our ideas about the good life. I didn't know who Jezebel was, or why we loathe her, or why she is the painted lady, or even that she was married to Ahab. (This also means I managed to spend most of a college semester studying *Moby-Dick* without knowing who the original Ahab was.) I was unfa-miliar with the second half of Jonah, ignorant of Ezekiel's valley of dry bones, unacquainted with the whore of Babylon. I don't want to sound like a theocratic crank, but I'm actually shocked that students aren't compelled to read huge chunks of the Bible in high school and college, the way they must read Shakespeare or the Constitution or Mark Twain. How else can they become literate in their own world?

That's my intellectual defense of reading the Bible. Now, a more personal one. As a lax, non-Hebrew-speaking Jew, I spent thirty-five years roboting through religious rituals. These rituals felt entirely

random—incomprehensible prayers honoring inexpicable holidays
that wove around the calendar like drunken sailors. None of it meant
anything to me. Now it does. Reading the Bible has joined me to Jewish life in a way I never thought possible. I can trace when this started
to the minute: It was when I read about Jacob blessing his grandsons
Ephraim and Manasseh, at the end of Genesis. I suddenly realized: Oh,
that's why I'm supposed to lay my hand on my son's head and bless him
in the name of Ephraim and Manasseh. This shock of recognition has
been followed by many more—when I came across the words of the
Shema, the most important Jewish prayer, in Deuteronomy; when I
read about the celebration of Passover in the book of Ezra; when I read
in Psalms the lyrics of Christian hymns I love to sing. Reading the
Shema in Deuteronomy did not make the existence of God more real to
me, but it did make me feel that I belonged. Its words were read and
spoken by my grandfather's grandfather's great-great-grandfather, and
his father, too, and so on back to the Judean desert. And now those
words are mine, too. I still don't believe Ephraim and Manasseh ever
existed, but I feel a sense of historical continuity, and a duty to that
history.

You surely notice that I'm not saying anything about belief. I began
the Bible as a hopeful, but indifferent, agnostic. I wished for a God, but
I didn't really care. I leave the Bible as a hopeless and angry agnostic.
I'm brokenhearted about God.

After reading about the genocides, the plagues, the murders, the
mass enslavements, the ruthless vengeance for minor sins (or no sin at
all), and all that smiting—every bit of it directly performed, authorized, or approved by God—I can only conclude that the God of the
Hebrew Bible, if He existed, was awful, cruel, and capricious. He gives
us moments of beauty—sublime beauty and grace!—but taken as a
whole, He is no God I want to obey, and no God I can love.

When I complain to religious friends about how much He dismays
me, I usually get one of two responses. Christians say, "Well, yes, but
this is all setup for the New Testament." To them, reading only the
Old Testament is like leaving halfway through a movie. I'm missing all
the redemption. If I want to find grace, forgiveness, and wonder, I have

to read and believe in the story of Jesus Christ, which explains and re-
deems all. But that doesn't work for me. I'm a Jew. I don't, and can't,
believe that Christ died for my sins. And even if he did, I still don't
think that would wash away God's epic crimes in the Old Testament.

The second response tends to come from Jews, who razz me for
missing the chief lesson of the Hebrew Bible: that we can't hope to
understand the ways of God. If He seems cruel or petty, that's because we can't fathom His plan for us. But I'm not buying that, either.
If God made me, He made me rational and quizzical. He has given me
the tools to think about Him. So I must submit Him to rational and
moral inquiry. And He fails that examination. Why would anyone
want to be ruled by a God who's so unmerciful, unjust, unforgiving,
and unloving?

Unfortunately, this line of reasoning seems to leave me with several
unappealing options: (1) believing in no god; (2) believing in the awful, vindictive god of the Bible; or (3) believing in a vague "creator"
who is not remotely attached to the events of the Bible, who didn't really do any of the deeds ascribed to him in the Bible, and who thus
can't be held responsible for them.

I am searching for a way out of this mess, and maybe I have found
one. I've spent most of my life avoiding the great questions of morality
and belief. I've been too busy getting the kids off to school and angling
for a promotion to spare much thought for the big questions. Reading
the Bible woke me up. Faced with its moral challenges, I had no choice
but to start scratching my head. Why would God kill the innocent
Egyptian children? And why would He delight in killing them? What
wrong did we do Him that He should send the Flood? Which of the
Ten Commandments do we actually need? I didn't become a better
person by reading the Bible. I'm not tithing or leaving gleanings in the
field or serving the halt and lame. But I am thinking.

And maybe that's my solution. I came to the Bible hoping to be inspired and awed. I have been, sometimes. But mostly I've ended up in
a yearlong argument with my Boss. This argument has weakened my
faith, and turned me against my God. Yet the argument itself represents a kind of belief, because it commits me to engaging with God. I

don't have the luxury that Christians do of writing off all the evil parts of the Old Testament. They've got Christ and the New Testament to fall back on. Jews have no such liberty. We have only one book. We're stuck with it. So what do we do? We argue with it, and try to fix it. I know I'm not the first person to realize that the Hebrew Bible is morally taxing. In some sense, the entire history of Judaism is an effort to grapple with its horror. Consider the passage in Deuteronomy stating that if you have a disobedient son, you can take him to the elders of the town and proclaim,

> *"This son of ours is disloyal and defiant; he does not heed us. He is a glutton and a drunkard." Thereupon the men of his town shall stone him to death. Thus you will sweep out evil from your midst.*

When I badgered my rabbi about this passage, she gave me a very convenient answer: "There is a lot in the Bible that not only do we not do, but rabbinic tradition says we *never* did—like stoning our children. . . . So what is it doing there? It is there for us to question, to study, and discuss." In other words, you don't have to believe the Bible, as long as you are willing to debate about it. A major purpose of Jewish commentary, of the Talmud and the Midrash, is to take the repellent stories of the Bible and make moral sense of them. God gave us the book, and then gave us 2,500 years to squabble about it.

What I've been doing, I think, is arguing with the Bible as it actually is, not as we want it to be. By reading the whole book, I have given myself a Bible that's vastly more interesting than the vanilla-pudding version I was fed by Sunday school teachers and the popular culture. The Bible's gatekeepers have attempted to dupe us into adopting a Bible with a straightforward morality and delightful heroes. The real book is messier, nastier, and infinitely more complex. In other words, it's much more like life.

The Bible has brought me no closer to God, if God means either belief in a deity acting in the world, or an experience of the transcendent. But perhaps I'm closer to God in the sense that the Bible has put me on high alert. As I read the book, I realized that the Bible's greatest heroes are not those who are most faithful, but those who are most contentious and doubtful: Moses negotiating with God at the burning bush, Gideon demanding divine proof before going to war, Job questioning God's own justice, Abraham demanding that God be merciful to the innocent of Sodom. They challenge God for his capriciousness, and demand justice, order, and morality, even when God refuses to provide any of these. Reading the Bible has given me a chance to start an argument with God about the most important questions there are, an argument that can last a lifetime.

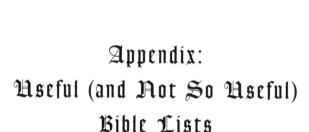

Appendix:
Useful (and Not So Useful)
Bible Lists

THE BIBLE'S TWELVE BEST PICKUP LINES

1. "Oh, give me of the kisses of your mouth, for your love is more delightful than wine" (Song of Songs 1:2).

2. "Lie with me."—Potiphar's wife to her slave, Joseph (Genesis 39:7).

3. "Praised be the Lord, the God of Israel, who sent you this day to meet me! And blessed your prudence."—David to his future wife, Abigail (1 Samuel 25:32–33). *An evangelical friend told me, "I use that line on Christian girls all the time. And it works."*

4. "What is your wish? It shall be granted you. And what is your request? Even to half the kingdom, it shall be fulfilled."—King Ahasuerus to Esther (Esther 6:6).

5. "There are sixty queens, and eighty concubines, and damsels without

number. Only one is my dove, my perfect one" (Song of Songs, 6:8–9).

6. "I saw that your time for love had arrived. So I spread My robe over you."—God to Jerusalem (Ezekiel 16:8).

7. "Let my beloved come to his garden and enjoy its luscious fruits" (Song of Songs, 4:16).

8. "Many women have done well, but you surpass them all." —husband to wife (Proverbs 31:29).

9. "Here, let me sleep with you," says Judah. "What will you pay for sleeping with me?" says Tamar, his daughter-in-law (Genesis 38:16).

10. "Come over here and partake of the meal, and dip your morsel in the vinegar."—Boaz to Ruth (Ruth 2:14).

11. "Your breasts are like two fawns, twins of a gazelle, browsing among the lilies" (Song of Songs, 4:5).

12. "Where are the men who came to you tonight? Bring them out to us, that we may be intimate with them."—townspeople of Sodom to Lot (Genesis 19:5).

GOD'S ELEVEN BEST MIRACLES
(AND ONE VERY LAME ONE)

1. The ten plagues: Blood, frogs, hail, boils, slaying of the firstborn, etc. Really, how could God top that? (Exodus 7–12).

2. Jonah and the whale: Three days and nights in a big fish, then spit up on land (Jonah 2).

3. The ark and the Philistines: The Philistines capture the ark of the covenant and leave it their temple overnight. When they come back in the morning, the statue of their god Dagon is lying on its face (1 Samuel 5).

4. Resurrection: Elijah lies down three times on the body of a dead boy and brings him back to life (1 Kings 17).

5. Parting of the Red Sea: Very cinematic! (Exodus 14).

6. The fiery furnace: King Nebuchadnezzar throws Daniel's three friends into a blast furnace. They—along with a mysterious fourth man—walk right out, unsinged (Daniel 3).

7. High noon: When Joshua fights the Amorites, the sun stops in the middle of the sky and stays there for a whole day (Joshua 10:13).

8. The Assyrian plague: The Assyrians are about to sack Jerusalem. King Hezekiah prays for relief, and that night a plague kills 185,000 enemy soldiers (2 Kings 19:35).

9. World's first IVF: Abraham and Sarah have a child when he is ninety-nine and she is ninety. Not such a miracle now, maybe, but it was miraculous back in the day (Genesis 17).

10. Elijah and the ravens: At God's order, ravens feed Elijah when he is hiding out in a cave (1 Kings 17:4–6).

11. The Temple renovation: When Joash renovates the Temple, the project comes in under budget (2 Chronicles 24:4–15).

The Very Lame One

1. The miracle of wicking fabric: To convince Gideon that he will be victorious in battle, the Lord makes a wool fleece wet. Gideon isn't persuaded and demands more proof, so the next night the Lord makes the fleece dry (Judges 6:36–40).

THIRTEEN SPECTACULAR MURDERS

1. Jael invites the fleeing General Sisera into her tent, gives him a glass of milk, puts him gently to sleep, then hammers a tent post through his brain (Judges 4).

2. Judge Ehud tells wicked King Eglon, "I have a message for you from God." Eglon agrees to meet with him privately, at which point Ehud stabs him so hard that "the filth came out" (Judges 3).

3. Shechem and all his townsmen are circumcised so that he can marry Dinah. When they're recovering from the surgery, Dinah's brothers show up and slaughter them (Genesis 6).

4. King Ahasuerus has Haman impaled on a stake seventy-five feet tall. Then Queen Esther does the same thing to Haman's ten sons (Esther 7–9).

5. After Daniel escapes the lions' den unharmed, Daniel's accusers—and their wives and children—are tossed into the den. "They had hardly reached the bottom of the den when the lions overpowered them and crushed their bones" (Daniel 6).

6. A gang surrounds a house and demands that the man inside come out to be raped. He sends out his concubine instead. "They raped her and abused her all night long till morning." She dies that day, at which point her husband chops her body into a dozen pieces and mails them throughout Israel (Judges 19).

7. Jezebel and Ahab have Naboth falsely accused of blasphemy and stoned to death, so they can steal his vineyard (1 Kings 21). But they get theirs, because in the next chapter . . .

8. Ahab is killed in battle by an arrow, and whores bathe in his blood (1 Kings 22). And a few chapters later . . .

9. Jezebel is thrown from a window by three eunuchs and trampled by horses. Then her corpse is eaten by dogs (2 Kings 9).

10. While he's fleeing a battle, David's rebellious son Absalom gets tangled in a tree by his long hair. David's soldiers stab him to death while he's hanging there (2 Samuel 18).

11. Shamgar slays 600 Philistines with an ox goad (Judges 3:31).

12. One-upping Shamgar, Samson slays 1,000 Philistines with the jaw-bone of an ass (Judges 15:15).

13. A woman in a town he is besieging drops a millstone on wicked King Abimelech's head. Abimelech begs his servant to stab him to death "that they may not say of me, 'A woman killed him'" (Judges 9).

THE NINE BEST PARTIES

1. The Persian king Ahasuerus's six-month party culminates in a weeklong feast, at which "the rule for drinking [is]: 'No restrictions!'" The drunken king demands that his wife dance for the guests, but she refuses (Esther 1).

2. Pharoah has a birthday banquet, during which he has his chief baker impaled, just as Joseph predicted (Genesis 40:15).

3. King Belshazzar of Babylon holds a grand party for 1,000 nobles. When he's falling-down drunk, he brings out the cups stolen from the Temple in Jerusalem so the guests can booze from them. Bad move. God's hand appears on the wall and writes that Belshazzar's days are numbered. He's killed that very night (Daniel 5).

4. After Aaron and the Israelites made the golden calf, "they sat down to eat and drink, and then rose to dance." This celebration ends badly: Moses arrives to bust up the festivities (Exodus 32).

5. Solomon's party at the dedication of the Temple lasts fourteen days, during which 22,000 oxen and 120,000 sheep are sacrificed (1 Kings 9).

6. Another party in Esther! After killing Haman, his sons, and 75,000 of their supporters, the Jews celebrate with "a day of feasting and merrymaking" (Esther 9).

7. Returned from exile in Babylon, the Jews rebuild the foundation

of the Temple, and rejoice with trumpets and cymbals, shouting, weeping, and singing (Ezra 3).

8. God orders a day of weeping and lamentation to prepare for a looming catastrophe, but the Israelites ignore him. "Instead there was rejoicing and merriment, killing of cattle and slaughtering of sheep, eating of meat and drinking of wine: 'Eat and drink, for tomorrow we die!'" (Isaiah 22).

9. When David brings the ark into Jerusalem, the band plays and he dances wildly before the ark, "leaping and whirling before the Lord" (2 Samuel 6).

MY FAVORITE PROSTITUTES

1. Rahab protects Joshua's scouts when they're spying on Jericho. She's the original hooker with a heart of gold—and she's an ancestor of Jesus (Joshua 2).

2. Tamar, the widow of Er and Onan, sleeps with her father-in-law, Judah, who pays her with his staff and seal (Genesis 38).

3. Two mothers each claim that a newborn is their son. Solomon finds the genuine mother by proposing to split the baby. The two moms are hookers (1 Kings 3).

4. Gomer. God tells the prophet Hosea, "Take yourself a wife of whoredom." *Pretty Woman*–style, he picks up Gomer and tries to make an honest woman of her (Hosea 1).

5. Jephthah's mother (Judges 11:1).

6. Moabite women. The Israelite men go "whoring" with them, and this really riles God (Numbers 25).

7. When Ahab is killed, the women who bathe in his blood are prostitutes (1 Kings 22).

8. During the time of bad King Rehoboam, Judah was swarming with "male temple prostitutes" (1 Kings 14:24).

9. Jeremiah says that Israel has "played the whore with many lovers" (Jeremiah 3:3).

10. According to Ezekiel, Judah is a hooker, "carr[ying] on her whoring so openly and flaunt[ing] her nakedness" (Ezekiel 16 and 23).

ELEVEN HEROES YOU DON'T WANT TO BE NAMED AFTER

1. Aaron: He makes the Golden Calf, then ducks responsibility. He tries to usurp the place of his brother Moses (Exodus).

2. Samson: A meathead. He's not merely a homicidal maniac; he's also a moron. Plus, he tortures small animals (Judges).

3. Sarah: No conscience. She happily defrauds Pharaoh and Abimelech. She vindictively, and savagely, has her servant Hagar and Hagar's son, Ishmael, exiled into the desert (Genesis).

4. Dinah: Innocent, but cursed. Her rape gives rise to the most shocking crime in Genesis (Genesis).

5. Levi: Tricks men into circumcision so he can murder them. Later seeks to murder his younger brother Joseph (Genesis).

6. Jacob: A con artist. Dupes his bighearted twin, Esau, twice; tricks his father Isaac and his uncle Laban, then sits by passively while his sons double-cross and murder innocents (Genesis).

7. Rebekah: The ultimate stage mother. She overwhelmingly favors her younger son Jacob, abuses sweet Esau, and gleefully cons her husband Isaac (Genesis).

8. Saul: Israel's first king was tall, handsome, and crazy (1 Samuel).

9. Isaac: A shiftless, easily fooled couch potato (Genesis).

10. Simeon: See Levi (Genesis).

11. Tamar: The *Flowers in the Attic* name. The first Tamar prostitutes herself to her father-in-law and gets pregnant by him. The second Tamar is raped by her own brother (Genesis; 2 Samuel).

NINE TRULY HELLACIOUS DIVINE PUNISHMENTS

1. Baldhead: Young boys mock the prophet Elisha, shouting, "Go away, baldhead! Go away, baldhead!" He curses the boys, at which point two bears rampage out of the woods and maul forty-two of them (2 Kings 2).

2. Preparation H: After the Philistines capture the ark of the covenant, they all get terrible hemorrhoids (1 Samuel 5–6).

3. Slaying of the firstborn: The last and worst of the ten plagues (Exodus 12).

4. Pillar of salt: Lot's wife, disobeying orders, turns around to look at Sodom's destruction and is salinated (Genesis 19).

5. Meat is murder: When the Israelites complain that they want meat instead of manna, a furious God sends a *The Birds*–like infestation of quail. As the greediest Israelites gorge themselves on the fowl, God strikes them down with a plague, killing them with the meat "still between their teeth" (Numbers 11).

6. Snakes on a plain: When the Israelites complain again about manna, God sends a plague of vipers (Numbers 21).

7. The earthquake: When Korah rebels, Moses proposes a showdown at which God will judge which of them is the true prophet. "The ground under [Korah and his supporters] split apart and the earth opened its mouth and swallowed them, with their households and all Korah's men and all their possessions. They went down alive

into the grave, with everything they owned; the earth closed over them" (Numbers 16).

8. Playing with fire: When Aaron's sons Nadab and Abihu present the wrong incense at the altar, God incinerates them (Leviticus 10).

9. Leprosy: Miriam criticizes Moses for marrying an African woman, so God eats away her skin with "snow white scales" (Numbers 12).

THE EIGHT TRIPPIEST AND MOST IMPORTANT DREAMS

1. Ezekiel dreams of beasts with four faces—human, ox, eagle, and lion. They have wings, spinning wheels for legs, and a sapphire throne over their heads (Ezekiel 1).

2. Joseph dreams that his brothers are sheaves of grain and stars bowing down to him (Genesis 37).

3. Daniel dreams of a beast with ten horns, including one horn with eyes and a mouth that speaks (Daniel 7).

4. Jacob dreams of a ladder up to heaven, with angels scurrying up and down it (Genesis 28).

5. Pharaoh dreams of seven gaunt cows eating seven fat ones, and seven parched ears of corn eating seven healthy ones (Genesis 41).

6. Zechariah has visions of a giant flying scroll and a woman in a lead-sheathed tub (Zechariah 5).

7. Nebuchadnezzar dreams of a huge statue that is crushed into dust (Daniel 2).

8. One of Gideon's soldiers dreams of a loaf of bread toppling the enemy's tents—a signal that Israel will be victorious in battle (Judges 7).

NINE WEIRD LAWS

I could reprint all of Leviticus and Deuteronomy here, but let me just give you a few favorites instead.

1. The no-polyblend rule: "You shall not put on cloth from a mixture of two kinds of material" (Leviticus 19).

2. The test for an adulteress: She must drink a cup of bitter water. If she's innocent, it won't harm her. If she is guilty, her abdomen will swell and her thigh will "sag" (Numbers 5).

3. The unsandaled one: If a man refuses to marry his brother's widow, she should pull off his sandal and "spit in his face." His house shall be known as "the family of the unsandaled one" (Deuteronomy 26).

4. A ball in the hand: If a woman grabs a man's testicles during a fight, her hand is to be cut off (Deuteronomy 26). You can see why they have this law, because . . .

5. . . . No one with damaged testicles can be admitted to the congregation (Deuteronomy 2).

6. If a priest diagnoses someone with leprosy, the leper's clothes shall be rent, "he shall cover over his upper lip, and he shall call out, 'Impure! Impure!'" (Leviticus 13).

7. If you find the body of a murder victim in the countryside and the killer is unknown, the elders of nearby towns measure the distance from the corpse to their village. The elders of the closest town then have to find a heifer—not just *any* heifer, but one that has never worked—break its neck, and wash their hands over the dead cow while declaring, "Our hands did not shed this blood" (Deuteronomy 21).

8. A soldier who has a nocturnal emission is unclean, and must leave the army until he can repurify himself (Deuteronomy 23).

9. If husband says his new wife is not a virgin, her parents must display the "evidence" at the gate of the city. If she's a virgin, he is to be fined and punished. If she's not, she's stoned to death (Deuteronomy 22).

THE SIX MOST IMPORTANT BUSINESS DEALS

1. The Cave of the Patriarchs: When Sarah dies in Hebron, Abraham pays 400 shekels to a Hittite to buy a grave site for her. This land became the "Cave of the Patriarchs" and Arabs and Jews are still fighting over it (Genesis 23).

2. The first case of eminent domain: King Ahab and Queen Jezebel covet Naboth's vineyard. (They want to plant a vegetable garden there.) They have him framed for blasphemy and stoned to death, and then seize his land (1 Kings 21).

3. Property rights for women: After their father dies, Noa and her four sisters petition Moses to be allowed to inherit his land. God and Moses decide that women without brothers can own land when their father dies (Numbers 27). This episode has been referred to as the world's first lawsuit.

4. Maoist economics: During the Egyptian famine, Joseph distributes grain to starving peasants, and seizes their land in return. He turns freeholders into sharecroppers, and transforms Egypt into a totalitarian command economy (Genesis 47).

5. She's my sister: Abraham and Sarah, by pretending that she is his unmarried sister, con first Pharaoh and later King Abimelech out of livestock and silver. So the first business deals in the Bible are swindles (Genesis 12 and 20).

6. Land for peace, take one: King Hiram of Tyre (Lebanon) supplies Solomon with gold and cedar wood for the Temple. In exchange, Solomon gives Hiram twenty Galilean towns. It's Israel's first land-for-peace deal, and it's a fiasco. Hiram thinks the towns are awful (1 Kings 9).

SIX ABUSES OF ANIMAL RIGHTS

1. Samson ties torches to the tails of 300 foxes and sets them loose in Philistine fields and orchards (Judges 15).

2. The first thing Noah does after he makes landfall is build an altar and sacrifice animals (Genesis 8:20).

3. The prophet Balaam beats his donkey when it refuses to move. An angel is blocking its way, but Balaam can't see the angel. Eventually the donkey complains and the angel appears to Balaam (Numbers 22).

4. David cuts the hamstrings of hundreds of the enemy's chariot horses (1 Chronicles 18).

5. At the party for the dedication of the Temple, Solomon sacrifices 22,000 oxen and 120,000 sheep (1 Kings 8).

6. The high priest Aaron puts his hand on the head of a goat, confesses all of Israel's sins to it, and exiles it to wilderness—as the "scapegoat" (Leviticus 16:2).

THE TEN MOST IMPORTANT MEALS

1. Eve's apple: It probably wasn't an apple, because apples don't grow where we think the Garden of Eden would have been. It might have been a pomegranate (Genesis 2).

2. Manna: "A fine flaky substance," which tasted like either olive oil or honey. Probably yummy for a couple of days, but the Israelites ate nothing else for forty years (Exodus 16).

3. Ezekiel's bread: He bakes it from wheat, barley, beans, lentils, millet, and farro, and lives on it for 430 days (Ezekiel 4). You can try it for yourself: Food for Life sells "Ezekiel 4:9" bread in yuppie markets everywhere.

4. Jacob's pottage: Esau sells Jacob his birthright for a bowl of red lentil stew and some bread (Genesis 25).

5. Quail: Sick of manna, the Israelites demand some meat for a change. Their complaints infuriate God, who decides to give them so much meat it will make them sick. A huge flock of quail kamikaze outside the camp, and the Israelites start to gorge themselves on the meat. God strikes the greedy ones with a plague, and they die with the flesh "still between their teeth" (Numbers 11).

6. David's cakes: When he brings the ark to Jerusalem, David gives all his subjects "a loaf of bread, a cake made in a pan, and a raisin cake" (2 Samuel 6).

7. Roasted grain and vinegar: Boaz and Ruth's first meal together (Ruth 2).

8. Abigail's fig cakes: When David threatens Abigail's husband, she buys him off with 200 fig cakes, as well as bread, raisins, mutton, and parched corn (1 Samuel 25).

9. Lion's honey: Samson kills a lion, and returns a year later to find bees swarming around the skeleton. He takes their honey and gives it as a present to his parents, but doesn't tell them where it came from (Judges 14).

10. Jael's milk: The fleeing General Sisera asks for water. Jael gives him milk instead. Then she murders him (Judges 5).

Acknowledgments

Good Book began as a project for *Slate* called "Blogging the Bible," and my first and greatest thanks go to Blogging the Bible's readers. When I started the blog in 2006, I found myself in the world's best Bible study group. Readers by the thousands e-mailed me to correct my theology, crack jokes, tell personal stories, retranslate key passages, damn me to hell, and proselytize me. That lively, contentious conversation not only kept me going through the Bible's dull portions—yes, I'm talking to *you*, Zephaniah and Micah!—but also made me appreciate and love the book more than I ever would have done on my own.

I'm not much of a God-thanker but thank God that I work at *Slate*, where I'm surrounded by the best colleagues imaginable. I'm particularly grateful to several of them. Jacob Weisberg encouraged me to do the blog, came up with the brilliant phrase "Blogging the Bible," and gave me time off to write the book. Julia Turner (and her mom) gave me the book title. Julia and Emily Yoffe also read and critiqued the manuscript, a thankless job. Brad Flora and David Sessions helped me enormously with the Bible lists. Jack Shafer lent me an inspirational CD of the book of Leviticus. June Thomas encouraged me to tour biblical Israel and write about it for *Slate*. Emily Bazelon edited my first blog entries and greatly enriched them. Sian Gibby, the best Jew I know, challenged me to think more carefully about the Torah.

Thanks to Kelly Mason, Mark White, Aryeh Tepper, Avis Miller, Robert Alter, Mark Dever, and Jacques Berlinerblau for advice on how to read the Bible. Abby Pilgrim was a marvelous scriptural guide, and I'm grateful to her parents for playing Bible trivia with me. Ian Stern, David Ilan, and Leor Ilan gave me a great biblical tour of the Holy Land. And big *Toda Rabas* to Josh Block for inviting me to Israel to begin with, and to Amiram Goldblum for being my host while I was there.

Sarah Chalfant is my ideal of an agent: equal parts editor, psychologist, and negotiator. Tim Duggan at HarperCollins is not merely a superb reader and editor, but also a mensch (unfortunately, not a word found in the Bible). Copy editor Susan Gamer gave the manuscript a great read, correcting errors, improving logic, refining jokes.

My parents, Paul and Judith Plotz, didn't give me a biblical education, and for that I am immensely grateful to them. Miriam and Eli Rosin are living proof that the Fifth Commandment should be amended to include in-laws. My daughter, Noa, asked me one hard question after another about the Bible, none more difficult than this: "Why are you writing the Bible again? There already is a Bible!" My son Jacob didn't ask me any questions about the Bible, but his exuberant sweetness reminded me of why we're commanded to go forth and multiply. And my son Gideon was born as I finished the book, allowing me to put my scripture reading to work by naming him after one of my new Bible heroes.

I must thank my wife, Hanna, for a boring reason: that she bought me a Bible and told me to write about it. And also for all the other reasons: like God at His best, she is wise, funny, just, loving, and merciful. But with Hanna, there's no smiting.